"Dr. Makary takes a deep dive into the real issues driving up the price of health care and explains how we can all take action to restore medicine to its noble mission." **—Don Berwick, MD, senior fellow, Institute for Healthcare Improvement**

"[*The Price We Pay*] is a fascinating look at people and communities throughout America—Dr. Makary blends reportage, research, and personal anecdotes about how money is really spent in healthcare, how we got to where we are today, and who is affected the most. I just started this one, and I already want to tell everyone to read it." **—*BookRiot*, "What to Read for #ScienceSeptember"**

"Brimming with true accounts that put faces on the numbers, *The Price We Pay* tours the landscape of contemporary American health care, with a generous sprinkling of hopeful counter-examples, or what the author calls 'disruptors.'" **—*Hopkins Medicine***

"[A] groundbreaking new treatise on why the cost of going to the doctor in the United States is spiraling out of control at an accelerating pace . . . [*The Price We Pay* is] remarkably enlightening on a number of levels as well as exceptionally infuriating on others . . . We are indeed in dire straits, but it is not hopeless. And I think you will agree if you decide to add this one to your reading list. Highly recommended." **—*Bowling Green Daily News***

"In this thoroughly reported primer Makary authoritatively and conversationally explains the money games of medicine . . . He found that working Americans feel that the system is stacked against them; it seems that they're right . . . Consider this book a powerful call to action for more information about health costs and for restoring the 'noble mission' of treating everyone with fairness and dignity." **—*Booklist* (starred review)**

P9-CSF-140

"I absolutely loved this book. Insightful, sharp, and essential reading—one of the top five books I've ever read." —Jay Newton-Small, *Time* magazine contributor and author of *Broad Influence*

"Marty Makary is a great storyteller, making accessible the business of medicine and the new ideas disrupting it without losing the important details. Everyone should read this book and then demand a more transparent and fair system." —Shantanu Agrawal, MD, chief health officer, Anthem, Inc.

"A valuable and illuminating read, full of intriguing insights into the use of decision-making in medicine and health care and how to make things work for all." —Cass Sunstein, coauthor of *Nudge* and professor at Harvard Law School

"Marty Makary is one of the great thought leaders in medicine, and his new book, *The Price We Pay*, brilliantly lifts the veil on the state of modern medicine and the new ideas that are disrupting it." —Senator William H. Frist, MD

"Over the course of decades, American health care lost the 'care' component and devolved into a big, wasteful business. In his new book, Marty Makary undertakes an extensive listening tour and astutely deconstructs how this occurred and what we need to do about it." —Eric Topol, MD, editor in chief of Medscape and author of *The Patient Will See You Now*

"Dr. Makary artfully sifts through complex data to shine light on a path for those seeking to build a better health care system." —Aneesh Chopra, president of CareJourney and former chief technology officer of the United States

"Marty Makary does a masterful job of describing the business arrangements of health care and their consequences in *The Price We Pay* . . . This book is a must-read for people struggling to find new ways to affect health care costs outside of a divisive political situation, in which governmental action on anything is becoming

increasingly difficult. Makary reminds us that simple awareness can lead to innovation and change. This reminder is badly needed in an industry that all too often bankrupts its customers."
—*Health Affairs*

"Plain talk from a surgeon and professor who has long studied health care issues and finds the American system badly in need of repair . . . He clearly demonstrates how medical care is secretive and predatory and why skyrocketing costs can be accounted for by the money games of medicine . . . Makary rightly takes the health care business to task, but he also offers a ray of hope that change can and will happen." —*Kirkus Reviews*

THE PRICE WE PAY

BY THE SAME AUTHOR

*Unaccountable: What Hospitals Won't Tell You and
How Transparency Can Revolutionize Health Care*

*Mama Maggie: The Untold Story of One Woman's Mission to Love the
Forgotten Children of Egypt's Garbage Slums*

THE PRICE WE PAY

WHAT BROKE AMERICAN HEALTH CARE—
AND HOW TO FIX IT

MARTY MAKARY, MD

BLOOMSBURY PUBLISHING

NEW YORK · LONDON · OXFORD · NEW DELHI · SYDNEY

BLOOMSBURY PUBLISHING
Bloomsbury Publishing Inc.
1385 Broadway, New York, NY 10018, USA

BLOOMSBURY, BLOOMSBURY PUBLISHING, and the Diana logo are
trademarks of Bloomsbury Publishing Plc

First published in the United States 2019
This edition published 2021
Copyright © Martin Makary, MD, 2019
Afterword © Martin Makary, MD, 2021

All rights reserved. No part of this publication may be reproduced or
transmitted in any form or by any means, electronic or mechanical,
including photocopying, recording, or any information storage or retrieval
system, without prior permission in writing from the publishers.

This a work of nonfiction. However, the names and identifying
characteristics of certain individuals have been changed to protect
their privacy, and dialogue has been reconstructed to the best of
the author's recollection.

This book is not intended to provide medical advice to individual readers.
To obtain medical advice the reader should consult a qualified
medical professional who will dispense advice based upon each
reader's medical history and current medical condition.

Bloomsbury Publishing Plc does not have any control over,
or responsibility for, any third-party websites referred to or in this book.
All internet addresses given in this book were correct at the time of
going to press. The author and publisher regret any inconvenience
caused if addresses have changed or sites have ceased to exist,
but can accept no responsibility for any such changes.

ISBN: HB: 978-1-63557-411-1; PB: 978-1-63557-591-0; EBOOK: 978-1-63557-412-8

LIBRARY OF CONGRESS CATALOGING-IN-PUBLICATION DATA IS AVAILABLE

2 4 6 8 10 9 7 5 3

Typeset by Westchester Publishing Services
Printed and bound in the U.S.A. by Berryville Graphics Inc., Berryville, Virginia

To find out more about our authors and books visit www.bloomsbury.com and
sign up for our newsletters.

Bloomsbury books may be purchased for business or promotional use.
For information on bulk purchases please contact Macmillan Corporate and
Premium Sales Department at specialmarkets@macmillan.com.

Dedicated to my father, whose compassion in caring for cancer patients has taught me that part of being a doctor is the responsibility to advocate for those who are most vulnerable

Contents

Preface

Sometimes when I sit down to write, I find myself staring at a blank screen. Before I know it, I'm buying toothpaste online. Writing this book was entirely different. As I traveled to see what American medicine looks like on the ground, I would rush back to my computer to write.

Over the past two years I visited 22 cities across America, listening to each of health care's stakeholders: hospital and insurance company leaders, policy makers, doctors and nurses and others. I've also sat with scores of patients—in living rooms, over dinner, at work—and they've shared with me, sometimes through tears, how the business of medicine ruined their lives. I spoke with numerous insiders who went into health care for noble reasons but found themselves caught up in a system they despise. I was also inspired by innovators who refused to accept the status quo, redesigning medical care and launching businesses aimed at disrupting health care by cutting through all its shenanigans.

My goal has been to understand health care and to examine it through the lens of its clinical mission of serving patients. Surprisingly, this exhilarating trip was not entirely different from my work as a surgeon. I've been "making rounds" on patients, but this time it was to see their wounds from the health care system rather than from surgery. Along the way, I learned what no health care textbook or classroom could have taught. I learned the business of medicine.

As I cared for patients back home, between my travels researching this book, I was often reminded of the deep trust people have in their doctor. Patients are willing to let me put a knife to their skin within minutes of meeting me, or to divulge secrets they've kept for a lifetime—just because I'm a doctor. In exchange for this trust, doctors like me promise to do our best to help, a contract articulated in the Hippocratic Oath. Similarly, most American hospitals were founded with a charter dedicating them to care for the sick and injured regardless of one's race, creed, or ability to pay. But tragically, that heritage of public trust is threatened today by a business model of price gouging and inappropriate care. However, a groundswell of doctors are saying, "No more." We must restore medicine to its noble mission.

For centuries, medicine was based on an intimate relationship between doctors and patients. But behind the scenes, a gigantic industry emerged: buying, selling, and trading our medical services. Health care industry stakeholders are playing a game, marking up the price of medical care, then secretly discounting it, depending on who's paying.

When a $69,000 bill hit one New York woman for a simple two-hour ER visit, she turned to my friend for help. She had only needed an IV and some basic tests, so she couldn't believe the price. My friend, a health care consultant, had a good relationship with the hospital's CEO so he met with him and told him about the two-hour visit in detail. "Guess how much your hospital charged?" my friend asked the CEO.

Cringing, the hospital CEO guessed $5,000, thinking he was guessing high. Then my friend showed him the itemized bill totaling $69,000. Embarrassed at how disconnected he was from his own hospital's billing practices, the CEO offered to forgive the bill.

This story reminded me that we don't have malicious leaders in health care; we have good people working in a fragmented system. The operations I do today use the same equipment, anesthetics, sutures, and paid staff that I used ten years ago. So how is it that health insurance costs have been skyrocketing? It's explained by the money games of medicine, loaded with middlemen, kickbacks, and hidden costs.

The profits are big but the casualties are great. Overtesting, over-diagnosing, and overtreatment are now commonplace in some areas of medicine.[1,2,3] And the prices are so high that patients can't pay the bills. About one in five Americans currently has medical debt in collections and half of patients with certain medical conditions, such as women with stage 4 breast cancer, now report being harassed by a collection agency for their medical bills.[4]

While patients are getting shaken down for inflated bills, the health care establishment conducts high-level panel discussions in gilded conference rooms discussing the issues in theoretical terms. I've been there. I sit on those panels too. But to understand what was *really* happening in health care, I shed my white coat and embarked on listening rounds across the country.

While these travels gave me the education of a lifetime, they also gave me new hope. I visited hospitals and start-ups charting new courses with fresh ideas. I met doctors, business leaders, insurance innovators, state legislators, millennials, and others fed up with the medical establishment and challenging it. This social movement has no formal name or membership, but is made up of people determined to put patients back at the center of medicine. They are working to make how you pay for medical care rational and fair instead of secretive and predatory. Using the simple principles of transparency and competition, they are showing us the way out of this mess. This book shines a light on many insider games of health care, but it will also introduce you to the innovators and disrupters working to save you money.

My favorite movie is *The Big Short*, a film about the financial crisis of 2007. Part of the reason I admire that movie is because it took an incredibly complicated problem and made it understandable by using stories and relatable examples. In this book, I want to do the same for American health care.

Before the Great Recession of 2007, Americans were being led to buy mortgages they didn't understand and could not afford. As I talked to families and business owners who purchased health care they didn't understand and couldn't afford, I began seeing ominous signs that health care has become another economic bubble.

A woman in California helped me appreciate the burden that our rising health care costs place on small businesses. To start her dry cleaning business, Jennifer had to pay $100,000 a year to get health insurance for herself and three employees.[5] Right off the bat, her small business was six figures in the hole. How many more garments does she now need to clean in order to be profitable? Jennifer's story illustrates one of the greatest risks to our economy: health care costs are increasingly suffocating business in America.[6]

The 2007 banking crisis resulted from complexity that kept onlookers confused. When people questioned banks being overleveraged and selling mortgages to people who couldn't afford them, financial experts responded by saying, "It's extremely complicated. Leave it to us." But the problem was simple: Banks were spending money on toxic assets with money they didn't have. Bad mortgages were bundled and sold on the market for more than they were worth. Credit ratings agencies, supposedly independent, received payments to prop up this house of cards. The result was a huge economic disaster.

Today, entrenched stakeholders in medicine fend off criticism by claiming these highly complex systems should be left to the experts. "You wouldn't understand . . . leave it to us."

But we *do* understand, and it's time to change the business of medicine. This book is my attempt to push back. We currently spend enough money to provide excellent health care to every American. We just need to cut the waste.

PART I
Gold Rush

CHAPTER 1

Health Fair

The Washington Monument, encircled by American flags, loomed tall and proud that sunny morning as I made the 20-minute drive through D.C. from my home in Virginia. I arrived at the office of Dr. Sridhar Chatrathi. He worked in Prince George's County, a predominantly African American suburb of Washington, D.C. I learn a lot from talking to community doctors like Chatrathi. In the lobby of his cardiology clinic, he welcomed me with a cheerful smile before ushering me into his office. Skipping the pleasantries, he got straight to the point. A fast-growing trend he was witnessing weighed on his conscience: doctors doing unnecessary vascular procedures.

"It's the Wild West," said Chatrathi. "Ballooning, stenting, and even lasering harmless plaques in leg arteries has spun completely out of control. It's a cash cow." He explained that within two miles of his office, there were four surgery centers doing these procedures all day long, every day.

"Ballooning" and "stenting" refer to the way doctors insert tiny inflatable devices or wire cages into arteries to spread open blockages that restrict blood flow. It's been going on for decades, but primarily in heart vessels. Such procedures can be lifesaving for someone experiencing a heart attack, but for most other patients, studies show stents provide no survival benefit. Because of that, heart stenting is in decline, replaced by better medications. In recent years there's also been a lot of public scrutiny of the practice.

A Baltimore cardiologist, Dr. Mark Midei, received a great deal of negative media attention for allegedly placing unnecessary heart stents in hundreds of patients.[1]

"The Midei headlines had a big impact on the field and sent a strong message to cardiologists," Chatrathi told me. "It helped clean up the practice of overstenting heart vessels."

Nonetheless, Chatrathi said, his peers—kings of a past era of stenting heart vessels—have found a new way to use their skills. Or perhaps I should say a new place: the legs. Ignoring guidelines of the U.S. Preventive Services Task Force that clearly state that there is no evidence to support screening for peripheral artery disease,[2,3] many of them do a test to see if there are any blockages in the leg arteries, and then follow up with a procedure to improve circulation. Heart stenting nationwide was on the decline. But leg is the new heart.

One thing puzzled me, though. It's not as if patients just book appointments to have cardiologists check out their leg circulation.

"Where are they finding all these patients?" I asked Chatrathi.

"In churches," he replied.

What!? I was confused. I'm a churchgoer, and I couldn't imagine doctors looking for customers in the pews. It's not as though doctors can just show up for worship services and offer the congregation surgery in the lobby afterward.

Chatrathi explained that churches hold community health fairs at which doctors show up and perform predatory screenings. I had to see this for myself. I tracked down an upcoming health fair at one of the churches in his area and a few weeks later went on another research field trip.

Once again, I let myself take in the scenery that morning as I cruised through our nation's capital. Though I'd been through D.C. countless times, I drove slowly, soaking in the stately surroundings. The Capitol dome stood graceful and white. I arrived at a church building where an African American congregation meets, minutes from the U.S. Capitol building. I walked inside and found a gathering of life and smiles.

A woman from a local cardiology group ripped a Velcro blood pressure cuff off an older woman's arm. "Let me do that again," she said warmly.

The congregants had turned into patients. It might seem like a selfless act of community service. After all, here were medical providers examining patients in a church filled with underserved minorities. But after talking to Dr. Chatrathi, I saw this scene in a different light. These medical providers weren't serving; they were prospecting.

The person from the cardiology group was conducting a test that measures how the blood flow in the legs compares to the blood flow in the arms. The rationale: Something might be wrong if the blood pressure is lower in the legs. It could be caused by a narrowing of the arteries, a plaque that slows blood flow. It might warrant further investigation.

There's just one problem with that notion: This test should not be performed unless a patient has serious symptoms, like crippling leg pain. For anyone else, it's likely to lead to medical care they don't need, which can be expensive and dangerous. That's exactly why independent medical experts do not recommend the type of peripheral vascular screening I witnessed that day at the church.

The dutiful patient being examined didn't seem to have any severe pain in her legs. In fact, the team seemed to be testing as many people as they could. The woman from the cardiology practice told the patient her reading was "borderline." She gave her instructions to follow up for ultrasound testing at the cardiology group's vascular center.

The medical provider convinced her that she cared only about her well-being, not telling her the other side of the story. The young woman administering the screening may have been unaware of national guidelines about this type of testing and, with good intentions, convinced herself that plaques are evil. And the woman being tested probably thought testing was good for her health. She would be responsible for a small portion of the cost, but all of us would pay for the rest of her bill through the Medicare program. The doctors stood to make a lot of money for each follow-up test that resulted from the church fair. Rather than showing up to help patients, this practice was panning for gold.

Attending the church outreach event that day offered me a fresh reminder that health screening can be a double-edged sword. It can be a powerful tool to detect disease and prevent tragedy. But it can also be a business model to recruit patients for treatments they don't need. In an instant, overscreening converts a community of average residents into a pool of patients. It's just one costly example of the medicalization of ordinary life.

Do You Have Leg Pain?

Doing leg procedures for people that don't need them is one form of unnecessary treatment. But the problem is even bigger. I worked with my Johns Hopkins colleagues to estimate the percentage of medical care that is unnecessary by sending an anonymous survey to a sample of 3,000 doctors across America and had 2,100 respond. The doctors replied that, on average, they believe 21% of everything done in medicine is unnecessary.[4] Breaking it down further, the doctors in that survey estimated that 22% of prescription medications, 25% of medical tests, and 11% of procedures are unnecessary. Literally billions of dollars are spent on care we don't need.

Public health crises can be divided into two types: naturally occurring and man-made. Many of the crises we face in medicine today are not naturally occurring viruses or other hazards from nature. They are manufactured, like the crisis of smoking, or opioid addiction, or antibiotic resistance. Similarly, too much medical care is a public health crisis that harms patients and wastes our health care dollars.

Even before meeting Dr. Chatrathi and attending the church health fair, I had become aware of unnecessary procedures on leg vessels from conversations I'd had with my friend Jim Black, chief of vascular surgery at Hopkins. When we were in the operating room together, he discussed the outlandish things some other doctors in the community had told his patients. Jim said some doctors justified these unnecessary procedures by telling patients it would improve their circulation. One doctor, he said, routinely told patients that the procedure would prevent an amputation in the future.

It's common for older patients to have some narrowing of leg arteries. The femoral leg artery is long, and some narrowing is normal. It's called peripheral artery disease. But the body usually adapts. If surgeons operated on every artery narrowing, we'd be operating multiple times on nearly everyone over 70 years old. But intervening with endovascular procedures is so easy and lucrative that cardiologists are not the only doctors to get into this unregulated area. Radiologists and vascular surgeons are also doing the procedures. Leg artery procedures can generate $100,000 in *one day* when a doctor owns the facility. By comparison, I earn about $2,000 per day doing cancer surgery. Doing a procedure pays well, but taking time to explain the importance of exercise, which increases leg circulation, pays poorly. I already knew our medical system gives incentives for us to perform procedures, whether patients need them or not. But the church health fair had vividly shown me just how prevalent unnecessary medical care had become.

Over the course of several conversations I had with Dr. Chatrathi, he explained the mammoth scale of the deceptive practice. Many private vascular centers in Washington, D.C., he said, are lining up a dozen or more patients per day.

"For the vast majority of cases they are doing, there is no evidence to support the procedure," Chatrathi said.

I asked Chatrathi how the doctors convince patients to undergo the procedures.

"They ask people, 'Do you have leg pain?'" he replied with a smirk.

I smirked too, knowing what all doctors know: Patients make decisions based on how we present options to them. We just give them a nudge.

Since my days as a medical student, I've seen doctors nudge patients for reasons good and bad. And we doctors are very good at nudging. We know the trigger words that steer patients. Every specialty has its phrases. For obstetricians, it's saying something like, "It might be safer for the baby." If an orthopedic surgeon is helping a patient decide between a knee replacement and a nonsurgical option, it's mentioning the joint is "bone on bone." The phrase "bone on bone" creates an image of grinding, like fingernails screeching on a chalkboard. Patients beg for it to stop. They choose surgery every time. And if a cardiologist tells a patient he has a "widowmaker" in his heart—an actual medical term used to describe a partially blocked artery—the patient does whatever it takes to address it. No one wants their spouse to become a widow.

Consider the simple presentation of a patient with early appendicitis. Three trials recently published in top journals show that treating the condition with antibiotics rather than surgery works 75% of the time.[5,6,7] And the evidence showed no increased risk of health problems for trying the antibiotic method.[8,9,10] More than 300,000 appendectomies are done in the United States each year, each with a hefty price tag. Most of these patients can be treated with antibiotics alone.[11] But whether patients choose surgery or a trial of antibiotics depends on how we surgeons present the options.

I see it in my own specialty of cancer surgery. Some old-school doctors have not learned minimally invasive methods, so they uniformly make large incisions on every patient to access the organs. If a patient asks one of these old-school doctors if an operation can be done with the minimally invasive method, the surgeon could refer the patient to a surgeon who could do it with small incisions. Or the old-school surgeon could drop the trigger phrase "If we use the minimally invasive method, there's a small chance we may not remove all the cancer." Guess what? Every patient chooses to be cut wide open.

Nudges from doctors can be as powerful as IV sedation. Sometimes we steer patients toward what's best for them. Sometimes we steer patients toward what's best for us. As Chatrathi discussed this phenomenon, we shared a sad smile. We knew how effective verbal triggers were. All a doctor has to do is suggest that a blockage could be causing the leg pain, and a patient becomes fixated on the idea and agrees to the procedure.

The recruiting line was simply "Do you have leg pain?" Here's a better question: Who *doesn't* have leg pain? Finding a Medicare patient in America without some leg pain is like finding a penguin in the desert. Leg pain is common in younger people, too. I tried yoga two weeks ago and I'm still limping.

Once a person admits to even the mildest leg cramp or stiffness or soreness, it triggers a chain of events. The patient might as well be picked up and placed on an assembly line. It starts with the test they did at the church fair—the ankle-brachial index test—to check the patient's leg circulation. If that warrants further checkup—and that's often a subjective call—the doctor will say: "Let's take a look with a handheld ultrasound probe." What follows is often another test: "Let's get a better look with a formal Doppler study." Next, since it looks a bit funny, "Let's do a diagnostic catheterization." They inject dye into the patient's leg vessels and shoot X-rays. "Good news," the doctor declares. "During the procedure, we found a small blockage that we ballooned open"—or stented, or zapped with a laser. "Come back in a few months for a follow-up to take another look." By the time they're done ringing the cash register, Medicare has spent approximately $10,000 per person, a cost that's passed along to every other American. Private insurance will pay up to triple that amount for the same procedure.

It may be a scam, but it's perfectly legal. The doctor carefully documents that the patient has a diagnosis of "claudication" to ensure that everything will be covered by insurance. Claudication is a rare type of debilitating leg pain that is subjective and nearly impossible to disprove. And even though doctors know that less than 5% of patients with this rare diagnosis benefit from surgery, inserting that single word once in a patient's chart guarantees the doctor will be paid in full and fend off any lawsuits. The crafty documentation sidesteps the national guidelines. In addition, the American College of Preventive Medicine has taken a stand against the screenings, warning that the false positives lead to unnecessary downstream tests, procedures, and psychological distress.[12]

As I spoke to Chatrathi, my mind was reeling. I had to pause to absorb what I was hearing: unsuspecting citizens were being systematically targeted for factory-style procedures. Their mistake? Wanting to take care of their health.

Telling the truth can get doctors in trouble with their peers.
I wanted Dr. Chatrathi to feel free to speak honestly, so I offered
to keep his name out of this book. He would have none of it.

"I don't want anonymity," he said. "That's the problem. We have
all been silent about all the waste in medicine, even as everyday
people pay higher and higher health care costs. Use my name. I'm
aware of the consequence to my practice. But it's time we as doctors
stand up to say what is right and wrong."

Digging Deeper

After several conversations with Chatrathi, I decided to bring up
the issue with my Johns Hopkins research team. At our next
meeting, I explained to them what I had learned. My team of ten
sat there listening in shock. Our group studies health care costs,
so this story struck a chord. Their outrage was palpable. It was
especially strong among the millennials, who I find have a low
tolerance for injustice.

Dr. Caitlin Hicks, our surgery department's newest hire, took a
special interest. She's a rock star. After graduating from Harvard
and the Cleveland Clinic, Hicks trained for 6 years at Johns
Hopkins to become a vascular surgeon. Everyone in our department had been impressed by her technical genius and research
productivity, and I was lucky to have her on my study team. As I
explained what I'd seen "in the field," Caitlin listened and main-
tained her composure, but I could tell she was seething. She had
heard of doctors making a ton of money by stretching the indications so they could balloon and stent leg vessels. Eventually she
spoke up, proposing we conduct a national study to see how prevalent the practice had become. She had written a hundred scientific articles as a medical student and trainee. Having Caitlin on
the case was a huge asset.

Our team eventually identified about 1,100 U.S. churches,
synagogues, and mosques that served as vascular screening
centers[13]—despite a scientific consensus that people should *not* be
screened this way for this disease.

Caitlin also worked on a national study of Medicare patients that revealed it was mostly minorities or people in low-income areas getting these procedures, even after accounting for contributing factors such as smoking or disease complexity.[14] We generated a county-by-county U.S. map showing where the procedure rate was highest. What we saw was infuriating. We were looking at a map of predatory screenings for unnecessary surgery. At our research meetings in my office, Caitlin and others on the team would present the findings in a scientific tone but get choked up when they considered what was happening to vulnerable Medicare patients. I admired their passion.

I decided to visit more church fairs, and I found that the D.C. city government promotes the events. It seems like every week in

Georgia

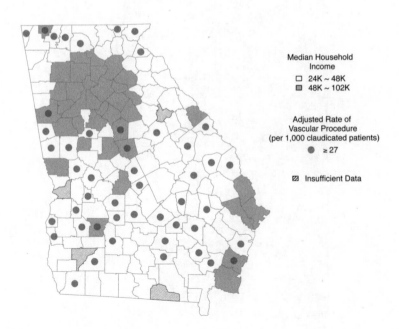

Median Household
Income
☐ 24K ~ 48K
▣ 48K ~ 102K

Adjusted Rate of
Vascular Procedure
(per 1,000 claudicated patients)
● ≥ 27

▨ Insufficient Data

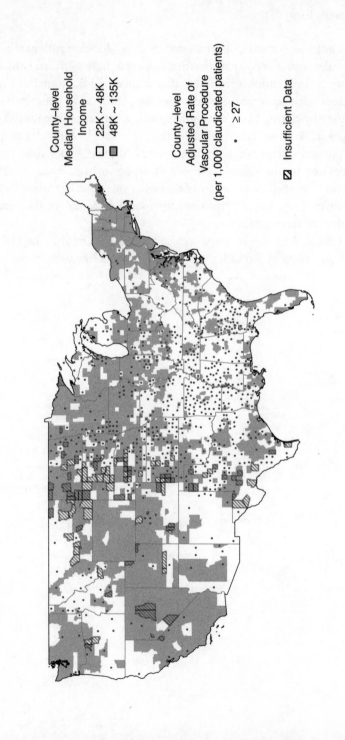

County-level
Median Household
Income

☐ 22K ~ 48K
▨ 48K ~ 135K

County-level
Adjusted Rate of
Vascular Procedure
(per 1,000 claudicated patients)

• ≥27

▨ Insufficient Data

the summer months, a local church offered community screening for leg circulation—and not just for leg circulation. My team found a host of other unwarranted health screenings, such as checking the carotid arteries in the neck and doing EKGs on people without heart symptoms.

One of the offending surgery centers had four full-time marketing employees. They recruited patients using the same tactic I'd witnessed at the church outreach event—by inviting people to see if they have poor blood flow in their legs. It's a scheme they undertake in churches, supermarkets, referring physician offices, and community health fairs. Some community residents receive spam mailings encouraging them to come in for screening.

One of the young members of our research team, Will Bruhn, insisted on joining me on my next church fair visit. One bright Saturday morning, we walked into a church plastered with signs advertising the free health fair. After signing in, we entered the fellowship hall, where table after table offered information about prenatal care, exercise programs, and a host of other topics. Then, over in the corner, we spotted him. A doctor sat in a chair with a Doppler ultrasound probe in his hand. He squeezed a generous dollop of lubricant onto the thigh of the woman sitting beside him, then ran the probe up and down her leg. When she got up, he handed her his card and the next person in line took a seat. It was like watching a round of speed dating.

Will and I got in line. We wanted to hear what the doctor was telling people. While waiting, we were presented with marketing materials. The images in the brochures showed a blockage in a leg artery and illustrated how a balloon or stent could open it up. When our turn came, the doctor refrained from doing an ultrasound, but he explained that he was helping people with varicose veins and checking for blockages in the leg arteries. Varicose veins are typically a cosmetic problem. But the pamphlets and posters at the church fair made them sound life-threatening.

For months, Caitlin, Will, and I continued to visit church health fairs, regrouping between visits with the whole team to study the magnitude of the problem and the broader cost implications. Will and I took photographs, conducted interviews, and documented the profit-driven screening. The research team produced figures, tables, and maps that described the predatory nature of the procedures. With every new piece of data, we got a clearer vision of the big picture—and it was distressing. With every trip to a church health fair, we were saddened to see happy, grateful people, mostly African Americans, being fleeced by white physicians and their staff. What we personally observed was consistent with what Caitlin's maps had indicated.

I wanted to see what the pastors thought about this. Did they know that the procedures being recommended at their church fairs were probably unnecessary? I returned to the first church where I had attended a fair, and the pastor graciously welcomed me into his cluttered office. He took a minute to introduce me to his wife, who helped run the church school and worked in an office a few feet from his.

We sat down and I explained to him what my team had witnessed locally and studied nationally. He was flabbergasted. "We don't know the medical science," he said. "We just wanted to serve our community and invite people into our church. Some churches do food giveaways. We always wanted to do more."

It's an admirable goal. It can be hard to get access to good care in low-income neighborhoods. A few times during the conversation, the pastor referred to the health fair as health "care." He talked about how people need health care and he wanted to help provide it. But after our conversation he said he felt used by the doctors he had been letting into his building. After that meeting, the pastor banned the vascular screening group from coming back to his church's health fairs.

Will Bruhn would go on to write studies on the harms and costs of overscreening, and Caitlin led a national effort to address predatory screening for peripheral vascular disease. Caitlin's standing in the field of vascular surgery enabled her to raise awareness and inspire medical students and residents to study the appropriateness of care as an academic field.[15] Ultimately, the experiences we gained helped us shape a national project that I'll explore further later in the book, called Improving Wisely, a multistakeholder collaborative aimed at addressing the issue of appropriateness in medicine.

Caitlin and I felt that we had a moral responsibility to do something with the physician-specific data from our research. We decided to send the list of outlier physicians to the Centers for Medicare & Medicaid Services (CMS) and to the Society for Vascular Surgery. We sent a letter to each with a list of the outliers by name and each physician's individual raw data. CMS responded by creating a new system to monitor for this egregious practice pattern, and the Society for Vascular Surgery launched a program to address the issue, placing Dr. Hicks as its leader.

We subsequently learned one of the physicians was arrested and others were reined in. Moreover, many doctors improved their practice patterns once the word was out that they were not practicing in a vacuum; i.e., that respected peers were looking at outlier data patterns. The idea of sharing data on outliers would spawn a successful national quality improvement initiative to reduce unnecessary and costly medical care, which I'll describe later in this book. What I would learn is that data transparency works.[16]

I reached out to more pastors in minority communities around the country and again took to the road to learn more. After attending a conference in Duck, North Carolina, where I spoke about the overscreenings targeting black churches, a hospital board member in the audience walked up and thanked me. His name was Bishop Kim Brown, pastor of Mt. Lebanon Baptist Church, a large, predominantly African American church serving the northern North Carolina and southern Virginia area. I shared more of my team's research findings with him. He was upset but not surprised, responding "This makes sense. Doctor groups and wellness companies are always calling us trying to get in our churches."

I assumed Bishop Brown was talking about church health fairs, but what he said next really shocked me. "Sometimes they want to come do health fairs, but sometimes they want to come in on Sunday after the service and set up a screening area," he said. The idea of the medical industry intruding on Sunday worship brought to mind the biblical account of Jesus throwing the merchants out of the temple.

I explained to him that some of these tests were unwarranted and done to create downstream business. Bishop Brown thanked me. "We are just trying to take care of our people," Bishop Brown told me. "Unless someone with expertise is honest with me, I don't know what to believe."

Getting Proximate

The business of medicine operates in even more disturbing ways. My next series of trips would teach me how the modern-day business model has even ventured into price gouging and predatory billing. Collectively, the two root issues driving health care's cost crisis—the appropriateness of care and pricing failures—would become increasingly vivid. In total, the many examples of clinical and administrative waste I witnessed violated everything my father, a cancer specialist, had taught me about being a good doctor. Yet every time I was tempted toward cynicism, I encountered people fighting back, innovators and visionaries who are disrupting health care to address these underlying problems and lower your health care costs. This book is my way of sharing their stories with you. By being proximate to the problem, they are charting a way forward.

After I left my meeting with the D.C. pastor, I drove home. Again, I passed the U.S. Capitol building. Though it was getting dark, I could still make out the flags around the Washington Monument flapping in the cool evening wind. At that moment Congress was meeting in a special session to talk about health care funding. As I passed the U.S. House of Representatives, I wondered if they had the slightest idea of what was truly crippling health care. The politicians debated how to *fund* health care, but what we really need to talk about is how to *fix* health care. While they made grand speeches and exchanged rhetorical fire calling for more funding, the business of medicine was humming just down the street, in the churches of our nation's capital.

If the politicians truly want to see why health care costs so much, perhaps they should suspend their arguments and take a field trip to the local churches. They would only have to travel two miles down the street.

CHAPTER 2

Welcome to the Game

My listening tour began locally with Henri, a master's degree student at George Washington University. Everything had gone well at the university's Parents' Weekend until Henri's dad, Adam, started getting chest pains while out for dinner. Adam was from France, so falling ill on the other side of the ocean created a crisis. Unfamiliar with the U.S. health care system, the *famille* was about to get an education.

Henri and his dad went to the closest emergency department, where the doctors discovered Adam had suffered a minor heart attack. The doctors stabilized him with medication and he spent a night in the facility. The next morning the doctors recommended a heart bypass operation—electively, that is, sometime in the coming weeks. Before Adam got discharged, a hospital representative came to his bedside to talk finances. He explained that the operation would cost $150,000.

Henri and his parents had no way to know whether this was a fair price. They called a family friend who put them in touch with a good heart surgeon in France. Over the phone, the French surgeon explained that the quality of the operation would be the same in France as it would be in the United States. The family timidly asked how much the operation would cost in France. "About 15,000 U.S. dollars," said the French surgeon.

Soon after, the local hospital representative who provided the $150,000 quote visited Henri's dad again to ask about their plans.

"Quite honestly, we are thinking of having the surgery in France for $15,000," Adam said.

Without hesitation, the hospital representative dropped the price to $50,000.

Alarmed at the sudden discount, Adam politely declined the offer and booked his flight to France. But as he walked out of the facility, the hospital representative approached him in the hallway one last time. Desperate to close the deal, the hospital official made a final offer: "Okay, we'll do it for $25,000."

Henri's family was disturbed by the ethics of a hospital that would try to charge $150,000 for something they would do for $25,000. They didn't expect a hospital to operate like a used car lot. Their trust had been shattered. I empathized with them. The hospital had tried to take advantage of them when they were vulnerable.

Adam had the surgery in France for $15,000 with a good outcome. "We loved our American doctors," Henri told me over a drink. "It was the business of medicine that turned us off."

The way the hospital haggled with Henri's family reminded me of Egypt's famous Khan el-Khalili bazaar, the largest open-air market in the world. The bazaar makes the floor of the Chicago Board of Trade look like a Presbyterian prayer group. It's a bustling shopping center for Egyptian locals and a tourist trap extraordinaire for any foreigner, especially if you wear a fanny pack. The millions of items of merchandise are sold without a price tag. Instead, the prices are set by how much merchants think they can get someone to pay.

The Arabic merchants are so good they have a global reputation for their sales tactics. They track your eyes to see what you look at twice and what makes you smile. If you ask the price of an alabaster replica of one of the famed Egyptian pyramids, they tell you it's $100. It may be worth $1. Some tourists fall into the trap and fork over the full price. Others nervously ask for a small discount and then pat themselves on the back for paying $90. The real wheeler-dealer shoppers counteroffer even lower and negotiate the price down to $50. They walk away bragging about their great deal. But it's the merchant who invariably wins. That's the markup and discount game.

At auto dealerships in the United States, you read the price on the windshield of a gleaming car and the salesperson says "I can talk to my manager about that." Then he or she drops the price and says "We're losing money on this sale to you." It's the same old dog and pony show.

Increasingly, we see the same markup and discount game in medicine. Hospital charges are notoriously inflated—and hard to pin to any actual costs. Each insurance company negotiates a different discount, which varies depending on who has the leverage. The result is that insured patients don't pay full price, unless their insurance carrier doesn't have a contract. Then they're "out-of-network" and face whatever the hospital decides to charge.

The only difference between the game in car sales and health care is the size of the margin. For the car dealer, getting people to pay sticker price can mean making 15% more off the sale. But for a hospital, gouging the sick and injured can mean making 1,000% more.

Henri's dad was lucky to get any price quote. In a study conducted by the University of Iowa, researchers called 101 U.S. hospitals and asked them what they would charge for the same type of heart bypass operation. Only about half of the hospitals—53 of them— would even provide the price. And for those hospitals that did, the average price was $151,271, just north of what Henri's dad was quoted. The range of prices was astounding, from $44,000 to $448,000. Did they use gold-plated surgical instruments? No. Was the center that charged ten times more the one with the best outcomes? Nope. Heart surgery outcomes are publicly available. The research showed no correlation between surgery price and quality.[1]

Would-be Robin Hoods

To understand the mystery of why some health care bills seem to defy logic, I asked my research team to dig deeper, to find out exactly how much medical bills were being marked up. It was an impressive group that took a deep dive into the national data. Medical students Angela Park and Tim Xu rose to the challenge and crunched numbers with the help of two of my Hopkins colleagues, Ge Bai, an accountant on faculty at the Johns Hopkins business school, and Jerry Anderson, a mentor of mine in our Department of Health Policy and Management.

The analysis revealed some markups to be 23 times higher than what was paid by Medicare (the government's insurance program) for the exact same service.[2] Were hospitals that tacked on giant markups simply located in poorer communities where patients were less likely to pay their bills? Our research found no association. It seemed strange that some hospitals just happened to have excessive prices while others did not.

I gently introduced the topic of markups with hospital leaders I met at conferences. Most had no idea how their markups compared to those of other hospitals. And many offered the simple explanation "We have to make up the cost of taking care of the uninsured."

But was that true? Were they really forced to upcharge some patients to compensate for charity care? They may have believed that explanation, but none of them could substantiate the claim with anything more than a hunch or an anecdote. We checked: the data did not support their assertion.

"It's a stupid game."

Every several months I am invited to a closed-door meeting of health care leaders who want to talk "big picture." Most of these gatherings convene with the lofty goal of fixing health care but quickly digress into pontificating about issues that account for less than 1% of health care costs. For example, we'll discuss ways to lower infection rates and hospital readmissions rather than tackling the leading drivers of our cost crisis. But one such meeting I attended was a refreshing exception.

This meeting, hosted by the Oliver Wyman Innovation Center, a global consulting firm, took place at a beautiful resort in Laguna

Beach, California. I was there with about 30 high-level executives from hospitals, insurance companies, and health care start-ups. The resort was perched on a cliff overlooking the ocean, so we enjoyed breathtaking views. Morning runs on the beach were followed by delectable breakfasts. But most refreshing was the honest conversation. Unlike most of these types of gatherings, this one was filled with straight talk without stakeholder agendas.

We got right to business. The group acknowledged the rising price of health care and began asking the hard questions. Maybe it was the off-the-record nature of the meeting, or maybe it was just the sea air and California sunshine, but these titans of health care spoke freely. Hospital officials confessed that they inflate bills more and more each year to generate more revenue since their insurance companies pay only part of the sticker prices. Insurers confessed they demand bigger and bigger discounts in their contracts with hospitals in order to keep up. Both acknowledged that they pass on higher hospital bills to the public in the form of higher insurance premiums.

It was a lively, civil, candid conversation. At one point, Dr. René Lerer, the president of the large insurance company GuideWell Florida Blue, silenced the room with his honesty: "Insurers fight for a bigger discount every time they renew a contract with a hospital. Then hospitals go around and inflate their prices. It's a game." He seemed disgusted by the markup-discount games everyone in health care has come to accept as standard operating procedure.

"We play it, you play it, we all play it. Let's not fool ourselves," he added. "It's a stupid game. We can do better."

If anyone had the authority to identify the problem, it was Dr. Lerer. He's been a practicing doctor and a health care executive, and he heads a well-regarded insurance company. I braced myself for backlash from the room, but an amazing thing happened: no one disagreed. Even if they didn't admit it, everyone knew it was a game.

One by one, people meekly began to try justifying markups and discounts. Some blamed other stakeholders in health care; others attributed the collateral damage to out-of-network patients. But one by one, like a round of whack-a-mole, Lerer shot down the excuses. "Yes, that's true," he'd say, "but it's still a game."

We discussed all kinds of issues that weekend, but they were all footnotes to the problem Dr. Lerer had named: whether we liked it or not, we were all playing "the game."

What does the game do? For one, it makes it nearly impossible for patients to know in advance what they will pay, but it enables insurance companies to have an agreed-upon discount rate on hospital bills. That discount rate is different for every hospital and a highly guarded trade secret. From talking to enough people in the industry, I learned that the secret discount that an insurance company gets ranges from 4 to 90%. But if you're paying cash, like Henri's dad, no one will tell you the discount given to insurance companies. With all the talk of addressing disparities in America, I'm amazed there can be radically different prices for the exact same medical care at the same facility by the same doctors and nurses.

Journalists have been busy trying to expose the game. A recent study found that the cost of a hospital bed alone during a routine childbirth can range from $1,000 to $12,000 per night. Johnny Harris, a journalist from Vox.com, read about the study and decided to shop around for the best deal before his wife gave birth. He called several hospitals to ask how much they would charge per night for his wife's delivery. He spent more than three hours on the phone getting put on hold and transferred. Finally, one hospital staff member told him he would not be able to find out the cost until *after* the baby had been born.[3] And that's for childbirth, one of the easier quotes to track down, since so many people are now asking.

Why couldn't Johnny get a price? A hospital's true costs are as mysterious as the curse of King Tut. There's good reason for the fog—it's lucrative.

I don't want to be too hard on people in the medical field (after all, I am one of them). My interactions with hospital leaders have been very positive. When it comes to pricing, I don't believe they're intentionally hiding what's available to them. Most of the time, the insurance companies don't let hospitals show their negotiated prices; they've made the hospital sign a nondisclosure clause in their operating agreement.[4] Plus, coming up with a price can be hard work for a hospital. Imagine trying to factor in the price of the janitor, the front desk person, the electricity, the malpractice insurance, the nurse's time, the supplies used, and all the rest. That's why smaller surgical centers are more likely to be able to produce a price (and, on average, a lower one). Hospitals, in order to ensure they have enough cash on hand on a macro level,

The book I'd like to write[5]

spend a lot of energy playing the markup and discount game. In fact, they are consumed by it. For example, if a hospital made $100 million the prior year, dialing up all bills by 5% as their expenses go up by 4% is a safe bet without having to accurately itemize every service. Hospitals use software called the "chargemaster" that automatically inflates prices to achieve a desired margin.

Markups are now so high that they are embarrassing for doctors and hospitals. It's only natural that the good people working at America's hospitals would react to questions by answering "That's to compensate for charity care," or "Don't worry, people are not expected to pay those prices." Given our research data, neither explanation seemed accurate, so I set out to explore each of these explanations in more detail.

Consider what happened to my friend Fred. He was skiing in Vail, Colorado, when he started to feel a little "off." After a few trips down the slopes, Fred developed a headache. He also felt a bit light-headed. To play it safe, he had his wife drive him to a nearby hospital. There, a triage nurse listened to his story, and then leaned in close. "You have a touch of altitude sickness," the nurse whispered. "We see it all the time. You didn't hear it from me, but I would suggest you go back to your hotel and drink some water."

Fred should have taken her advice. Instead, he decided to see the doctor. Within an hour, the doctor delivered the same diagnosis the nurse had given: altitude sickness. They gave Fred a whiff of oxygen and discharged him. A few weeks later, Fred's brief trip to the hospital was a fading memory. That's when he got a bill for $11,000. Suddenly he was light-headed again.

He was outraged for good reason. My hospital in Baltimore, for example, would charge $800 for the same service. Why was the bill marked up? Did the hospital by the Vail ski resort take care of so many low-income and uninsured skiers that it had to make up for all its charity care? No, Fred was the victim of a business model that has become all too common in American medicine: price gouging.

Desperate for Honest Pricing

When discussing astronomical medical costs, hospital CEOs often tell me, "Marty, nobody pays those chargemaster prices." They point out that insurance companies have discounts. "Those are just the sticker prices. You wouldn't ever be asked to pay that price." But as I researched the issue, I discovered categories of people who are explicitly and sternly told they must pay those inflated sticker prices.

The Amish, who have a large community near my childhood hometown in Pennsylvania, believe in paying their bills in full. As a student rotating at a hospital in that area, I saw Amish people show up in the ICU with bags of cash. Their community would pool funds from their farmer's market to pay medical expenses.

My colleague Jerry Anderson has done research on markups and has become a go-to person for some of the Amish leaders in America. One day an Amish leader in Indiana called Jerry, begging him for help in negotiating a bill for a man in his community. The man's child had complications at birth and the hospital charged the man—in effect, the Amish community—a million dollars for services that would have cost less than $300,000 if a private insurer was paying. Jerry told the Amish leader to send him the bill because he was going to be seeing the head of the hospital at a reception in Washington, D.C. At the event, Jerry quickly made the case to the head of the hospital, and the price was reduced to less than $200,000. Ironically, it turns out that the Amish had helped build the hospital. If Jerry hadn't gotten involved, the Amish community would have rounded up all its cash and somehow managed to pay the bill in full, paying five times what it cost the hospital to provide the service.

I decided to take a road trip into Amish country to learn more. Will joined me for the trip. We began our day at the Amish Farmers Market in a town called Bird-in-Hand, Pennsylvania, deep in the heart of Amish country. Half of the Amish people we interviewed said that when they or a relative gets a serious sickness, they take the Amtrak train to Mexico. Why? Because the medical quality is good and the prices are fair and disclosed up front. Will and I interviewed dozens more Amish people, everyone from those who sold us sticky buns to those stepping out of their horse and buggy. I couldn't believe what I was hearing. Our next stop was the local Amtrak train station where we learned that some trains are half-full of Amish people taking the six-day ride to Mexico for medical care. Mexican hospitals even advertise in the Amtrak magazine. It's incredible how far people will go for honest medical pricing. Uninsured patients who make too much money to qualify for Medicaid also get hit with the inflated sticker price. If they don't pay up, they get sent to collections, which means they're hassled by debt collectors and have their credit ruined. Debt collectors can be ruthless and often violate consumer protection laws.

Then there are the "surprise" bills—bills for costs a patient presumed were covered by insurance but were not. About half of these bills are for lab work, facility charges, or imaging tests.[6] The other half of surprise bills are generated by doctors working behind the scenes, such as pathologists or radiologists, who may be out of your insurance network, meaning they don't have a negotiated discount rate with your insurance company. The same could be true for your emergency room physician, or the lab that processes your blood tests, or the anesthesiologist who puts you to sleep. Your primary surgeon or obstetrician may be in-network, but you could have an out-of-network doctor put in your epidural or perform the pediatric hearing test on your newborn. You may not realize that a doctor or lab didn't have a discount contract with your insurance company until weeks later. And those surprise bills are issued at the inflated sticker price.

Surprise bills are common. In 2015, the Consumer Reports National Research Center estimated that 30% of Americans received a surprise medical bill. But just three years later, another study found it was about double that figure. The University of Chicago reported that 57% of Americans received a surprise bill in the previous year.[7] Another study of New Mexico residents found that more than half of people who had gone to the emergency room got a surprise bill.[8]

The concept of a surprise bill really bothered me as a physician. Ever since my eager high school days when I accompanied my physician father to his clinic as an observer, I saw how preparing patients for the unexpected was part of the art of medicine. Dad explained to leukemia patients up front everything they might experience in the course of their treatments. The modern-day surprise bills of medicine seem to violate a heritage of honest doctoring.

Genius

True geniuses are rare. But every few years, one shows up in my office. Tim Xu, the John Hopkins medical student I mentioned above, is one of them. He asked if he could observe my research team meetings. But unlike other students, Tim didn't just sit there. He first looked up, read, and nearly memorized all 200-plus articles I have ever written in the medical literature. During the meeting discussion, he chimed in with deep insights and corrected errors with catlike reflexes. Every time the young gun rattled off formulas, theories, and article citations in seconds without hesitation, I could barely keep up. Tim blew all of us away. "I've heard about super geniuses like him," said Dr. Susan Hutfless, a Harvard grad and PhD statistician on my team, after a meeting Tim attended.

Before coming to Hopkins medical school, Tim graduated summa cum laude from Vanderbilt, earned a master's at Cambridge in mathematics, and started a genomics company. In his free time during medical school, he completed the health care management track at the consulting firm McKinsey & Company. I think Tim was bored in medical school. His massive brain probably explains why he had the time to publish ten research studies with my research team as a medical student.

One day at our research meeting Tim proposed a highly mathematical study of medical bills to understand how they are being marked up. He was the right man for this study. Over the next several weeks, Tim showed me data on the complexities of medical bill inflation, pointing out the randomness of price setting and the stratagems for hiking charges. Tim was the lead author on our study that found that emergency room bills were marked up a lot more than what the internal medicine department charged for the same services.[9] Tim and Angela also conducted a similar study of cancer care, which yielded similar findings. The markups certainly did not correlate with the amount of free medical care the hospital was providing, or with how poor the patient population was.

The game is absurd. Think of the problem of being out-of-network. The recommended solution is to join the network. The game proposes a solution that exists only because it created the problem in the first place. The network is both the firefighter and the blaze. It's the savior and bogeyman, the police officer and perpetrator. We have come to accept this as standard operating procedure in the business of medicine. But somebody needs to ask: Did anyone ever intend things to get this bad? While networks served a purpose, they are now the very reason we have surprise bills and lives ruined by financial toxicity.

After Tim wrote his momentous papers on price markups, he mentioned to me that he had one more rotation to complete before finishing medical school. He was going to be working in a hospital's emergency room. This would be great, I thought. Tim did a study looking at the big picture and gave us a global perspective in his study. Now he could zoom in to the granular level, examining the problem from inside a single emergency department. I couldn't wait for Tim to get to the bottom of it. I told him to talk to emergency department doctors and business people in charge of billing to see if he could discern any rhyme or reason for the markups on emergency room bills. He eagerly agreed to investigate it from the inside.

A few month later we exchanged text messages:

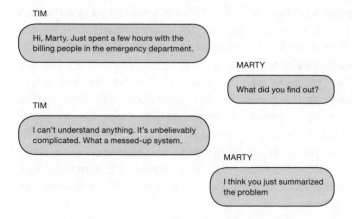

TIM

Hi, Marty. Just spent a few hours with the billing people in the emergency department.

MARTY

What did you find out?

TIM

I can't understand anything. It's unbelievably complicated. What a messed-up system.

MARTY

I think you just summarized the problem

If a genius like Tim can't understand how medical bills are created, the average patient doesn't stand a chance.

Who Gets Played

Ron and Heather, close friends of my sister and her husband, are among those who fell prey to the game. One day when I stopped by my sister's house, I bumped into them when they were over for dinner. They heard I was writing a book on the cost crisis in medicine and told me about the time Heather went to the Washington Hospital Center, a prominent Washington, D.C., hospital, for a small skin growth on her finger. Months later, she got smacked with a $10,000 bill. It included an $87 charge for blankets. No, these were not handwoven Persian shrouds. They were ordinary soft white coverlets such as one finds in a hotel room.

Heather sent me the bill. I had a tough time deciphering it. But one thing was easy to see: they had put her under general anesthesia for a minor procedure on her finger.

"Why did you have general anesthesia to remove a skin tag on your finger?" I asked Heather. They had basically shaved something off her finger—closer to a haircut than a medical operation.

"I don't know," Heather told me. "We thought it was going to be done by simply numbing the area. I was shocked. Someone came in just before they took me into surgery and said, 'We are going to be doing general anesthesia,' even though I told them I didn't want general anesthesia." Nevertheless, in her frightened and intimidated state, general anesthesia is what she got.

The couple have six children and had about the same income as the average American household, about $59,000. Their $10,000 bill was devastating.

I called the hospital on Heather's behalf and asked them to explain to me, a surgeon, why was general anesthesia required for a procedure that could have been done with local numbing medication? And why did her blankets cost $87?

The representative who picked up the phone insisted that Heather and I complete a patient privacy authorization form, which we did. They accept these forms only by fax. (For younger readers, a fax machine is a device that humans used in the last century to transmit photocopies across telephone lines.)

Once I called to confirm that the authorization form had been received, I requested an itemized bill. I was told this had to be done in writing by ground mail. (For young readers, ground mail was a way people sent written documents, like letters, from the 1600s through the late twentieth century.)

Two months after I sent my letter requesting an itemized bill by ground mail, I received in my mailbox a letter from the hospital explaining that there is a $25 fee to receive a copy of the itemized bill. The letter went on to explain that the request had to be sent by mail (no self-addressed envelope was included) and that the $25 had to be paid with a paper check. (For younger readers, paper checks are pieces of paper on which one person designates an amount of money to be withdrawn from their bank account and given to another person).

After months of forms and delays, I finally had the itemized bill in my hand and authorization to speak for my friend Heather. I'm a patient person, but by this time I was feeling irritated. I let the billing representative have it. I went on a 15-minute rant, citing the unnecessary general anesthesia and the needless hassle even to get the itemized bill, let alone have a conversation about it.

She stayed so silent that I thought I might be getting through to her. But then, like an Olympic boxer playing possum, she perked up and said, "The law allows us to charge whatever we want. If we want to charge a million dollars, she has to pay it."

I reminded the representative that the hospital, a nonprofit facility, was price-gouging a woman in the community for medical care that was excessive. I asked them to reduce the bill to the Medicare allowable amount of $750. She transferred me to her supervisor, who repeated her party line position. As I was getting ready to escalate the issue to the hospital CEO and board members to educate them, Heather, threatened by bill collectors, paid the amount in full to avoid further damage to her credit rating.

Heather is not alone. *Half* of metastatic (Stage 4) breast cancer patients in the United States report being pursued by a collection agency for their medical bills, according to a large study conducted in 41 states.[10] As a cancer surgeon, hearing the details made me sick to my stomach. Is this what the noble profession of cancer care has become? Is this really how our society now treats breast cancer patients at the end of their life?

The game is out of control, and that's yet another reason health care costs so much. Hospitals and insurance companies spend a ton of money playing the game—the staff, the infrastructure, the subcontractors. In addition to the collection side, hospitals and insurers have small armies of business people who negotiate discounts. Doctors and nurses don't see these people. Their offices are off campus, even tucked away in the tallest skyscrapers in some big cities. Some doctors complain about the growth in hospital administration. But hospitals have to hire a lot of business people to participate in the game.

We see the game at work when we see hospital prices rocket up year after year. Consider joint replacement surgery. Medicare pays less than $13,000 for the standard operation, yet one in six U.S. hospitals charge more than $90,000 for it. And the prices go up year after year,[11] even though it's the same people doing the surgery. How does one explain this price variation and these price spikes in just one year?[12]

The game creates a giant middle layer of health care: the repricing industry, dedicated to negotiating bills among three or four parties after care is delivered. As I learned when attending one of their conferences, it has thousands of consultants and vendors, and well-paid middlemen. The bureaucracy on the hospital side is also large. One study found that for every ten doctors, the average

The Surge of Medical Prices for Joint Replacement Surgery

MEDICAL CENTER	PRICE*	CHANGE FROM PRIOR YEAR
St. Francis Medical Center, Trenton, NJ	$135.4K	+76.8%
Lutheran Medical Center, Brooklyn, NY	$115.0K	+55.5%
Highland Hospital, Leominster, MA	$114.1K	+43.2%
Community Howard Regional Health, Kokomo, IN	$79.2K	+73.6%
Arrowhead Regional Medical Center, Colton, CA	$96.3K	+42.6%

*2016 prices; Medicare pays 13K for the same procedure

U.S. hospital has seven nonclinical full-time-equivalent (FTE) staff working on billing and insurance functions.[13] Health care has been one of the leading drivers of job growth in the United States, a trend that has made it the leading industry in the U.S. economy. But is this industry of new hires who are "playing the game" generating a product? Is this game making a meaningful contribution to our country's GDP? Or is it a bubble?

Although the game gets scant attention in the news or in health reform debates, it explains many health care trends. It's the reason hospitals are on a buying spree, snapping up private practices and other hospitals.[14] It explains insurance company mergers. The players need power when they clash in the markup-discount game. It explains why health care stakeholders spent $514 million lobbying Congress in 2016. They need to keep their footing on the playing field.

These middlemen have nothing to do with removing a tumor, hammering in a hip replacement, sewing a pancreas, or comforting a patient. Yet their will often prevails over the providers of all of these services. This mammoth behind-the-scenes industry has created tens of thousands of millionaires. When people wonder why health care costs so much in the United States, they must remember that the cost of the giant repricing industry is built into the cost of medical services. The question no one in the health care establishment has been asking is: Do we really need it?

A Carrot

The American people are hungry for *real* prices, not the inflated "chargemaster" prices. Making real prices public would infuse much-needed competition into health care's bloated $3.5 trillion market. To manage rising hospital prices, insurers have responded by designing plans with higher deductibles and copays. But that's not real relief. For too long, the black box of real prices has been protected as a trade secret, resulting in medical centers competing on the level of better parking and NFL game day billboards rather than on quality and value.

The absence of real prices also fuels the problem of surprise bills and predatory billing. Conversely, predatory billing practices are rare in the few health care sectors that have already adopted real price transparency, including cosmetic surgery, in vitro fertilization, and LASIK surgery. In these markets, true competition has resulted in a global reduction in prices over time and has appropriately rewarded high-quality physicians. As Congress and many states consider new legislation to rein in surprise bills, they should consider how transparency of real prices could address the underlying root problem.

Critics of real price transparency have argued that patients do not use price information when choosing where to go for their care and, when they do, they may sometimes choose the most expensive service because they are not paying for it. But asking how many patients will shop for care using price information is not the right question because proxy shoppers[15]—self-insured employers, health plans, and some patients who pay out of pocket—will use real price information to drive the market for everyone.

Proxy shoppers are common in other businesses. Think about what happens in the grocery business. Only some customers at a grocery store look at the price of produce and comparison shop, oranges to oranges, with other stores. Yet those who aggressively comparison shop create the demand for grocery stores to keep their prices competitive in order to retain the business of the small fraction who price shop, which in turn benefits all shoppers.

Critics also argue that prices are impossible to produce for emergency care. But no one is suggesting you are quoted a price if you are shot in the chest. Sixty percent of medical care is shoppable, representing a large opportunity for competition to reward centers with high quality and fair prices.

The debate over what percentage of patients will use pricing information has been a distracting argument used by special interests. The issue is not how many people will look at prices. It's whether we as a country will empower proxy shoppers to drive value in health care.

Once real prices are available, Google should consider putting a hospital's average "markup" on a hospital's information card when a person searches a hospital. And hospital ratings organizations such as *U.S. News* and Medicare's 5-star rating program should factor a hospital's price quality and predatory billing practices when calculating a rank score. Given the heavy toll on patients, and its downstream impact on patients avoiding care in the future, financial harm should be considered a complication of medical care.

When you go to a restaurant and ask for a menu, you might be alarmed if the waiter or waitress were to respond by asking, "Who's your employer?" If you then learned that the prices on your menu were much higher than those on menus given to other customers, you'd conclude it's a dysfunctional market. Yet this is exactly what happens when you need medical care in our status quo system today.

But some smart people are now disrupting that status quo. Adam Russo is CEO of a Boston business that is self-insured— that is, his company directly pays for his employees' medical bills. He's one example of a proxy shopper. By virtue of his business, a consulting firm that reviews the medical bills of its clients, he sees wide variation in medical prices for common services in the Boston area. In particular, he observed that the cost of a standard uncomplicated baby delivery in Boston ranged from $8,000 to $40,000. The least expensive and the most expensive hospitals have the same quality. So Adam, a business leader who likes to try new ideas, decided to give any employee who delivers at one of the $8,000 hospitals (like South Shore hospital), free diapers and wipes for a year! Guess where every pregnant employee of his started going for their prenatal care? The $8,000 hospitals. Even though they had the ability to go to any hospital and have it fully covered by the company. The women didn't price shop, they only quality shopped. Adam successfully demonstrated the power of proxy buyers empowered with price information.

An American Revolution?

"I don't understand how a hospital can welcome a patient and then turn around and put them in medical bankruptcy." Dr. Keith

Smith, an anesthesiologist and health care reformer, spoke these words to a grassroots gathering of doctors a few years ago. About 100 people from 10 states attended, at the historic Skirvin Hotel in downtown Oklahoma City. I had flown down to join them and learn more. This was the first medical "tea party" meeting of its kind, and the group later became what is now called the Free Market Medical Association.

Dr. Smith's damning statement resonated. The atmosphere in the room suddenly felt heavy. We sat in silence, reflecting on how far our profession had deviated from its noble heritage. We had gone into medicine to take care of the sick and injured, not to take advantage of them. Smith is a soft-spoken man with a disarming Southern drawl. But he becomes animated when discussing the lack of transparency in health care.

This was my first time meeting Smith. He had invited me to this impromptu conference to discuss how to change the game. Innovators like Smith are rewriting the rulebook in favor of patients. The message that greets visitors to the website for the Surgery Center of Oklahoma, which Smith leads, is simple—but it's revolutionary in the health care industry: "You can and should know the price."

Honest pricing is like kryptonite to the game. The website for Smith's surgery center features an interactive menu of their prices for common procedures.

There is no game being played at Smith's surgery center. Everyone gets one fair price, whether it's an insurance company paying, an employer paying directly for their employees' health care, or an individual patient paying out of pocket.

Smith is a free market champion. His convictions about transparent pricing stem in part from studying free market competition. He and his colleagues have treated hundreds of people from outside the United States, including patients from Canada, Mexico, and Japan. What would make a Japanese person fly to Oklahoma City for treatment? It's American medicine with price transparency. Furthermore, because his surgery center is honest with their pricing, Smith believes patients are more trusting and satisfied.

Smith has not only attracted increased business with this simple idea, he has also saved the millions of dollars in overhead that's usually required to play the game with insurers. As a matter of principle, the hospital carves out resources for free care, which is part of their mission to the community. His surgery center is especially popular among employers who self-fund their employee's medical care, since they are protected from price gouging.

As you can imagine, his surgery center in Oklahoma has enemies. Some feel threatened by Smith's price transparency model, especially if it becomes contagious. It could force competing medical centers to show prices and compete in a real marketplace. Many people at the conference said they've been bullied by insurance companies and hospitals in their area for showing their prices. Insurance companies like having secret discounts and networks.[16] Those secret discounts are what insurance companies sell to employers who are essentially buying hospital services in bulk through an insurance company. Hospitals, in turn, rely on insurance companies to send them a steady stream of business. The self-preservation efforts of the stakeholders are so strong that California lawmakers had to pass a law to prevent insurance companies from retaliating against hospitals that disclose prices.

I had been sharing what I learned from Smith with other doctors and hospital officials when speaking at medical conferences. Frequently, someone in the audience would ask one important question: Is price transparency good for a medical group's business?

I asked my research team to study the few medical groups in the country that have gone from the old way of doing business—giving patients sticker shock after their surgery—to doing business with full price transparency. Our study was led by Dr. Ambar Mehta, an inquisitive Hopkins medical student who is now a surgical resident at Columbia University Medical Center in New York City. His findings were dramatic. Centers that initiated full price transparency saw a 50% increase in patient volume, a 30% increase in revenue, and an increase in patient satisfaction.[17] People are sick and tired of the game.

Two brilliant minds—David Goldhill, a business genius and author of *Catastrophic Care* and the *Atlantic* cover story "How American Health Care Killed My Father," and Mike Botta, a young, enthusiastic Harvard health economics PhD—are taking things one step further. They created an impressive website where doctors can post real cash prices for medical services—an online marketplace where consumers can schedule an in-person consultation or talk directly with a doctor virtually and on demand. I've joined their effort, called Sesame (SesameCare.com)—a new medical marketplace that is rapidly growing nationwide.

It's ironic that the federal government already has a mandatory disclosure rule for the real out-of-pocket costs people incur at a vulnerable time in their lives. But it's not a rule for health care—it's for funeral homes. The Funeral Rule,[18] enacted by the Federal Trade Commission in 1984, requires funeral providers to offer itemized pricing information to consumers before they purchase any services. The rationale is that consumers in a distressing situation should have honest pricing information, a rule that should also apply to the living, not just the dead.

As a surgeon, I can tell you firsthand that patients and their families are also vulnerable when they seek medical care. There should be no excuse for taking advantage of them. But American health care is so crazy that as long as you are alive, you are susceptible to being taken advantage of by the game. Ironically, once you're dead, federal law protects you.

CHAPTER 3

Carlsbad

We boarded the single-propeller plane on a beautiful West Texas afternoon. The sun heated the tarmac and glinted off the wings of the tiny aircraft. The young pilot instructed us to buckle up, and moments later, the eight-seater wobbled into the air. After two hours of flying over the desert, we landed on a small airstrip in Carlsbad, New Mexico. Upon arrival, nobody checked our credentials. This remote outpost seemed long forgotten by the TSA.

The town of 25,000 had no Uber or Lyft. Its little airport had no rental car company. Fortunately, I'd called ahead. The hotel couldn't help me, so I'd phoned City Hall. They gave me a number for Betty, a local resident recruited by the city government to give people rides. Suggested fee: $2. I was relieved we didn't have to resort to Plan B: walking to our hotel through the desert with our luggage. My medical student, Will Bruhn, had joined me for the journey.

I hear from hundreds of patients each year who have been harmed or ripped off by the medical system. But the hardships faced by a woman named Jennifer and other Carlsbad patients were unlike anything I'd ever heard. Will and I had traveled all this way to talk to patients like Jennifer, a mother of four young children, two of whom had special needs.

Before we flew to Carlsbad, Jennifer had explained her situation to me over the phone. Her three-week-old baby girl became sick and had to be rushed to Carlsbad Medical Center, the town's only hospital. Even though Jennifer and her husband had health insurance, her deductible was high and they couldn't afford to pay the hospital's inflated medical bill. The hospital didn't work with her or negotiate. Instead, the hospital sued her, won a judgment, and garnished her husband's wages—meaning they took money from his paycheck without his permission.

Not long after, her five-year-old daughter came down with the flu. Again, Jennifer had to go to Carlsbad Medical Center, where they gave her little girl IV fluids and a nebulizer breathing treatment. The child improved, but the IV became infected. The infection turned into sepsis, a life-threatening condition in which an infection spreads through the blood to multiple organs.

Jennifer explained to me that the pediatrician documented in her daughter's medical record that the hospital had caused the infection. Regardless, the family got stuck with a huge bill. Jennifer and her husband couldn't afford to pay the $2,400 portion not covered by insurance. Again, the hospital didn't work with the couple to help settle the bill—as medical facilities often do in these types of cases. Instead, the hospital sued them again. And they garnished Jennifer's husband's paycheck a second time.

On the phone before our trip, I had asked Jennifer if she knew anyone else who has been sued and had their paycheck garnished by the hospital. "Lots," she said.

Examining online court records, it was clear Jennifer wasn't the only person being sued by Carlsbad Medical Center. Hundreds of cases, maybe even thousands, were showing up on the local judicial docket. I told Will about Jennifer's story and the court records. Intrigued and alarmed, Will and I went to Carlsbad to check it out.

When our plane landed in Carlsbad, the pilot opened our door and personally grabbed our bags out of the cargo bin. We walked right off the runway to the parking lot, where Betty awaited with a giant smile.

"Well, you guys must be Marty and Will!" she said with a friendliness reminiscent of a recent visit to Minnesota. On the drive, the three of us began a fun conversation about Carlsbad. She pointed out the Walmart and City Hall and we observed a string of homes and storefronts that looked like classic Americana. The town reminded me of my hometown in rural Pennsylvania.

"What are you fine young gentlemen doing here? Are you visiting the caverns?" Betty asked, referring to the famous Carlsbad Caverns National Park.

"We're actually here to learn about the billing practices of Carlsbad Medical Center," I told her.

Betty went silent. Her peppy mood disappeared. I asked what she knew about the subject.

She told us her own story about dealing with the hospital's inflated bills and legal threats, even as a city employee with good insurance. She told me it's so bad that the city encourages its workers to drive more than an hour to the hospital in Roswell, the next town over, to avoid Carlsbad Medical Center.

She talked our ears off for the 20-minute ride before dropping us off at our hotel. I reached into my pocket to pay for our ride— four bucks for the two of us. I found a $20 bill and told her to keep the change. She thanked us profusely.

As we were checking into our hotel, the receptionist asked if we were there to visit the caverns.

"No, we're here to learn about the billing practices of the hospital," I said.

The receptionist froze. She motioned us over to a corner of the reception counter and in hushed tones unloaded her own family's story, pausing every few minutes to make sure we wouldn't name her as a source. We agreed to keep it off the record.

Her daughter—I'll call her Tina—worked as a housekeeper at Carlsbad Medical Center. One day, Tina developed an allergic reaction and went to the facility, where she received a steroid injection, a nebulizer treatment, and an IV. Tina was in the hospital for only a few hours but was billed thousands of dollars. From her description of her bill, it sounded as if she was charged about double what we would charge for the same service at Johns Hopkins. Tina was a single mom and worked a minimum wage job. She had health insurance, but the bill was below her deductible and much more than she could afford. She got sued—by the same hospital that employed her! The hospital won a judgment and garnished her wages—so her pay went from about $7.50 to $5.00 an hour to pay off the debt. The hotel receptionist said she had to watch her daughter's kids so that she could take on a second retail job and, later, a third job as a waitress. Tina eventually stopped working at the hospital. When she switched jobs, her garnishment was transferred to her waitressing job.

Tina's relationship with the hospital, which was both her employer and her debt collector, reminded me of the stories from my hometown in the northeastern coal country. In the 1800s, coal was king, yet the prosperous coal companies charged miners for their shovels. A miner could work months to pay off the cost of his shovel. If it broke, the miner would be charged for another at full retail price. All along, the miner ate food from the only company store near the mine. Company stores were known for high prices, since there was no competition in the remote mining areas. After a few months of hard labor, a miner might have no net income and instead *owe* money to the company for working there.

According to a Kaiser Family Foundation study, it's common for Americans to go through hardships like Tina's. The study found that 70% of them are cutting back on food, clothing, or other basic needs to pay medical bills.[1] The study also found 58% have taken an extra job or worked more hours to pay a medical bill, and 41% have borrowed money from friends or family to pay a bill. It's so bad that in a West Health Institute–University of Chicago nation-wide study, more respondents feared the cost of treating a serious illness than feared becoming ill.[2]

Will and I had been in Carlsbad, New Mexico, for only two hours and already two people we randomly met had shared nightmare stories of the hospital going after them. We went to our rooms, threw our bags down, cleaned up a bit, and then embarked on a trip with Betty to the courthouse.

The Courthouse

Most courthouses aren't hospitable, and the one in Carlsbad was no exception. After getting scolded by a security guard for not removing our belts, we went to the clerk's office and faced an intimidating row of bank-teller-type windows with a woman behind one of them. She gave us a "What do you want?" look as she began to speak. The thick glass muted her voice. I tried to talk in sound bites though tiny air holes in the glass, explaining that we wanted to review any available court records of the hospital suing patients. Her confusion about what we wanted quickly turned to frustration. She finally hit a button that projected her voice through a loudspeaker.

"You're here to do what again? Are you lawyers in a case?" she said with a stern look.

We introduced ourselves and explained that we were looking into Carlsbad Medical Center's practice of suing its patients. Suddenly something clicked. She buzzed us through a nearby door. The hostile atmosphere dissolved. She warmly shook our hands.

"Gentlemen, nice to meet you. So you're here to help people sued by Carlsbad hospital?"

We told her yes and politely explained how we wanted to find out how often the hospital sued its patients and garnished their wages. As I spoke, I noticed a handful of courthouse staffers sitting at their desks, eavesdropping.

The woman who let us in nodded. Another clerk mumbled "Oh, yes, thank you." One by one, the five women who worked in the clerk's office came to meet us.

"Carlsbad Medical Center is like 95% of the lawsuits here at the courthouse," said the clerk who handled civil cases.

"They go after everyone: old people, disabled people, people who can't pay, the insured, the uninsured, and they garnish their wages," added another administrator, a pleasant middle-aged woman who walked over to join the conversation. "They even garnished an old man's 401(k) retirement dividends."

"They went after my relative and garnished her wages," another court employee said.

A secretary for one of the judges came over. One of her family members was charged for simply going to the hospital, even though they never made it past the waiting room, leaving before getting any services.

The lady who buzzed us in the security door piled on another story. "We just had an old man here with one leg, in a wheelchair from a car accident. The insurance company paid the hospital about $300,000, but the hospital billed the man for another $300,000, and then went after him."

Almost every employee had a financial horror story about Carlsbad Medical Center. Moreover, they all had stories of other community members that had been sued and had their wages garnished.

Will and I dug into the court records and found thousands of garnishment cases. The hospital had won nearly every one. We estimated that about one in five people in that small town had been sued by the local hospital and had their wages garnished. The hospital was holding Carlsbad's citizens hostage to predatory billing practices.

I examined the copy of the medical bill from one lawsuit involving the medical center, but all the line items were blacked out. The charges and prices—so often inflated—had been redacted.

"Is that what the judge sees?" I asked the clerk. "Or can the judge see the line items that are blacked out here?"

"No, that's exactly the bill the judge sees."

"Well, how can the judge determine if the prices are appropriate?"

The clerk shrugged. "When the hospital alleges that a bill was not paid, it doesn't have to explain. The judge has little choice but to allow the garnishment."

The personal experiences of everyone we met in Carlsbad seemed consistent with what we saw in these court records—pay your bill in full, or you'll be served with a lawsuit and your wages will be garnished.

It's easy to look at the thousands of cases, long list of names on a docket, and forget these are people whose lives are being wrecked by predatory practices. Will and I looked up some of the locals involved in these Carlsbad Medical Center lawsuits and set out on house calls.

Hannah

Hannah was a high school teacher whose school was a short walk from our hotel. A geologist, she was two courses away from getting her PhD, and she had moved to Carlsbad to work for an oil company. After being laid off when oil prices dropped, she picked up the teaching gig at the University of New Mexico High School. She met us in her classroom as the alarm sounded and her students dispersed at the end of the day. After Will and I walked in, 31-year-old Hannah graciously pulled up small desk chairs and we sat around a table.

Hannah's bright smile faded as she explained how she had been sued multiple times by Carlsbad Medical Center and had her paycheck garnished, savings depleted, credit score cut in half. Fighting the hospital had also consumed every naptime for two years as she raised two babies.

It started when she noticed a small rubbery spot on her right leg just below her knee. Almost like a clot. She pointed it out to me on her leg and described what it felt like. I had seen these small superficial lumps before and knew that in the absence of leg swelling, they don't need any formal testing. I've treated these by recommending compression stockings, maybe an ibuprofen. Hannah knew that too, because she had previously had the problem and it went away. But this time she was pregnant and concerned the lump could dislodge and present a danger to the baby. I knew it wasn't dangerous but understood why a concerned mother-to-be would want to get it checked out.

The doctor at Carlsbad Medical Center did an ultrasound, even though one is not medically required for superficial clots below the knee. The charge for the ultrasound alone was $1,200. (It's $300 at Johns Hopkins.) The hospital did other tests with similarly inflated charges, then swiftly sued her for the full amount. Embarrassingly, she was served with the lawsuit at school by the sheriff's deputy. She called Carlsbad Medical Center ten times to straighten out the bill but never got it resolved.

"I've always had good insurance and documented everything," she explained. But each time Hannah got a bill, she became entrapped in a finger-pointing game between the hospital billing department, their collections agency, and her insurer. She could not get basic answers to her questions: Can I get an itemized bill? What does insurance pay? And what am I responsible for paying? The fog of the three-way war enabled the collectors and the hospital's law firm to simply answer her questions with "We can't answer your question, you just need to pay."

Hannah showed us folders of detailed records she kept of her dozens of requests to see an itemized bill. The fog of war was lucrative for everyone except Hannah. She discovered that the Carlsbad Medical Center never actually sent the bill to her insurance company. Hannah presented a letter to the judge on her court date, explaining the situation in detail. Her medical bill was voided. The law firm representing the hospital was in Missouri and did not need to show up in court because it was considered small claims.

Another time, Hannah got sued for going to the hospital on a weekend and getting an antibiotic for a urinary tract infection. There was no other way for her to get the prescription. She got only a prescription, no treatment, so I estimated the ER visit could cost $400. But the hospital charged five times that and swiftly sued Hannah for the full amount.

"I've always paid all my bills on time, but I just couldn't make sense of the bills," she explained. "I called dozens of times trying to resolve the many bills sent to me. Each time they would transfer me to someone else, the calls would disconnect, or I was put on hold for over 30 minutes. No one could help me. Every time my babies would nap, I would be on the phone. It's been horrible."

Hannah's final experience with Carlsbad's billing department came when she was pregnant. On a few occasions she experienced some nausea and abdominal pain and went to the hospital to get it checked out, as directed by her obstetrician. At 20 weeks' gestation, she walked in to Carlsbad Medical Center, where a doctor did an ultrasound on the baby and checked her cervix, and the nurse put in an IV for a few hours of hydration.

The hospital hit her with a massive bill, one I carefully reviewed and would deem outlandish. Five weeks later, when the same thing happened, she drove more than an hour through the desert to a hospital in Roswell, the next town over, where they did the exact same things but charged one fifteenth the amount of the Carlsbad bill. She was able to pay the Roswell bill on the spot. At Carlsbad, she had had to set up a payment plan: $25 a month for years.

How could one hospital charge 15 times more than another hospital for the exact same services? I drove to the Roswell hospital to find out what was different about it and how the town was different from Carlsbad. It turns out not much is different. It's just that Roswell doesn't jack up their prices 15-fold, then take legal action to essentially shake down patients for their last penny. I checked to see if Roswell hospital has ever sued a patient and garnished their wages. The answer was no. Two towns, two hospitals—one ruining the lives of the people they serve, the other loyal to the mission of medicine.

Hannah described to me how her town's hospital ruined her family's life, taking her credit score from 700 to 400 and adding lawsuit guilty pleas to their legal record. That's a public record that sticks with a person. Buying a home became almost impossible, and at one point her credit card stopped working because of her low credit score. She was not shaken down by the hospital for an unpaid liver transplant bill, a month in the ICU, or anything like that. On the contrary, she sought medical help for minor things—a blood clot on one occasion, a pregnancy scare on another, a urinary tract infection on another—none of which required a hospital stay.

In that empty classroom that day, Hannah cried. "I would rather die driving to Roswell than go to the Carlsbad Medical Center," she said.

Rent-a-Center

Our next meeting was at the town's Rent-a-Center, one of those stores where you can rent anything from couches to televisions. On our drive there, we passed seven dollar stores, including Dollar General, Dollar Tree, and Family Dollar, all of which were large. It was a long way from Laguna Beach or Manhattan, where experts discuss health care over gourmet appetizers.

Rent-a-Center saleswomen Luz Tatum had suggested we meet her at work during the lull just after lunch. Entering the store, we spotted a woman with a moving dolly in the back of the store.

"Hi, my name is Marty, and this is Will. Are you Luz?"

"She should be back any minute from lunch. Is there something I can help you with?"

"That's okay, we'll wait for Luz."

"Wait," she said, "are you the guys here to talk to her about medical bills?"

After we said "yes," this younger woman, who wore a lifting brace around her torso and asked to remain anonymous, shared four stories about how Carlsbad Medical Center sued her (a single mom) as well as other loved ones. The prices they charged sounded massively inflated to me. Will and I would occasionally glance at each other, apparently thinking the same thing—this was unbelievable. Almost every person we talked to in that town had experienced the hospital's shock-and-awe billing practices.

Raised in rural Oklahoma, Will told me that being in Carlsbad reminded him of home. As we sat in the Rent-a-Center waiting for Luz, Will tried to reconcile what he was seeing with his ideals. "I thought hospitals were a refuge for the sick and injured—that's why I went into medicine," he said. "But the hospital here is deliberately ruining lives."

When Luz showed up, she welcomed us to sit on one of the leather couches for rent in the showroom. Luz was a Hispanic American in her forties who felt very comfortable navigating the large showroom floor. After we sat down, she began to tell us her story. She has a medical condition known as chronic nausea that on occasion requires IV hydration and antinausea meds. In 2017, the first time Luz went to Carlsbad Medical Center for treatment, they charged her $3,000 for the few hours of care she received.

Luz made only about $500 a week and had a high-deductible insurance plan. She called the Carlsbad billing department and was told she had to come in person to talk about a payment plan. By the time she could get a day off from Rent-a-Center, the hospital had already sued her for $3,000. She got served the papers by the local sheriff's department.

The next time Luz needed treatment, she drove to a hospital in the next town over. They charged her $600 for the same treatment. Carlsbad Medical Center was not only overcharging her, they were suing her when she couldn't pay the bill.

These inflated medical bills cause incredible hardships. Luz is a single mom with a five-year-old son. She also needed money to repair her 1995 Mercury Cougar, but Carlsbad Medical Center had garnished her near minimum wage income pay by 50%. The car mechanic wanted $800, but Luz didn't have the money. He kept the car for the six weeks it took her to round up the money. She walked to work.

"It's hard for a single mom," she told me, showing me a photo of her son. He was adorable and reminded me of my nephew. They were roughly the same age. But sitting on that couch in the Rent-a-Center, I realized how different my life was from hers.

There are two Americas—the one I live in and the one I was now observing. Research shows that six out of every ten Americans have less than $1,000 in savings[3] and about half of them have no savings.[4] As I stood there in the Rent-a-Center, I was grateful for the opportunities I've had in life. Also, I was reminded that the health insurance deductibles so often discussed in our health policy circles may seem inconsequential to wealthy people and to decision makers in the policy world, but they are crushing many Americans.

Luz's story made me want to do something. I called Cori Cook, a lawyer who specializes in medical billing practices. I've partnered with Cori on other projects. I asked her how much a hospital could garnish from a minimum wage worker. She said it varied by state but is limited to 25% in New Mexico.[5] Luz told me that when she was promoted to sales manager she got a raise to about $600 a week, which was garnished down to $350. Others told me their paychecks were docked by 70%. It's easy for the people who garnish wages to break the law, Cori said. Cori was so disturbed by what we had discovered that she offered to provide free legal help to the people we met.

Soon after her lawsuit and wage garnishment, Luz received a surprise bill from the hospital for $68. She didn't know what it was for, especially after her most recent garnishment. But the bill said if she didn't pay it in ten days it would increase from $68 to $389. In my opinion, this was a clear example of bullying. In what business does the interest rate on a bill go up by 20% per day? Was medicine ever intended to be like this, where a patient comes to a doctor for medical care and the hospital turns around and sues them, garnishes their wages, ruins their credit history, and even gets the town's sheriff's deputy to serve them papers at their home? The people I met in Carlsbad were not criminals or fugitives from the law. They were hardworking Americans with health insurance. They got sick and went to a doctor, were treated, and a few hours later went home. Their problem was that they lived in a town with a hospital that forgot the Hippocratic Oath to do no harm.

The Cop and the Teacher

It's sobering to be on the ground and see how our health care system treats patients. In Carlsbad, it felt like no one was safe from the hospital's predatory practices—not even a police officer and his wife, a fifth grade teacher.

Will and I sat in the living room of Officer Mike Shott and his wife, Meghan, listening to their story as their two kids rummaged through toys and their two-year-old explored the art of walking. In October 2016, with a jabbing pain in his side and worried he might have appendicitis, Mike had gone to the Carlsbad Medical Center's emergency room. The doctors ordered a CT scan. It's debatable whether he needed it in the first place, but when they did it, the technicians didn't inject the dye that made it possible to see the appendicitis, so they had to do another CT scan, this time with dye.

Although it was their mistake, Carlsbad Medical Center charged Mike for both CT scans. And it gets worse. At Johns Hopkins, the scan would cost $487. Mike got charged $13,000 for each scan. It turned out Mike didn't have appendicitis. The doctor said the pain could have been from his heavy police belt. Before Mike and Meghan could even sort out the bills, the hospital sued him. This created a unique problem for Mike. As a police officer, he has to appear before the judges in the same court where he was being sued. The lawsuit could ruin his professional reputation, so the couple tapped their savings to pay the full hospital bill.

Mike is not the only cop who's been at the mercy of the hospital. He said the same thing has happened to at least three of his colleagues. All of them are insured by the city.

Mike and Meghan pay their bills on time. Together they make more than $100,000 a year. But their plight with Carlsbad Medical Center got even worse when Meghan delivered their youngest baby. As they told me the rest of the story I kept thinking, *You can't make this stuff up.*

Meghan had maxed out their deductible that year, and she delivered her child before the end of that policy year. But the hospital submitted the bill late, so it didn't get applied to the year in which she had met her deductible. The insurance company stuck Meghan with the full cost.

Meghan made dozens of calls to the hospital and insurance company to correct this simple, obvious mistake. But she kept getting the fog-of-war business model. "This is non-negotiable," one billing representative told her. Then, being the Carlsbad Medical Center, they sued her. At this point, I had come to expect it, even though this isn't how most hospitals treat their patients. The bill collectors told Meghan there was no need for her to show up in court. But she's married to a cop. She knew that if she didn't show up, the judge would find for the plaintiff by default. Overall, Meghan estimates that she spent 100 hours disputing her bills, all the while taking care of her young children and working as a teacher. They paid the bill to avoid garnishment. But they had to max out their credit cards to stay afloat.

On that trip to Carlsbad, we spoke with seven patients who had had their wages garnished. All were hardworking and insured. Several didn't understand the legal system well enough to know that they had even been sued until they noticed their paycheck had been garnished. I talked to a few doctors at the hospital and they had no idea their patients were being sued. When I showed the doctors what I had learned about the predatory billing practices, they said they detested what was happening. I realized that if this practice is to change, it will require doctors and everyday Americans to ask their local hospitals to end the practice of suing low-income patients and garnishing their wages. And the next time you hear health care experts say that no one is expected to pay the full price of an inflated medical bill in America, you can tell them to take a trip to Carlsbad, New Mexico, and talk to Luz, Meghan and Mike, Jennifer, Hannah, and the countless others there that I didn't get a chance to meet.

The Judge

I wondered what the judges at the Carlsbad courthouse thought about this problem. Their dockets are stuffed with cases in which

Carlsbad Medical Center has sued patients. Surely, they notice the trend. I reached out to the judges while we were visiting and by phone in the weeks after our trip. I tried through intermediaries but heard nothing. Then I left a voicemail for one, telling her I was a researcher at Johns Hopkins University trying to understand the practice of hospitals suing patients. The next day, Judge Lisa Riley called me back. "You're from Johns Hopkins? How did you find out about Carlsbad?" she asked in bewilderment.

I explained how our investigation had led to this point and told her about talking to the many good people of Carlsbad who were getting sued. I asked if it was true that 95% of the civil cases in her courthouse had been filed by the hospital going after patients.

"Well yeah, it's a lot of work." Judge Riley's voice had a soft tone, as if she appreciated my interest in the lawsuit epidemic. "My focus is criminal cases, but the lawsuits from the hospital are a burden on our limited administrative capacity."

"The employees in your courthouse said they and their family members have also been sued," I said. "Are you aware of that?"

Yes, she knew. And that's when the judge said something that shocked me, even after all I'd heard from other Carlsbad residents: "My husband and I have both been sued by the hospital."

I almost dropped the phone. "You're the judge and you've been sued by the hospital in your own court?"

"Yes, and my husband, on separate occasions, for different medical bills. I always thought it was well known in our town that the hospital sues everybody."

Clearly, the Carlsbad Medical Center had a shoot-first-and-look-second approach. I talked to Judge Riley for half an hour and learned how helpless patients were when the hospital sued them. In the legal cases, judges can see a reference to the services provided but the itemized details are redacted. They just see a total amount owed that's called "bad debt." That's not a fair term when it's an inflated bill that may be in dispute. It also makes it hard to spot price gouging. She said she didn't know the prices were marked up so high, although the judges suspected that a quick checkup in the emergency room should be closer to $500 than $5,000.

I told the judge the stories of the patients we had interviewed. She seemed impressed that our team had taken an interest. But

I didn't see what else I could do. As a doctor, I was outraged. I thought back to my conversations with hospital CEOs about how they mark up bills with outrageously high charges. "Marty, nobody pays those high prices," they would tell me. Insurance companies get them good rates, they claimed. But by going out to the front lines I learned that many people pay a heavy price for the high prices they are charged.

On the last day I was in Carlsbad, I was having dinner at Yellow Brix, a well-known restaurant in town. Will and I were sitting down with a nurse named Misti and her husband, learning how Misti had been bombarded with bills and sued by the hospital. She stopped short when she noticed someone in the corner of her eye. The hospital's head surgeon had just entered the restaurant. A good doctor, he was well liked in the community, she whispered. He also happened to be on the board of the hospital—the group of clinicians and community leaders who oversee the facility's finances and quality.

I wanted to get his thoughts on his hospital filing these lawsuits. I asked Misti if it would be okay for me to introduce myself to him. "I suppose," she said.

Dr. Murugan Athigaman passed our table and I introduced myself. I mentioned that I had heard good things about him from a patient. He smiled and thanked me for the compliment. I told him I'm also a surgeon. He asked me where, and I told him Johns Hopkins. He wondered what I was doing in town, and I explained that I was researching hospital billing and had heard that Carlsbad hospital has a track record of suing patients who couldn't pay their bills. I asked him whether he was aware of the hospital's suing anyone. He said "no" and seemed shocked. I told him how many cases I had found at the courthouse and asked him to please ask his hospital to stop suing patients.

I contacted Carlsbad hospital and asked them about the thousands of lawsuits they filed against patients. They replied with an email saying that they work closely with patients on payment arrangements but "may take action to collect payment from those patients who seem to have the means to pay for the care received. This is always the last resort, after numerous other attempts to resolve the bill, and each case is individually evaluated." It was classic corporate speak, disconnected from what I saw on the ground. I also reached out multiple times to the hospital's parent company, Community Health Systems.

After multiple attempts, I finally heard back from them, a company I learned was investor-owned and publicly traded on Wall Street. They told me that they investigated the cases I sent to them. They eventually dismissed some egregious bills but pushed back on others, claiming they reached out many times to the same patients who told me they had never heard from the hospital and that the hospital wouldn't take their calls. The company told me they would change the criteria they use to sue patients to reduce the number of lawsuits they file. But it wasn't all out of the kindness of their hearts. It took my calling my friend Elizabeth Cohen at CNN and inviting her to Carlsbad to meet the people I described above. Elizabeth did an exposé on CNN that got the hospital's attention (and was praised by people in the community).[6]

I would later learn that Community Health Systems was a financial mess in jeopardy of going out of business. Their stock price went from $17.68 four years prior to $1.88 per share when I submitted this book for publication.

My team's discoveries in New Mexico motivated me to launch a national study of predatory billing and wage garnishment to see just how common it was. Carlsbad Medical Center violated everything doctors consider sacred about making hospitals a safe haven for the sick. But that was not the case in Roswell, the next town over, about an hour away. The Roswell hospital seemed to represent what's honest and fair about medicine. So were there more hospitals like Carlsbad out there? I took that question to my team at Hopkins, and we applied the same scientific research methodology to hospital lawsuits that we would use to study cancer. Our findings were surprising. They also validated our concerns. We discovered that Carlsbad Medical Center was not alone.

CHAPTER 4

Two Americas

After returning from New Mexico, I called a special meeting of my Hopkins research team in my office. My team is a bunch of young guns, a diverse group of 24- to 35-year-olds from all over the country, representing a wide range of medical specialties, but all with a passion for studying health care costs, public health, and vulnerable populations. With all ten of them seated around the meeting table, Will and I began to tell them the dramatic stories of the people we met in Carlsbad. We showed the group the picture of Hannah crying in her classroom with a stack of medical bills and lawsuits. We showed them a picture of Jennifer's small home with random cinder blocks in the front yard. Heidi Overton, a surgeon working on her PhD with me, was particularly distressed by the stories. She was from New Mexico and had lived in Carlsbad. Will and I continued to talk about the people we met in Carlsbad. We explained how their hometown hospital harassed them with predatory billing and aggressive lawyers.

The team couldn't believe it. Some peppered me with questions, wanting more details. I have asked my team to tackle a lot of big issues in the past, but I don't remember anything that has gotten them more fired up than this.

I presented to them my fundamental research question: "How many hospitals in America are like Carlsbad, and how many are like Roswell?" In other words, how many sue people and garnish wages and how many don't? The entire plane ride home from Carlsbad, the question had echoed in my mind.

The PhDs on my team proposed a series of studies to nail down the magnitude of the problem. Some of the millennials were talking activism. For Heidi, it was personal. She even had plans to move back to New Mexico after completing her surgical residency and PhD. She couldn't believe this was happening in her home state and told the team she would do anything to stop these lawsuits against well-meaning, hardworking Americans. "I went into medicine to help people, not ruin their lives financially," Heidi said with a stern expression.

We started by checking to see if Carlsbad Medical Center was part of a larger system of hospitals that sued patients elsewhere, too. Indeed, Carlsbad Medical Center was owned by Community Health Systems. According to its website, this enterprise owned 119 hospitals in 20 states. We looked at online court records to see whether any of their other hospitals were suing its patients with such vigor. We started with Missouri, where the chain has three facilities. Sure enough, the facilities are plaintiffs in hundreds of lawsuits against individuals, and the cases appeared to be related to their medical care.

We broadened the search, checking out the chain's hospitals in all the states where Community Health Systems operated. Online court records showed the company's hospitals were filing thousands of lawsuits against patients in many of the states.

One of the difficulties of doing this type of research is that these lawsuits are filed in state courts, and they are divided by county. Lucky for us, Virginia court data can be found online for the entire state. That means it's consolidated and easier to search. We were able to pull up every civil case filed for each year going back several years.

Some of the research questions were obvious: How many hospitals sue patients, and how many lawsuits were filed? But we also wanted to know the characteristics of the hospitals. Are they all for-profit hospitals, like Community Health Systems? Or do nonprofits also sue patients and garnish wages?

The results of our analysis were alarming. At the top of the list of hospitals that sue was Mary Washington Hospital in Fredericksburg, an hour south of my home. In 2017 alone the hospital sued more than 4,300 patients and garnished the wages of 1,756, the court records showed.[1] In some cases the court required the patient to provide their personal bank information—routing number and account number—so that the hospital could pull money directly from a checking or savings account. Sometimes the hospital had filed more than a dozen lawsuits per day. I couldn't believe it! There was a Carlsbad Medical Center in my own backyard. I wanted to go to Fredericksburg to learn more. Will, Heidi, and Tina insisted on joining me.

Driving into Fredericksburg, it's easy to see why "timeless" is the city's tagline. Colonial-era mansions line the streets. The historic downtown, which boasts more than 350 buildings from the 18th and 19th centuries, looked gorgeous that beautiful summer morning. The small courthouse was a few miles from George Washington's boyhood home at Ferry Farm. As we walked into the renovated courthouse building, we noticed a flat-screen TV right outside the courtroom that was scrolling through the 100-plus names of people being sued by the hospital that day. We stepped into the courtroom and saw roughly 50 people sitting anxiously, waiting to be called forward by the judge. A Hispanic man in worn clothing by the name of Mr. Ortiz was at the stand when we walked in.

A cold-sounding judge was pressing him. "Do you or do you not owe the hospital this money?" the judge asked repeatedly. Each time, Mr. Ortiz stammered to explain his situation. Each time, the judge would hammer back the same question.

Eventually Mr. Ortiz stopped trying to explain and said, "No, I do not owe this money." The judge set up a hearing for next month, and Mr. Ortiz walked out of the courtroom visibly shaken.

We were able to catch Mr. Ortiz outside the courtroom and he agreed to tell us his whole story. He's a 50-year-old man from Guatemala who works for himself as a landscaper. His wife has been disabled and in a wheelchair for 20 years, so she is not able to contribute to the support of their household.

Four months earlier, he had some dizziness and decided to go to the Mary Washington Hospital emergency department. The doctors did a series of minor tests and found nothing wrong. But they were still concerned, so they decided to hospitalize Mr. Ortiz for four days, doing countless tests and blood work panels. Eventually, after everything came out clean, they discharged him and referred him to an ear specialist. Mr. Ortiz saw the specialist the next day and was told it was a common ear infection and that it would go away within a week or two. A few weeks later, Mr. Ortiz received a bill in the mail from Mary Washington for $14,000.

For months Mr. Ortiz has tried to talk to Mary Washington about the bill but said he received no help, which led to his having to defend himself in court that morning. We saw many other stories much like Mr. Ortiz's: a single uninsured mother being sued, an army veteran harassed by collection agencies, an elderly widow being dunned for her deceased husband's medical bills.

We had pulled up to the courthouse as stoic academic researchers with surveys and notebooks in hand, ready to gather data. But we left that courthouse feeling emotionally distraught, like people who had just witnessed a social injustice.

In total, our research revealed that over the last five years, Mary Washington Hospital had filed more than 24,200 lawsuits against patients, the equivalent of one lawsuit for every resident of the city (Fredericksburg has a population of 25,000 by census and is surrounded by large farming areas). The hospital's website boasts that they rank #2 in quality. I'm not sure about the quality, but they appear to rank #1 in suing patients in the state.

Ironically, their website also boasted, "Our not-for-profit status drives us to be the kind of organization that provides care to those in need regardless of their ability to pay." Wait a minute. They will take care of you regardless of your ability to pay, but if you don't, they sue the socks off you? Even though the hospital bears their family name, I'm not sure George Washington or his mother, Mary, would be proud. After I called their hospital CEO to verify the high number of lawsuits his hospital filed, the statement on their website suddenly disappeared and instead it now reads "Because

of our not-for-profit status, we file reports with the IRS to demonstrate our income and spending."

Keep in mind that most hospitals that sue patients are not
shaking people down for fair market prices. I searched Mary Washington's pricing data through the American Hospital Directory
database. They mark up their bills many times higher than what
Medicare would pay for the same services.

Within a couple of weeks, my research team had crunched the
numbers for all the hospital lawsuits in Virginia. The good news
was the majority of hospitals didn't sue any patients in 2017, a
finding that restored our faith in the leaders of American hospitals. However, the 37% of hospitals that did sue filed over 20,000
lawsuits against patients that one year alone.

Carlsbad Medical Center was no lone wolf. Each of the cases my
team pulled represented an American worker or family—like the
teacher and cop and Rent-a-Center employee I had met back in
New Mexico. These patients would have no way of knowing
whether their local hospital was the type that sued its patients
for not paying inflated bills. Hospitals warn patients with dozens
of signs about X-ray radiation all over the radiology area. I wish
these hospitals would warn patients about being sued with the
same level of concern: WARNING: HOSPITAL LIKELY TO SUE.

Surprisingly, nonprofit hospitals were more likely to sue patients
than Virginia's few for-profit hospitals.[2] My team and I also gathered more information on the patients being sued. People in rural
areas were just as vulnerable as those in urban and suburban parts
of the state. Our study showed where the patients who had their
wages garnished were employed. At the top of the list was Walmart,
with about 450 employees from Virginia who had their wages
garnished in 2017. Other employers ranking high were Lowe's
home centers, the U.S. Postal Service, Perdue Farms, and two area
supermarket chains, Kroger and Food Lion.

I contacted some of these patients from Virginia and heard
stories identical to those of the full-time workers we'd encountered
in New Mexico. Here were hardworking Americans with health
insurance who made too little money to afford inflated hospital
bills but made too much to qualify for Medicaid. These were not

one-percenters. These people were within the income range of the average American worker, who makes about $18 an hour, according to the Bureau of Labor Statistics.[3] I asked my team to reach out to Walmart and other employers to let them know what we were finding. Employers needed to know how often their workers' paychecks were being docked.

One day I happened to share some of our findings with a lawyer I met at a birthday party for a mutual friend. I told her how blown away I was by how some hospitals had stooped to this level, and how proud I was of the hospitals that didn't. She didn't share my outrage. "What's wrong with garnishing wages if someone doesn't pay their debt?" she argued.

I get it. Hospitals have a right to get paid for the work that they do. And patients have an obligation to pay for services received. But let's also put things into context with some key facts. Hospitals are marking up their bills by 2 to 23 times what Medicare would pay for the same services.[4] Further, our research showed that hospitals playing the pernicious markup game were also the most likely to sue. Of the many sued patients with whom I spoke, not one had a cosmetic procedure like a breast augmentation and refused to pay. These were basic medical services for sick and injured folks.

Also, many of the hospitals filing lawsuits were nonprofits. They enjoy huge tax benefits because they claim to the IRS that they provide charitable care to the community. Yet in some cases, they were pulling the trigger on lawsuits without providing discounts or payment plans. Even when these medical facilities did offer payment plans, they were often for the full bill, which is typically marked up three- to fivefold. If a bill is inflated, do we really believe that paying the inflated amount over five years at zero interest is fair? Plus, these bills that lead to lawsuits are peanuts for the hospitals. For many hospitals, it represented less than 1% of their overall revenue. Suing patients did not appear to be associated with a hospital's need for cash. Advocate Aurora Health sued many patients the same year that their CEOs' salaries doubled by $11 million.

I decided to pay a visit to Mary Washington Hospital. I wondered whether the doctors working there knew the hospital's legal team

was giving their patients this follow-up "treatment." After all, the
Carlsbad doctors hadn't known. And why would doctors know
about it? The clinical side of a hospital is typically walled off from
the operation's billing side.

At Mary Washington, I headed for the cafeteria. I wanted to
grab lunch and chat up doctors. It's hard to work up an appetite in
a hospital cafeteria. Hospitals are supposed to promote healthful
foods, but the flavorless, processed, overcooked, carb-laden food
they serve is a constant on hospital menus. And of course, they
always have Jell-O. I've eaten in hospital cafeterias in the north,
south, east, and west, and Jell-O is always available. After studying
the epidemic of hospitals suing patients, it was time for some
emotional eating. I skipped the antibiotic-injected chicken and
grabbed a limp slice of pizza and a piece of cake.

After forcing down this uninspired lunch, I started hunting for
doctors to interview. I can spot doctors a mile away. Of course the
obvious sign is the white coat. If it's waist length, that's a medical
student. Midthigh or knee, you've got a resident or doctor. From
there, my eyes go to the pockets. If they're stuffed, it's probably a
resident carrying around paperwork, prescribing pads, and pens.
If there's a banana or one of those little bottles of 5-hour Energy
in the pocket, that's a resident. If the pockets are empty, it might be
a surgeon. If there's a stethoscope, that person is probably in internal
medicine or a cardiologist. A dermatologist carries a penlight.

I sidled up to a couple of doctors and introduced myself as a
surgeon at Johns Hopkins. I said that I was doing a study on hospital
billing practices and it had come to my attention that their hospital
sued a lot of its patients and garnished their wages. At that point, one
of them did a double-take and I could see his mental wheels turning.

"Mary Washington is actually one of the most aggressive in the
country," I told them.

"No one intended the system to be this messed up," one of the
doctors told me. "The games have gone too far."

My research team and I continued our analysis of these medical
lawsuits. A few weeks later I raised the topic from the stage in front

of a few hundred people at a medical conference. The audience
included doctors from all over the country. I had a hard time not
getting emotional as I presented our research and shared the
shocking stories of patients whose lives were ruined by our medical
system. I urged those in attendance to call on their hospital leaders
and board members to stop the predatory billing and suing of
insured low-income patients.

"These are *our* patients," I explained. "These are not the patients
of our hospital billing departments. These people came to us as
doctors because they were sick or injured, and we should respond
in the spirit of the Hippocratic Oath." In the audience, every head
nodded. I asked them the same question that Dr. Keith Smith
from Oklahoma had posed to me: "How can we take an oath, treat
a patient, and then allow their lives to be ruined financially?" One
doctor approached me afterward, fired up. He wasn't going to stand
for this type of treatment of patients, he told me. He committed to
go back to his hospital and talk to his leadership to ensure they
are not part of the problem.

Within a few months, Will, Angela, Heidi, Tina, and other
medical students with whom they had been talking approached
me and said they wanted to take action. They wanted to rally other
students, doctors, nurses, and concerned citizens about these
issues in an effort they referred to as the Restoring Medicine Project.
Their website, RestoringMedicine.org, gives people ranging from
doctors to community members the resources they can use to
address predatory billing, suing, medical overscreenings, and other
unfair health care practices in their communities.

I reached out to Mary Washington Hospital's CEO, Dr. Mike
McDermott, and CFO, Sean Barden, and had a chance to speak
with them. I asked them about the 24,200 lawsuits their hospital
filed against patients. McDermott said the number of cases was
"probably correct." He said that going to court was a last resort.
"We only get to the legal action side if we are unable to establish
communication, if the patient or their families have been unrespon-
sive to all of our efforts to establish communication with them,"
McDermott said. "We have [financial aid] programs for patients
and families who have higher incomes who find themselves in

unusual and catastrophic situations where they are unable to make payments," he said.

But their earnest responses to my questions did not correlate with what I was seeing on the ground. For example, Lisa Lester, a woman I met at the courthouse, was sued by Mary Washington one month after her husband died in March 2018. Lisa applied for the hospital's financial aid to help pay his $10,000 bill but told me she didn't get any help. Lisa said she was getting harassed and threatened by hospital collections people when she was in the midst of her grieving. "They make it impossible to get financial aid," she said.

The hospital executives were cordial when I spoke with them, but their reasonable-sounding approach was disconnected from the ugliness I saw in the courthouse. They seemed entirely disconnected from people like Wanda Brooks, a 52-year-old African American woman who went to Mary Washington with a headache and got billed more than $8,000 for both a head CT and a head MRI. Wanda's employer, an assisted living facility, had insisted she have the hospital check her even though the single mom knew she was simply exhausted from working 16-hour shifts. Both the CT and MRI were normal, and probably neither was necessary based on the symptoms she described to me. Certainly one normal scan would negate the need for the other in working up a headache.

Standing with me outside the courthouse on her trial day, Wanda explained that she had no way of knowing that she didn't need both scans. Faced with the bill, Wanda said she applied for Mary Washington's financial aid but was denied because she was told she earns too much (she earns approximately $25,000/year). The hospital then sued her and started garnishing her wages four months after her headache. According to Wanda, the hospital garnished half of her two-week paycheck, chopping it from $1,200 to $600. Wanda's eyes welled with tears as she told me how the lawsuit and garnishment caused sleepless nights and made it hard to pay for essentials like food and rent. It also crushed her credit score. This was right before Christmas and I couldn't help imagining how tough the garnishment made it for her to buy gifts for her son.

Others I met at the courthouse said they had to pay higher mortgage payments after their FICA scores got hurt by medical bills. In looking at Wanda's records, I saw that she had been billed for both the CT and MRI at a rate about four to five times higher than the Medicare allowable amount. I asked the hospital's CEO, a radiologist, how much a head CT or MRI costs at Mary Washington. He wasn't sure. I asked him to consider helping Wanda with her bill and he said he would gladly review it.

But Wanda's court day was looming. I offered to be an expert in her case. On her court date, the judge called her name. I approached the bench with her. Then something funny happened. The judge did a double take of her paperwork and said, "I've never seen this before, but your case has been canceled." She was so nervous bracing for the worst, she didn't process what he was saying. He then said, "Go on, you're all set." We embraced as she walked out of the courtroom, elated.

On the way out, I approached more patients appearing in court that day and offered to be their pro bono expert. Every time the hospital saw my name listed on a case as the expert, the case was canceled before I could argue it. Judges began asking me who am I and what I was doing in their small town. I explained that I'm a physician and believed, based on my research, that patients were being overcharged by their local hospital. I explained that hospitals historically have been a safe haven for the sick but that aggressive billing was now eroding the public trust between the medical profession and the community, some whom now avoid care for fear of price gouging. I also explained that wage garnishment has a rocky legal basis. I told one judge, "If I mow your lawn for 30 minutes and send you a bill for $8,000, you would say that you are not required to pay because there is no valid contract." Even consent forms where patients sign their financial life away in the emergency department are invalid because people are under duress and can't be expected to understand the unilateral terms.

After this frustrating experience, I called a dozen journalist friends at all the major news outlets and told them about the national trend I had discovered. They were shocked. I met with many of them and shared the data that my team had found on hospitals engaging in what I call predatory billing. Many journalists I met with ran stories on hospitals suing patients, creating public accountability for hospitals. I invited Selena Simmons-Duffin from NPR to join me in Fredericksburg, Virginia, to see what I was seeing. She documented the patient stories from that courthouse and my team's work there—a story ran on NPR. Within a week, Mary Washington Hospital announced it would stop all lawsuits against patients.[5]

My team and I continue to fight for patients on every level. In addition to educating patients, we urge state legislators and governors to do what four other states have done and ban wage garnishment for unpaid medical bills. My team has argued to members of congress that an IRS tax-free designation is not appropriate for hospitals that provide no charity care and instead sue low-income patients for inflated bills. I also took a few patients to the White House where they told their story directly to the president and Secretary Azar. I argued that half of U.S. women with stage 4 breast cancer are now being harassed by medical debt collectors. Secretary Azar called it a disgrace and instructed his staff to work hard on a bipartisan solution that would provide relief for Americans gouged by overpriced and surprise bills. Shortly thereafter, he announced initiatives aimed at curbing egregious medical billing and increasing price transparency. What started as a spark in New Mexico was now a national movement for more honest health care.

The Great Divide

As I traveled across America for this book, what I saw was not a Republican/Democrat divide or a conservative/liberal divide. Instead, I felt a widespread sentiment among low and middle-income workers that the system was stacked against them, controlled by the powerful elite who make the rules.

Honest, hardworking Americans feel helpless against a ruling class who use power and access to their favor, creating fine print and laws to give themselves the upper hand. The folks I met often pointed out how the process of appealing a hospital bill or an insurance company denial was too complex and utterly exhausting.

I heard from farmers, small business owners, and even hospital workers who have been sued by hospitals. With intense frustration, they told me that it's not a level playing field. For some, crying foul paid off and got them some measure of justice. But many others left defeated, feeling the system was "rigged against the little guy," as one factory worker in Ohio put it. Some people were not formally educated on the issues, yet they eloquently argued for transparency and accountability. Sometimes they pointed out how health care is lumped in with other industries in which the rules are made by powerful elites. For example, one woman from Texas complained to me that incredibly profitable oil companies pay no taxes, yet she must struggle to pay hers. A man from Georgia asserted that we have two justice systems, one for the powerful wealthy establishment and another one for lower- and middle-income Americans. "When the rich rob people, their company pays a fine that doesn't affect them," a Midwestern farmer said. "If *I* rob someone, I go to jail," said one mechanic in Carlsbad. "Everyone is fed up with a system where people use their power to take advantage of the little people." Some respondents saw hope in President Trump's anti-establishment style, which helped me better understand how he swept elections.

You'd think the hospital leaders in the audience where I spoke might contest what I had discovered in our research, but the truth was that most of these conference attendees were unaware of it. As I began discussing how the hospital bill markup game left patients holding the bag, heads nodded in acknowledgment. But when I added that some hospitals sue patients and garnish their minimum wage paycheck, hospital executives would come up to me immediately after my talk and say "That's terrible" and "We don't do that." Others would turn to their colleague and say, "We don't do that, do we?" Without even knowing whether their hospitals sues low-income patients, many hospital executives from around the country condemned it, and would even come up to me to tell me they were personally repulsed by the idea.

Again and again, I observed this irony of hospital leaders appalled by the idea of lawsuits filed against patients without realizing their own hospitals engaged in just such predatory practices. Clearly, there is a disconnect.

At another conference of a large hospital system, a hospital board chair told me, "Marty, we forgive patients who can't pay." The look on his face was earnest as he told me that the hospital's mission was to serve. He told me they took their inspiration from the example of one of the Catholic saints. This guy really seemed to care about patients and to be proud of his hospital's charitable mission. But when I looked up court records online for the flagship hospital in his chain, there were ample cases of his hospital suing patients and garnishing their wages. When I circled back with him weeks later, he was clearly disappointed in his own hospital.

I heard that some large faith-based hospital systems never sued patients, so I reached out to them. Over the phone, I explained to one of the systems' vice presidents what I had seen nationally. I asked him if they sued patients. "We don't sue patients," he quickly replied, disgusted at the very idea.

The vice president told me that he left his lucrative corporate job because the values of the health care system transcended typical corporate values. "People here believe in what we do," he said. "And what we do is help people." On its website, his hospital chain bragged about its charity care. Again, I felt inspired by the conversation. But when I did a routine fact check for this book, emailing him to confirm his quote, he changed his message from "We don't sue patients" to "We advocate for our patients."

The change made me suspicious. So I looked up his hospital's court records. It turns out that they had in fact sued many patients. In one case, his hospital pursued wage garnishment against a patient all the way into her bankruptcy. The judge finally stepped in to side with the patient.

Just before I submitted this book for print, I discovered cases in which my own hospital had sued low-income patients to garnish their wages. I was extremely disappointed to learn this. But at the same time, I was inspired by the hospital's response to change its ways once it came to light before the hospital's clinical leaders.

Throughout the 1960s, the Internal Revenue Service gave tax-exempt status to nonprofit hospitals on the condition that these hospitals provide free or highly discounted care to patients that could not afford it. Obviously, this tax break is of tremendous financial benefit to the facilities. Nonprofit hospitals are expected to provide charity care and to avoid predatory billing practices. The exemption from paying taxes was to be permitted so long as the hospital "operated to the extent of its financial ability for those not able to pay for the services rendered and not exclusively for those who are able and expected to pay."[6]

In 1969, the IRS became less clear on what qualifies a hospital for tax exemption.[7] It created the "community benefit standard," which recognizes the "promotion of health" as in and of itself a charitable purpose. Hospitals were no longer required to have a demonstrated level of charity care to become tax exempt. This new lower standard created debate about the minimum requirement to establish a "community benefit."

In 2014, the IRS required nonprofit hospitals to have a written financial assistance policy that would clearly indicate exactly who was eligible for free or discounted care at their facility. The IRS mandated that nonprofit hospitals should not engage in "extraordinary collection actions" on unpaid debts until the hospital makes "reasonable efforts" to determine if an individual is eligible for financial assistance.

In a subsequent correspondence with the hospital's VP, he emphasized that his hospital had a financial aid process for all patients. I responded by telling him that merely offering a financial aid process was a matter of federal law—a requirement for all hospitals mandated by the Affordable Care Act. I asked him to advocate for his hospital to please stop suing patients and start forgiving them when possible, or at least limiting collections to the Medicare allowable amount when patients couldn't pay.

A few months later I visited another hospital system that touted its merciful approach with patients. Before the gathering the hospital's C-suite leaders told me they care for people the way Jesus Christ did. When patients struggle financially, they work out a payment plan, they said, or even forgive the bill. I felt inspired.

Then we looked up the hospital's legal filings and found that this hospital system had sued hundreds of patients. We looked at one of the judgments against a husband and wife whose debt ballooned because of interest and court fees. It went from $783 for the principal, plus $291 for interest and $176 for court fees up to a total of $1,252. And the judgment drew interest at 9%.

The interest and court fees amounted to 60% of the principal. That sounds less like a hospital that's there to serve and more like a payday lender that's trying to hound a patient in debt. Those aren't quite loan shark interest rates, but if you're asking "What would Jesus do?" I'm pretty sure this ain't it.

I was starting to feel like a cop who had seen so much crime he lost his faith in the system. But I knew the truth. Most U.S. hospitals care for patients without suing them and garnishing their wages. What's more, some hospitals forgive patients who can't pay without making them feel like fugitives. I wanted to visit one of these great American hospitals and find out how they can afford to do it. I would soon find one in rural Nebraska.

A Breath of Fresh Nebraska Air

I met Michael Hansen at the annual meeting of the Nebraska Hospital Association, where I spoke about health care transparency. Mike, the mild-mannered and affable CEO of a rural Nebraska hospital, was the association's board chair, and he liked my message of fairness and transparency in hospital pricing. He approached me after my talk and invited me to visit his hospital. Within a few months, we had planned a time for me to go and see his hospital in Columbus, Nebraska, 70 miles west of Omaha, bang in the middle of the heartland.

I landed at the Omaha airport and immediately saw a big Omaha Steaks shop in the airport terminal. This was beef country. Mike picked me up and we drove a little over an hour, past cornfield after cornfield. As we arrived in Columbus, a town of about 25,000 people, he pointed out the Cargill and ADM food factory and processing centers. This was a blue-collar town built on corn. Ag was king in rural Nebraska. Throughout our drive, Mike educated me on the life of the typical Nebraska farmer.

He pulled up to the Ramada Inn, where I checked in and dropped off my bags. Even though it was the nicest hotel in town, the room cost a fraction of what you'd pay for the best rooms in the big city. From there, we went to the hospital, an average-sized facility on 80 acres of land. Mike pointed out the $20 million wellness center they had built to promote fitness, where they also have a bike share program, cooking classes, and many walking and running events, as well as events for people with disabilities. We also went to the surgery center and clinics, conveniently scattered around the hospital to make pulling up and parking easier.

"In-hospital care is not health care," Mike explained. "In-hospital care is about 14% of health care. The rest is determined by social determinants of health, behaviors, and choices."

Mike was proud of the way his hospital interacts with its community. For example, he explained how their occupational and physical therapists partner with 850 businesses in town to promote healthy living and prevention. This seemed to be medical nirvana.

Mike and I discussed his hospital's finances. As I suspected from the tour, they were doing well. While many hospitals have a 3 or 4% profit margin, his had been in the range of 10 to 15% over the past several years. Most hospitals claim they make good money on privately insured patients but lose money on their Medicaid and Medicare patients. I had to ask Mike whether his payer mix explained the healthy profits. Perhaps the hospital had only a few patients covered by government plans.

"That's what everyone asks me when they hear we have a strong margin," he said. "But no, 50% of our patients are Medicare or Medicaid."

What? Hospitals usually claim they can't get by on what the government pays through Medicare or Medicaid. Columbus Community Hospital proved they could.

The other half of the hospital's patients are mostly covered by the dominant insurance company in the state. The company pays the hospital about what it charges, which is close to the lowest prices in the state, he said.

Mike said the hospital doesn't waste its time and resources playing price games with insurance companies. There is pretty much one price per procedure, which anyone can look up on his hospital website. He offers every insurance company a minimum discount of 4%, no exceptions: "We don't play that game where one insurance carrier gets a secret 20% discount and the other one gets a 5% discount."

The flat 4% discount means that out-of-network patients don't get outrageous bills. But was there a catch? Did Mike's hospital take care of a lot of wealthy people? Did it have a big donor, or few uninsured patients? It didn't. The average income in Columbus was about $26,000. It's a farming and blue-collar town of food processing and some steel workers. Columbus Community Hospital was the only hospital around, so it takes care of everyone, including those who are uninsured. There was no alternative "safety net" hospital subsidized to take the poorest patients.

Mike reduced his costs by keeping his middle management to essential personnel while investing in the people who worked there with good pay and benefits. At a time when hospitals struggle to staff their wards with nurses and doctors, Mike had set up extra rotations for nursing and medical students and residents. The best of them were drawn to the place by its positive culture, making recruitment and retention easier and less costly. While the average turnover rate in Nebraska hospitals is 19%, Columbus Community Hospital has steadily averaged an 11% turnover rate.

I brought up the lawsuits. "I've discovered that about one third of hospitals in some parts of the country sue patients for unpaid medical bills and have the court garnish their wages."

"That's wrong," Mike said, almost before I could finish my sentence. "Any nonprofit hospital should spend about 5% of its money on taking care of people who can't pay. Our goal is to spend a bit more than that." Mike described two complex cancer operations they had recently performed on undocumented patients, as well as babies they had delivered for free, without blaming the mothers for their inability to pay. It's one thing for a hospital to eat the cost of someone who comes into their emergency room. But it's another when a hospital approves elective surgery when they know the patient will be unable to pay. That's real charity care.

If patients need a payment plan, Mike works a deal with the local bank to give them a low-interest loan. The hospital backs the debt, so if the patient defaults, it falls on the hospital, not the patient. I pressed Mike to see how far his hospital would go to collect an unpaid bill and he said they do a lot to be reasonable and help people, mostly by offering to work with patients by giving them a discount and putting them on a payment plan.

As I thanked Mike and his wife, Colette, for hosting me during my stay in Columbus, Nebraska, I realized that his hospital's success had huge implications for health care. A well-run hospital can be profitable even when half its bills are paid by Medicare and Medicaid. It doesn't have to overcharge its patients. And it doesn't have to sue them when they can't pay. When people ask me if I'm optimistic about the future of health care, I say "yes," and I think about hospital executives like Mike and places like Columbus Community Hospital. It's a reminder that there are a lot of inspiring people who are keeping hospitals true to their great mission.

CHAPTER 5

The Ride

When I was growing up in rural Pennsylvania, there wasn't a lot of exciting stuff to do. There was no movie theater, and the oh-so-quiet library wasn't for me. But the town had an ambulance. The day I turned 16, I became a certified EMT, spending nights at the volunteer ambulance station along with my friend and class-mate Rick Hebert. For a teenager, flipping those lights and sirens on and watching the road ahead clear was a power trip like no other. At the sound of the station alarm, I transformed from a socially awkward teen to Moses parting the Red Sea. Flipping on the lights and sirens offered a rush so enticing that Rick and I were sometimes known to use them while transporting a nursing home patient to a scheduled rheumatology appointment.

A few times we responded to a crash scene where things looked so terrible we'd radio the dispatch center to send the helicopter, the mother of all emergency vehicles. We would stand in awe of "the bird," as we called it, slick, dark blue, and chalked with medical emblems. Medics and nurses would land, hop out in jumpsuits and flight helmets, and scoop up a patient as if it were a Navy SEAL extraction. Heroic and inspiring.

Our local hospital, Geisinger, owned the helicopter. That meant the reasonable $800 to $2,000 cost of the helicopter ride would be added to the patient's hospital bill and covered by insurance. For decades, hospitals charged reasonable prices for helicopter flights based on their true equipment, fuel, and personnel costs.

Some hospitals, including Geisinger, even took a loss some years on their helicopter programs. The loss was inconsequential because the complex patients flown in were high utilizers and profitable. For decades, that was how the business of air ambulances worked in America.

But over time, investors moved in and radically changed the ecosystem. They saw big profits if they could buy the air ambulance service from the hospital and bill the patient directly. That is, if the hospital didn't own the helicopter, the transport would not be on the hospital bill and often not be covered by insurance—the patient would be responsible for the bill. Injured patients began opening surprise bills having no idea that the trip in the bird wasn't covered by their insurance. Even when insurance would cover part of the bill, the helicopter's new private owner could go after the patient directly for the difference, a practice known as "balance billing."

Air ambulance bills began to inflate and superinflate and super-hyperinflate. We're talking tens of thousands of dollars for a short ride and even hundreds of thousands of dollars in some cases. Between 2007 and 2016 alone, the average price of an air ambulance transport charged by one company went from $13,000 to $50,000.[1] With big money on the table, it was off to the races. Private equity firms began buying air ambulance services from hospitals and setting up shop all over America, regardless of need. The number of air ambulance companies increased by 1,000% from the 1980s to 2017. In Ohio, EMTs began observing multiple helicopters landing at the same car accident site, each jockeying for the business to transport patients. In one instance, seven helicopters arrived at a car accident scene, apparently looking for customers. For-profit medical flight companies swooped in and set up shop around busy hospitals. For example, in 2015, Vanderbilt Medical Center found themselves surrounded by for-profit helicopter companies and, after losing market share, sold their program operations to one of them. As a result, bills from Vanderbilt Life Flight no longer appear on your hospital bill. Instead they come from the for-profit company that is considered out-of-network. The air ambulance industry has become big business in America.

Small-Town America

People living in rural states are getting hit the hardest. Sitting at home in Montana, John felt a stomach cramp one day. It was a little worse than the bellyache of everyday life. At his local hospital, the doctors told him, "This could be serious. We are going to transfer you to the big city where they can take care of you." About eight hours later, afraid and with no other options explained to him, he was wheeled off to the elevator, where the nurse hit the H button (for helipad). A helicopter pilot was there to greet him. He was loaded on the chopper for a 30-minute ride to the city.

When he arrived at the city hospital, he was peppered with medical questions and assigned to wait in the emergency room. The beds were full, so they placed him on a stretcher in the hall. There he waited several more hours until that hospital's on-call specialist saw him. He repeated the battery of tests and then hours later explained that John had no real reason to be in the hospital. He told him he could go home.

"How do I get home?" he asked his nurse after the doctor left. An army of discharge planners came to his bedside and offered to call his wife for him or pay for a cab ride to the local bus station. He called his wife and said, "Honey, I'm fine, and they say I can go home. Can you come pick me up?" Early the next morning, his wife drove several hours to get him. Meanwhile in the hospital, a nurse, doctor, social worker, and unit coordinator would all repeatedly ask John for the exact time that his ride would arrive. They needed his hospital bed.

A few months later, John received a flurry of bills totaling almost $400,000. He called his insurance company and got scolded for flying to a hospital that was out-of-network, a designation of which he was unaware. He was told that the $60,000 helicopter bill was not covered. Soon after, collection agencies began harassing him with calls and threats. He called the numbers on the bills but was merely offered a 10% discount if he paid in cash immediately. They also told him about a financial aid program that let him pay in monthly installments of $5,000—you know, the kind of pocket change most people have around.

John had read a recent news story about a Johns Hopkins study I led on hospital markups and called to tell me about his dire situation. "What did I do wrong?" he asked. I looked over John's bills and was able to quickly discern that he hadn't needed half of the stuff listed on his bills. Also, his helicopter ride should have cost 10% of what he was billed. I told him about "the game." Sadly, the collectors had called and threatened him often enough that he had decided to dip into his retirement savings to pay the bill.

Medical centers and air ambulance companies price-gouge in hopes that naïve and frightened patients, employers, or payers will fork over the entire bill's charge in a moment of weakness. You may think it's good for insurance companies to just pay the inflated bills outright. But that money has to come from somewhere. Insurers pass inflated air ambulance prices on to everyone else in the form of higher premiums.

It seemed that health care was simultaneously saving and destroying lives.

John is just one of many patients and families who have had their lives wrecked by an air ambulance bill. Take the case of Hugh Sparks of Plano, Texas. Hugh and his son stopped by the side of the road to take photographs, but Hugh got too close to a rattler that dug its fangs into his wrist. They drove to the nearest hospital, where he was treated with antivenom.[2] But the doctor there recommended transferring him to a larger hospital in Abilene, Texas, about 50 miles away.

Hugh was worried that an air ambulance would be expensive, but the medical workers insisted he take it. They didn't offer a ground ambulance option and wouldn't let his son drive him. A helicopter whisked him to the bigger facility, where he spent three days wondering if he might die.

Hugh survived the bite, but months later, he felt he might die again when he got a bill for $43,514 from the air ambulance company. His Blue Cross Blue Shield insurance paid $13,827. The air ambulance company turned around and billed him for the $29,687 balance. He said he felt a "slow, boiling anger" when he opened the bill. "That was actually more traumatic than when I realized I was bitten by a rattlesnake," he said.

Out-of-network price gouging has become so lucrative that air ambulance companies hustle to grow their business. Pilots can't just listen to police scanners and dispatch themselves. Instead, they rely on medical professionals to summon them. As a result, for-profit air ambulance programs have become aggressive in their quest to win referrals from EMTs, paramedics, nurses, and emergency physicians.

Talking to people on the ground, I discovered air ambulance companies have flown in pizzas to please emergency room staffers. That's what you call a special delivery for your pepperoni pie. And they give away cool flight helmets. As a teenage EMT, I could only dream of having my own life flight helmet. Some companies have built helipads for hospitals and installed activation buttons so doctors or nurses can rapidly summon a helicopter for a hospital-to-hospital transport. As for-profit air ambulance companies expanded, they started paying paramedics, nurses, and doctors to become advisers, with informal agreements to promote the company to first responders and other medical professionals.

A Glimmer of Hope

In talking to a lot of experts about air ambulance price gouging, I heard from a few of them how Dirk Visser and a few doctors are shaking up the industry for the good. I met up with Visser in his office in Missoula, Montana. A pleasant Montana gentleman, he was low-key but confident. He explained how people in rural areas are hit the hardest by hyperinflated air ambulance bills.

Dirk runs a large third party administrator—that's a company that manages employee benefits for companies that self-fund their medical care. In other words, he's on the receiving end of a lot of these helicopter bills, processing them for the plans his company administers. He's seen it all. Dirk told me of one patient who was flown from Montana to a rehab facility in Florida by one air transport company. They flew him on a 1978 Lear 7 jet and charged $630,000. "The plane itself only sells for $350,000!" Dirk told me.

As we talked, he kept one-upping himself with the egregious price gouging stories.

Dirk had seen so many abuses he decided to do something about it. He and his colleague Jeff Frazier founded a company called Sentinel Air Medical Alliance. The company is committed to price transparency and to putting a stop to the air ambulance rip-offs. They use the power of the free market to give patients a fair price, up front, with no games.

"Marty, you can let people know that we'll transport any patient from any point A to any point B within the continental U.S. for under $20,000," Visser told me.

A fair price never to exceed $20,000? Sounds reasonable. Wow, talk about a market force!

I then spent some time with his colleague Jeff Frazier, who runs the day-to-day operations of Sentinel Air. Jeff has the perfect combination of skills and experience to disrupt the air ambulance industry. He spent more than two decades flying helicopters for the United States Coast Guard and worked as a commercial pilot for TWA. He's also a finance expert. But maybe his greatest advantage is that he spent several years running his own air ambulance company. He knows the business cold, so he can see through the schemes and loopholes companies use to take advantage of patients.

Frazier first got an inkling that the industry was ripe for disruption when he flew medical helicopters as a pilot. It seemed that, well, not every flight was a true emergency. During one patient transport, the patient asked if someone had a camera so he could take pictures. Another asked if Frazier could hover over his house so he see what it looked like from the air. One "patient" asked if Jeff could find a herd of elk because he and a buddy were going hunting the following week. "I got the sense we were not snatching people from the jaws of death," Frazier told me.

Frazier was on to something. Most people see air ambulances only when they arrive at the scene of an accident. We get the impression that these flights are used just in dire emergencies and are a rarity. But that's not the case. Eighty percent of the more than half a million air ambulance flights a year (1,300 per day) in the United States are *not* emergencies but are much more like routine transfers. In other words, most of the time, these helicopters are taking stabilized patients from one facility to another—just as I took nursing home patients to the hospital as a teenage ambulance driver. "Many of those trips could be done at a much lower cost with a ground ambulance," said Frazier.

Even among so-called emergency flights, there appears to be a lot of waste. An analysis by the University of Arizona of more than 5,200 trauma patients concluded that "nearly one-third of patients transferred by helicopter were minimally injured."[3]

Frazier's Sentinel Air Medical Alliance fights the predatory tactics of the air ambulance industry in several ways. They have put together a network of air ambulance providers all over the country who are willing to bid for jobs so consumers can get a fair price. Most transports aren't emergencies, so Sentinel's staff can quickly make calls to get a reasonable rate. That's how Sentinel Air guarantees that a customer can get anywhere in the United States, coast to coast, for a reasonable price, never to exceed $20,000.

Not every air ambulance patient gets hit with an inflated bill. Patients covered by Medicare and Medicaid, aka the government payers, make up a large percentage of air ambulance flights. The law doesn't allow companies to bill Medicare or Medicaid patients for anything above what the government pays. It's only non-Medicare, non-Medicaid patients who are affected by price gouging.

Sentinel Air sometimes represents patients and insurance companies who are hit with unfair charges, stepping in to negotiate with air ambulance companies. Since they know the real costs of helicopters, staff and fuel, they get right down to the numbers. Some of the markups they've seen make drug markups looks like peanuts. In one case, an 18-year-old girl with cystic fibrosis was traveling with her family in Ixtapa, Mexico, and needed to get home to Chicago. The air ambulance plane had to land in Houston for fuel, where the patient went into respiratory distress. The girl probably should have been rushed to a hospital in Houston, but the air ambulance service kept her on the plane to Chicago. The doctor who reviewed the case for Sentinel said it was borderline malpractice. The patient died a couple of days later.

It's a long way from Ixtapa to Chicago, so you would expect a large bill. But the air ambulance company charged a whopping $382,000. I went online to see how far I could fly on a private Lear jet for that price. It turns out that for $382,000 I could fly a private plane to China and back five times.

For the family who lost their 18-year-old daughter, Sentinel price-checked the company that charged $382,000 by calling and asking for a quote for the same aircraft and crew for the same two flights. The company quoted a total of about $54,000. The $382,000, Frazier said, is what they can get when they do business using the element of surprise. While there are many social injustices in this world, the reason I'm so appalled at predatory medical billing is that it's done to people when they are at their most vulnerable.

In another case, a young man suffered brain injuries in a freak accident when a tree fell on his car. He spent a month in the hospital and then needed to go to Atlanta, Georgia, for rehabilitation. The air ambulance company brokered, or outsourced, the flight and charged $150,000 just as a broker fee (by comparison, the Sentinel broker fee is $750). When Sentinel called to get a quote for the same flight, with the same craft and crew, the company said it would do it for $14,300.

With their industry knowledge, Sentinel calculates the true aircraft, crew, maintenance, and fuel costs to shed light on inflated bills. Hearing Visser and Frazier describe how they are challenging a nontransparent industry in health care, I was amazed at their boldness. Even though both of them live in bear country, they don't seem to believe in the "Don't poke the bear" rule. As you would expect, Sentinel is hitting a nerve by cutting into the industry's profits. That's why one of the industry giants is suing Sentinel, on the grounds of defamation for calling out their unfair prices.

Visser has spent hundreds of thousands of dollars fighting this lawsuit. And the lawsuit has been revealing. In one deposition statement, the CEO of the air ambulance company argued that whatever amount they charge, the bill should be paid in full, even if it is $1 million.

The U.S. Government Accountability Office exposed the alarming air ambulance industry practices in a 2017 report. The price inflation may have been the most disturbing finding. Companies charge patients a lift-off fee and then a price per mile. Between 2010 and 2014 the median prices for an air ambulance doubled, from about $15,000 to about $30,000 per transport. Some companies average much more today and the trend is continuing upward. Charges by Air Methods, the country's largest air ambulance company, increased from $13,000 in 2007 to $49,800 in 2016, said the government report. That's a 283% increase in ten years.

Three large companies control 75% of the helicopters in the business, government investigators found. The companies are for-profit and often owned by private equity firms. "Investors see profit opportunities in the industry," investigators wrote.

Air ambulance companies claim they lose money from government payments, so they charge insured patients more to make up for it. One air ambulance provider had contracts with fewer than 10 out of approximately 1,000 private insurance companies. That means 99% of its patients are out-of-network. Going after the patient for the balance above what insurance may pay is a profitable tactic, browbeating either the insurance company or the patient to pay up.

The costs to run an air ambulance business are high, and fixed, the government report said. Air Methods said it requires 13 people to maintain 24/7 readiness—4 pilots, 4 paramedics, 4 nurses, and a mechanic. The average cost per transport was between $6,000 and $13,000 in 2016, according to the 8 providers who spoke to the GAO. A typical Medicare payment is about $6,500, and Medicaid and self-pay reimbursements are even lower, according to the providers.

Frazier can cut through the industry's excuses for its high prices because he knows how they play the game. He said Medicare's reimbursement rates are enough to cover the cost of most air ambulance flights. In 2004, Medicare used the industry's numbers to set favorable rates, he said. And you can see the air ambulance industry liked the rates because of the incredible increase in companies, he said. Back in the 1980s, there were fewer than 100 air ambulance helicopters nationwide. In 2016, there were

1,045. When I asked experts how many air ambulance helicopters we need in the United States to ensure the safe and rapid transport of critical patients, they said we probably need about 600.

The reason our country has so many helicopters is because there's money to be made, said Frazier, not because people are suddenly having more medical emergencies. Air ambulance companies were setting up across the street from one another. The Dallas–Fort Worth area alone has 24, while the neighboring Rio Grande Valley, a migrant farm worker area, has none.

Dr. Abernathy

I wanted to hear the truth about the industry from someone who really knew, so I reached out to Dr. Michael Abernathy, professor of emergency medicine at the University of Wisconsin School of Medicine and director of the hospital's medical flight program. He knows the industry and its money games. Dr. Abernathy's medical flight program has been retained by the hospital and does not gouge anyone.

"We operate in the black and we charge less than half of what the others charge," he told me in a long phone conversation. "In fact, our hospital's air ambulance prices are in the lowest 15th percentile in the country." Dr. Abernathy explained that after private companies moved into the market, they added a $30,000 "lift-off" fee in addition to a per mile fee. He added that some for-profit companies are good and fair: Boston Med Flight and Acadian, among others. He even described how Sentara, a Virginia-based hospital system, operated their high-quality program at a loss to serve their community. But, he added, many air ambulance companies are charging more than they should.

Dr. Abernathy said the state of Wisconsin does "a pretty good job with 13 helicopters." The nearby state of Missouri has 37, he said, even though both states have roughly the same population (12 million), same size (65,000 versus 69,000 square miles) and same flying conditions (lots of snow). I asked Dr. Abernathy why

the big difference in the number of helicopters. "Medicaid reim-
burses better in Missouri," he said.

Dr. Abernathy also pointed out that Medicare and Medicaid do
not pay based on quality, which drives many for-profit companies
to use old planes and staff with bare-bones training. His medical
flight team at the University of Wisconsin, a nonprofit operation, flies "state-of-the-art twin-engine birds, has excellent crew
training, and includes a physician on each flight. Other companies fly 30-year-old single-engine AS350 and Bell 206 aircraft,
with little training and no physician on board. Both get paid the
same."

A *Consumer Reports* analysis suggests Dr. Abernathy may be on
to something. Based on their review of National Transportation
Safety Board data about air ambulance accidents between 2010 and
2016, *Consumer Reports* concluded the nonprofit companies were
safer.[4] A 2014 study published in the *Journal of Trauma and Acute
Care Surgery* found that of 139 crashes, 118 involved for-profit
operators.[5]

Breaking It Down

I realized that the growth of air ambulance is facilitated by the
portability of the business. Imagine you had a burger shop and
noticed that business would be better in the next town. Moving a
brick-and-mortar store involves acquiring new property, moving,
hiring new employees, and the bureaucracy of permits, utilities,
and other paperwork. Now, if your business was a food cart without
government regulation or permits, you could home in on the profit
centers. That's how the air ambulance business works. The
industry claims it needs all these air ambulances, but that's not
true, said Dr. Abernathy, and I trust his judgment. Dr. Abernathy
has flown more hours on air ambulances than any other physician
in the country.

The excess number of helicopters in some states means each
aircraft gets fewer flights. Frazier said it's true that most of the
costs are fixed, and he broke them down for me. The fuel and the

equipment and staff are about $160,000 per month for one heli-copter. If you have a lot of flights, the cost per flight is lower than if you have a few flights. If a company has 40 flights per month, each flight will be about $4,750. Medicare pays an average of $6,200 per flight, so that's a handsome profit if a company gets enough flights. If the company gets half as many flights, the cost per flight will be about twice as much. Then the Medicare reim-bursement doesn't cut it.

Now that air ambulances have flooded the market, to make their profits, companies need to push for more flights and higher prices. How do they bring in all those flights? They staff their flights with local doctors, nurses, and EMTs who work in the facilities. When they work shifts outside their ambulance jobs, and someone needs a transport, they remain loyal to their air ambulance company.

The undisclosed conflicts of interest create an unfair situation for patients. Frazier compared it to a scenario in which you're driving down the road and your car stalls. A sheriff calls a tow truck for you, which takes you five miles down the road to the nearest town. Then the tow truck driver says you owe him $5,000, and if you don't pay it he'll send you to collections and put a lien on your house. Then a few days later you see the sheriff off duty driving the tow truck, and you realize the sheriff works on the side for the tow truck company.

It seems that profiteering air ambulance companies strive to avoid having patients shop for a fair price. Sentinel's process of getting bids, when the patient's condition allows them to take an hour to collect bids from multiple air ambulance companies, uses the free market principle. Hence the market prevents companies from exploiting patients with inflated charges.

The folks at Sentinel Air gave three case studies to federal government investigators. Each one compared the "market" rate to the "surprise" rate:

Example 1: The company American Medflight flew a patient from Ely, Nevada, to Salt Lake City, Utah, in a 1978 Piper Chey-enne turboprop airplane. That's 213 miles. American Medflight charged $55,155 for the flight. (Frazier said that's about 17% of the cost of the aircraft.) Sentinel contacted American Medflight and asked for a quote for a patient transport from Ely to Salt Lake City. The company said it would do the flight, using the same aircraft and crew, for $7,200.

Frazier said the lower price is actually market rate. You must assume the company still profits with this more reasonable fee, he said. But when the company had no market participation, it could charge 766% of the market rate. Frazier sent American Medflight's original bill and its drastically lower quote to the GAO.

Example 2: REACH Air Medical flew a patient 232 miles from Elko to Reno, Nevada. The company charged $65,000. Sentinel contacted REACH and asked for a quote for the same service. The company said it would do it for $13,000. In that case, the company's charges were 500% of the market rate, he said.

Example 3: Airlift Northwest used a Lear jet to take a patient from Juneau, Alaska, to Seattle, Washington. It charged $101,388. Sentinel called the company and got a quote, for the same flight, of $22,950. Airlift's charges were 422% of the market rate.

Frazier said there's an easy explanation for the large gap between billed charges and the bids on the same flights: customer choice. "Providers knew that if they failed to provide a competitive quote, the customer would contract with another service," Frazier wrote to the investigators. "In other words, the quoted rates are the *market* prices for the above transports."

Many companies hide their prices from consumers, Frazier told the government investigators. He provided an air ambulance consent form that patients have to sign making them responsible for the payment for the flight. The companies know how much each flight costs, he said, but they don't give a price to patients when they make them sign the legal paperwork. "Air ambulance providers go to great lengths to conceal their billed charges, operating costs, and the availability of other providers," Frazier wrote to investigators. "Again, the last thing they want to do is participate in a market."

Frazier's letter cited an ABC News story in which a company was asked why it didn't inform patients about the cost of their services. The company said: "Some have asked why we don't include pricing on our release forms and the truth is because the number one focus of family and loved ones in these traumatic situations is on making clinical decisions so their loved ones survive. That's their number one focus—and it's our number one focus too."

At best, that response is disingenuous. At worst it's downright dishonest, because most air ambulance flights are not actual emergencies. Also, medical providers can't think only about the physical well-being of patients. Ripping them off hurts them, too. And the industry doesn't let things go if a bill is unpaid. Air ambulance patients who can't pay their bills often get hounded by collectors and air ambulance companies place liens on their homes.

Because of the growing uproar by everyday Americans who have been gouged with no legal recourse, legislators have been getting an earful. Several states have investigated the air ambulance industry on behalf of consumers. Patients and consumer advocates confronted the companies at a Maryland Insurance Administration hearing.

Lori Parks-Murphy submitted her story in writing for the hearing. In 2014, her husband was flown from Meritus Medical Center in Hagerstown to the hospital where I work, Johns Hopkins Hospital. Air Methods charged $42,863 for the 63-mile journey— more than his bill for an entire week at the hospital. The company billed the couple $37,756 for the amount their insurance wouldn't pay.

Air Methods is a publicly traded company that had more than $1 billion in revenue in 2014, Parks-Murphy wrote in her statement. Its average bill is in the range of $40,000. In her case, the charges don't reflect the cost of services, and the company refused to substantiate them. "These companies charge exorbitant fees because they can," she wrote. "It is outrageous that these air ambulance companies profit from the pain and suffering of critically ill patients."

Officials from two air ambulance companies at the hearing, Air Methods and PHI, used the same old excuses defending their charges. They said the high prices are a result of the cost of keeping their fleet at the ready around the clock. Also, Medicare and

Medicaid rates don't cover their costs, and when private insurers don't pay the full price, the companies have to turn to consumers. "Our intent is never to gouge patients," said an accountant for Air Methods.

Industry insiders gave federal investigators three suggestions for addressing the high prices. Congress could change the Airline Deregulation Act to allow states to have an oversight role. Medicare could raise its rates for air ambulance services. Or the Transportation Department could collect data, for investigations or to make the public more aware of prices. The government investigators recommended that the Secretary of Transportation:

- Post air ambulance complaints online, including those related to balance billing.
- Make complaint information public; for instance, the number of complaints per company.
- See if there's other data that could help check unfair or deceptive practices by the companies.
- Consider requiring the companies to inform patients about their prices and insurance contracts.

Unfortunately, air ambulances companies are only one example of how a wealthy class of businesspeople has figured out how to gouge ordinary Americans at a time when they are most vulnerable. Free markets rely on price transparency, which is not only absent with air ambulance transports, but the payments to referring first responders, nurses, and doctors are unknown to the people who get stuck with the bill. If you think this problem affects only those being transported and their loved ones, remember that when health insurance companies are given these bills, they often pay them and pass the cost on to you in the form of higher health insurance premiums, especially in rural areas.

It's not just air ambulances that are preying on patients at a scary time in their lives. Some *ground* ambulances are doing the same. More and more people are risking their lives by taking the popular ridesharing services Uber or Lyft to the hospital even for medical emergencies. Why would they take a gamble on a much slower form of transportation? They're desperate to avoid the predatory billing of ground ambulance companies.

My friend Jill risked her life to avoid the money games of a ground ambulance. She had watched her brother go through a nightmare fight with their local ambulance company after he received a surprise $8,000 bill for a short lift to the hospital. After that, she vowed to avoid an ambulance at any cost. Then, a year later when she felt deathly sick and started vomiting, she called Lyft to take her to Inova Fairfax hospital. Curled up in the fetal position in the back seat, she arrived, and noted seven other Uber and Lyft cars also dropping off patients like her, bent over in pain.

On her suggestion, I drove to Inova Fairfax hospital myself, where I used to work in the emergency room as a trauma resident, and saw what she was talking about. Instead of the ambulances I remember clustered around the emergency room drop-off area, now there was a gathering of Uber and Lyft cars dropping people off.

We need to restore trust in health care services starting with more honest, transparent, and fair billing practices. It may take an act of Congress to end kickbacks and institute patient protections in the air ambulance business. But state lawmakers could take immediate action to protect consumers. If they can't control the prices, at the very least they could publicize them. How about a law requiring air ambulances to tell patients how much their flight is going to cost? Or a database that would track and publicly report each company's charges per flight? The database could also name the person who made the decision to summon the air ambulance company, so that hidden conflicts of interest could be revealed. If patients are going to be taken for a ride, at least they have a right to know how much the ride will cost them.

What I find most inspiring about the work to disrupt the predatory billing practices of the industry is the voices of the many doctors who are standing up for patients. It's an advocacy that's intrinsic to the profession of doctoring, perhaps known best to pediatricians but close to the heart of any compassionate doctor who cares for the defenseless and vulnerable.

Air and ground ambulances are still saving lives, as they were when I was an EMT, but today their bills are putting patients into a state of shock. My hometown ground ambulance company remains a volunteer community service and my hometown hospital of Geisinger decided not to play the air ambulance out-of-network price gouging game. The hospital never sold their helicopters to a private equity group. Instead, they continue to charge fair prices and include them on the hospital bill. Most admirably, they run their air ambulance program to serve patients rather than investors.

PART II
Improving Wisely

CHAPTER 6

Woman in Labor

Sweating profusely, her legs up in stirrups, Ebony's groans and screams flooded the emergency room. She was in the middle of another contraction. She was in the worst pain of her life, but it just another day on the job to the staff at the Florida hospital. After each agonizing push, Ebony fell into a micronap. Like calm water between crashing waves, the brief pause between contractions provided a moment of peace: her labor was progressing.

The obstetrician on call (I'll call him Dr. Dinner) had just completed his scheduled office visits for the day. Dr. Dinner had a routine. When on call, he finished seeing patients in his office by two o'clock. Then he would head to the hospital and perform a C-section on any woman in labor, whether she needed it or not. That way, Dr. Dinner made it home by five.

Doctors agree that, when possible, vaginal deliveries are ideal for both mother and baby. Even Dr. Dinner would agree. My OB/GYN colleagues at Hopkins explained the reasons. As the baby moves through the birth canal, contractions compress and expunge fluid from the lungs, promoting healthy breathing. In addition to the pain of major surgery and a longer recovery, C-sections can lead to surgical complications like infections. In some cases, the C-section scarring can change the contours of the mother's cervix and other anatomy, reducing chances of her having a vaginal delivery in the future. In rare cases, it can cause chronic pain. One

of our pediatric gastrointestinal doctors told me C-sections nega-
tively affect the bacterial balance in babies' GI tracts.

But letting labor progress naturally can take hours. No doctor
wants to get called out in the middle of the night. Instead, Dr. Dinner
used what we in medicine call the "one-hammer approach."
C-sections all around. By 2:15 in the afternoon, Dr. Dinner walked
up to Ebony and uttered that famous phrase that nudges moms
worldwide toward a C-section: "It might be safer for the baby."

I know nudging. A trigger phrase like that can be as powerful
as IV sedation.

Ebony responded to Dr. Dinner's nudge and the staff prepared
the operating room. If she hadn't agreed to the C-section,
Dr. Dinner had another line he frequently dropped: "If the baby
dies, you don't want to be responsible, do you?"

By four o'clock, Ebony's baby was delivered by C-section. Per his
routine, Dr. Dinner went home in time for supper with his family.

If only Ebony could have seen Dr. Dinner's pattern, his 95%
C-section rate, she would have known the truth: that his recommendation was in neither her nor her baby's best interest. Some
states publish their hospitals' C-section rates, but even those statistics wouldn't warn Ebony about Dr. Dinner. The overall hospital
C-section rate would be much lower than Dr. Dinner's because
most doctors perform the operations sparingly, in accordance with
best practices.

As I learned about Dr. Dinner's routine from staff who worked
with him, I knew that he broke no law. If you reviewed his individual C-section cases and challenged his judgment, he could
easily push back, pointing out his subjective bedside impressions
that would be impossible to verify. He could also produce the
consent forms Ebony signed—she agreed to the C-section and its
potential complications. No dummy, Dr. Dinner was keenly aware
of the litigiousness of obstetrics, so he would also have tight documentation to justify what he did. He knows his uniform approach
to delivering babies is immune to malpractice charges. He is
also immune to insurance scrutiny, since insurance companies
examine only deviations in the care of an individual patient, not
patterns based on groups of patients.

A Hole in the Data

As I thought about Dr. Dinner's pattern of unnecessary C-sections, I realized that the ways we measure the quality of health care can be deceiving. We spend a ton of money measuring quality. A study in the journal *Health Affairs* found that we as a country spend $15.4 billion per year on collecting and reporting our current set of quality metrics. That's the equivalent of giving every physician in America a part-time personal assistant.

But our methods of measuring quality are flawed. We focus on the results of a procedure, not on whether the procedure was appropriate. Hospitals track how often C-section patients get an infection or bounce back to the hospital after discharge, but they are not evaluating the most important question: Did the patient even need the surgery in the first place?

Dr. Dinner's "complication rates" were probably superb. As we surgeons know, if you are operating on healthy people who don't need surgery, your complication rate will be close to zero. Meanwhile all kinds of unnecessary procedures are never questioned. Our health care system measures the quality of knee replacement surgery by infection and readmission rates, even though both events are rare. At the same time, orthopedic knee surgeons have suggested that as many as one third of knee replacements are unnecessary.[1] That data point is missing from the quality formula, and the miss is a big one.

In my own specialty, pancreas surgery, most doctors exercise sound judgment in deciding when to operate. But there are others who are far less selective. Despite this wide disparity, all of us are measured by our complication rates. When I go to policy conferences and hear experts say "The only important thing in health care is outcomes," I feel torn. I want to agree with them, but I know the subtleties involved in how the starting population is defined. If you have unnecessary surgery with no complications, that's not a great outcome.

The health care system also measures quality by analyzing the process of doing an operation. Hospitals and regulators monitor how often hospitals administer antibiotics before surgery. They look at how hospitals take steps to prevent blood clots. They look at whether urinary catheters are removed within two days of surgery. I'm not criticizing these metrics. I've written that they should be publicly reported, and each measure that has been reported to the public has improved significantly over time. But let's not fool ourselves. None of them would flag Dr. Dinner. None of them would address what should be the fundamental question: Did the patient need the surgery?

We tend to lump everyone together by focusing on a hospital's overall quality. But that fails to address the variation that exists between types of treatment. In my pancreatic surgery specialty, the readmission rate is off-the-charts high (approximately 30%). That statistic holds true for me and all five of my partners, because that's the nature of pancreatic surgery. For some reason, when God made the pancreas, he didn't surround the organ with a capsule to protect it as he did with other organs. Cutting and manipulating the pancreas during surgery often causes it to leak at a high rate. It doesn't matter who performs the surgery or how delicately the surgeon works. Following the operation, leaks are anticipated.

My partners and I do more pancreas operations than any other group in the country. We use sound criteria and, given the type of surgery, we have great results that are frequently cited in journals and textbooks. But due to the way we currently measure quality, our specialty's unavoidably high readmission rate adversely affects the hospital's overall readmission rate. This one-size-fits-all approach would mistake what my partners and I do for subpar work.

The case of Dr. Dinner also exposes how our traditional way of measuring hospital quality misses issues of individual performance and their patterns.

Cindy

Recently, while catching a flight to Florida, I was exhausted, entirely ready to board my plane and relax. Unfortunately, the crankiest flight attendant on the planet happened to be on my plane. As I stepped on board, Cindy demanded I gate-check my small laptop bag. She claimed there was no room, but I could see there was plenty of space, especially in first class, where I was planning to enjoy my free upgrade. I asked if the flight included a drink service. "There is no time!" the attendant barked. I asked her for some water, which she plunked down on my tray half an hour later with a roll of the eyes. I felt like a FedEx package on a cargo plane.

The other flight attendant on board was kind and thoughtful. "I'm sorry about her," she apologized. "She's been here a long time," she whispered as she offered to get me a drink.

The next day the airline sent me an email asking for feedback on the service I had received during my flight. Seeing that the survey was general, asking me to rate my overall flight experience, I didn't complete it. I didn't want to complain and risk getting the good flight attendant in trouble. It hit me that performance data at the group level may have no effect on an employee who's causing problems. Yet that's what we do in health care every day—we feed group data to individual staff, then wonder why it's not having an impact.

Imagine that Cindy's supervisor informed her that the entire airline ranks below average in customer satisfaction. Or even if he said it was her individual flight crew. Would that information change her behavior? Probably not. She could easily dismiss the results and say "It must be other flight attendants bringing us down," or "My customers are more difficult because they fly out of some of the world's most frustrating airports."

Now imagine that the same rude flight attendant's supervisor tells her that her individual customer satisfaction score ranks at the very bottom, in the first percentile of the airline's 10,000 flight attendants. Then the supervisor informs her that her scores will be reviewed again every six months. That would change her behavior. Cindy might even start offering passengers an extra pack of pretzels.

That flight home reminded me of what should be a central tenet of measuring quality across any industry: data must produce meaningful results so people will be prompted to take action.

I often visit hospitals and hear "We collect all this data, now what do we do with it?" Administrators deliver organizational-level data to doctors and nurses and expect it to somehow transform behavior. That doesn't work. However, showing how individual doctors are performing can be formative and typically leads to rapid improvement. I've seen it happen many times.

Competitive by Nature

When I traveled to Providence St. John's Hospital in Santa Monica, California, I witnessed the dramatic effects of switching from group to individual data. In January 2017, the hospital's C-section rate for first-time deliveries was the highest among 12 hospitals in the region. Dr. Jon Matsunaga, chair of the OB/GYN department, didn't like how his hospital's statistics compared. Knowing that their patients were no different from the others', Matsunaga decided to get a handle on the data. The hospital began using peer benchmarking: they compared doctors to one another.

He showed each doctor in his department his or her C-section rate, and something magical happened. Immediately, the C-section rate plummeted. Within a matter of months, he reduced the hospital's C-section rate by half. Now Providence St. John's Hospital held the lowest ranking out of the dozen hospitals in the region. Dr. Matsunaga's leadership proved a critical prerequisite, but it was the power of peer benchmarking, with usable data, that resulted in thousands of healthier moms and babies in Southern California.

I asked Dr. Matsunaga how the obstetricians with the highest C-section rates changed their ways so quickly. He recognized that the doctors had allowed competing priorities to override what's best for the patient. He found that once he started sharing data among the doctors, it made them much less likely to nudge patients toward a C-section.

In the larger scheme of things, Dr. Matsunaga's intervention truly improved health outcomes, far beyond reducing complications per operation. His work redesigning the way doctors are managed had a greater impact on the community's health than any new medication or new technology in the field that year. Data, when used properly, can be incredibly powerful.

In a different case, a New York hospital asked me to analyze C-section rates for each doctor in a group that shared the same call schedule. Somehow one had an extremely high C-section rate compared to the others. I produced the doctor-specific data so each could see how he or she compared to their peers.

Based on the performance of the group, I showed an upper boundary of what would be considered acceptable. That way each doctor wouldn't feel pressure to be right at the middle. The focus was on the outliers whose rate went beyond the threshold—far beyond in the one case. The hospital leadership presented the reports to the doctors.

A few months later I sat in a conference room with a handful of this hospital's leaders. I asked them how the data was being received. "Most all of our obstetricians were pleased to see their data was in the reasonable range," one said.

"But," he continued, "our outlier doctor, the guy with the 60% C-section rate, he gave us an earful. He argued that his patients are sicker. He claims he is an expert on high-risk pregnancies, and because he is the best in his field, he gets the hardest cases within a poorer population."

I've heard those claims before. We agreed to do homework. I returned to Hopkins to talk with my obstetrics colleagues. They didn't buy the doctor's excuses. They treat a lot of high-risk patients from inner-city Baltimore and still have a C-section rate under 30%.

I asked the hospital leaders to ask the doctor what he considers to be a high C-section rate, given the complexity of his patients. 50%? 80%?

When I took a closer look at this doctor's data, I saw his patients were about the same as those of his peers. That was to be expected. It wouldn't make sense for him to get all the complex cases. The deliveries were random, based on whichever doctor was on call at the time.

Then I noticed something peculiar in the data. This doctor's C-section rate wasn't especially high on most days of the week. But on Fridays, it shot up to 80%. Were all the high-risk women coming in exclusively on Fridays? Maybe all these C-sections had more to do with this doctor's desire to enjoy his weekend.

I showed the hospital leaders the Friday phenomenon. They smiled and said, "Thank you very much." When they went back and showed the doctor his C-section rate broken down by day of the week, he quickly changed his tune. He no longer claimed his patients were more complex. He responded, "Okay, I'll see what I can do."

Seeing my own performance data has also helped me improve. At Hopkins, Dr. Caitlin Hicks, the surgeon on my team, teamed up with one of our anesthesiologists, Dr. Steve Frank, to tackle the problem of unnecessary blood transfusions. The problem was that doctors were sometimes ordering blood on patients who did not meet the laboratory criteria. The criteria were well established and based on many studies, including one in the *New England Journal of Medicine* from 20 years ago, but getting doctors to follow the evidence was a daily struggle at our hospital. So Drs. Hicks and Frank decided to be creative and harness the competitive nature of a doctor's personality. They began sending us regular reports on how our personal blood transfusion rates compared to those of others in our department. The result was dramatic. They saw an immediate reduction in unnecessary transfusions. One of the quarterly reports showed that my rate was higher than those of four of my partners who do pancreas surgery. I didn't like being an outlier without any justifiable explanation. It was the kick I needed to get back in step. The next time an anesthesiologist started hanging a bag of blood during surgery, I stopped him and asked whether the patient's blood level was low enough to meet the criteria in the national guidelines. He said "no," and that he had just assumed I might want the transfusion. I nixed it, sparing the patient unnecessary risks of a transfusion. The power of peer benchmarking became real to me.

Hard Work Ahead

After I got back from Florida, I talked to my research team about Dr. Dinner. We discussed ways to measure patterns of individual doctors' performance and evaluate the appropriateness of care. We knew our methods would have to be clinically smart so they'd be fair to physicians, tailored to their specialty and unique types of patients. We also had to make sure we collaborated with a diverse group of physicians who practice in the specialty being measured. Community physicians, not just academic physicians, had to be included. They have a unique vantage point, and after all, they deliver most of the medical care in the United States.

Measuring appropriateness would become a focus of our research team. We studied patterns of performance. They showed the style of doctors' practices, their threshold to intervene, and the degree of risk they take. Patterns are what we talk about in our surgical locker rooms and lounges. They are how we describe doctors who are following best practices and doctors who need help. They are what doctors like me use to find our own highest standard of medical care.

There's one strong reason that practice patterns have not been used to measure clinical appropriateness and waste in health care: this kind of study is hard work. Constructing measures that are smart and don't unfairly label great doctors as bad ones requires an intense understanding of the specialty, treatment algorithms, medical codes used, and an appreciation for doctors who may treat complex populations.

It also requires a good deal of time to establish consensus around thresholds of what constitutes an outlier, and a good deal of boldness to challenge outdated practice styles. It would take digging into the clinical nuances and areas of waste in countless clinical scenarios. Thousands of practicing doctors would need to contribute. Daunted by the project's scope, I considered retreating and instead simply writing philosophical pieces in the medical journals. But executing these objectives could make medicine more precise and less costly.

Soon after I presented the goal of measuring patterns to my research team, I spoke at the national health insurance conference put on by America's Health Insurance Plans (AHIP), where I outlined how using pattern data could allow for the measurement of the appropriateness of medical care. I concluded by suggesting we measure patterns of overuse. Susan Dentzer from the Robert Wood Johnson Foundation, the largest philanthropy in health care, was in the audience. She approached me after my speech. "Marty," she said, "I get it. Let's talk."

Susan previously worked as the editor in chief of *Health Affairs*, the nation's leading health policy journal. She knew the issues. Thanks to Susan, Anne Weiss, and Emmy Ganos at the RWJ Foundation, I soon had a large grant to create a new generation of quality measures. We would finally be able to measure appropriateness of care.

The RWJ Foundation had already funded the Choosing Wisely program, a national collaborative that challenged every medical specialty to list five tests or treatments that are usually unnecessary. For example, one of the consensus recommendations is not to use a DEXA bone scan in women under 65 to screen for osteoporosis. Another Choosing Wisely recommendation is to avoid a CT scan or MRI of the head in a child with a simple febrile seizure. Choosing Wisely has done an impressive job of raising awareness among both doctors and patients about the problem of overtreatment. The consensus recommendations can be found at ChoosingWisely.org.

Remarkably, the Choosing Wisely project created a new conversation in medicine about overuse. Eighty medical specialty associations participated and changed the culture of medicine. The next step would be to go beyond awareness and move to meaningful quality metrics. My charge from the foundation was to pick an area of medicine in which data transparency could be used to reduce unnecessary procedures and lower health care costs.

We called this new program Improving Wisely.

CHAPTER 7

Dear Doctor

The usual odorless, tasteless cubed cantaloupe made its standard appearance in the back of the Marriott Marquis meeting room, but this was no typical meeting. I was in Washington, D.C., with the top leadership of an association of skin cancer surgeons called the American College of Mohs Surgery. If you're not one of the millions of patients a year who get skin cancer, you may not have heard of Mohs surgery. But the technique—developed in the 1930s by Dr. Frederic E. Mohs[1]—is a big reason skin cancer is much more manageable today.

I had heard that the Mohs surgeons were interested in addressing overtreatment. And months earlier, I'd connected with the association's president, Dr. John Albertini, by phone. I had told him how my Hopkins team and I wanted to work with specialty associations to identify ways to measure the appropriateness of medical care. Right away, he got it. He even one-upped me, telling me about something else he saw doctors doing that troubled him.

To enable me to understand the problem, Albertini had to explain the technicalities of Mohs surgery. In this specialty, the doctor's role is unique because the doctor acts as surgeon, pathologist, and reconstructive specialist all during the same procedure. The goal is to excise all the skin cancer while minimizing the amount of healthy flesh that gets removed. A Mohs surgeon starts by cutting out the cancer in a block of tissue and examining it under the microscope. It might be a sliver of flesh or an inch-square cube. If the tissue block has cancer cells on the edge, that means the surgeon didn't remove all the cancer. It's what we surgeons call a "positive margin." The surgeon goes back to the patient and removes an additional sliver of tissue at that location. Each tissue block removed is referred to as a "stage" of the surgery. The Mohs surgery breakthrough is removing all the visible cancer while preserving as much normal skin as possible. In the old days, skin cancer surgery disfigured patients because doctors took so much flesh at once.

Here's where things get interesting. Mohs surgery typically takes one or two precise stages. On rare occasions, a third stage may be necessary. Surgeons get paid well for Mohs procedures. And it turns out that they get paid per stage. Cut a little extra here and there and you get a bigger paycheck, whether the extra cuts are necessary or not. As a surgeon, I was familiar with these types of financial "carrots" lying around the operating room.

Albertini explained that over the last several years, the association's leadership had heard multiple reports that some doctors appear to be doing the operation in too many stages. It may be that the doctors need further training. Or they could be motivated by money. Albertini proposed a pattern we could examine for the Improving Wisely project. We could look at the average number of stages each surgeon used during the procedures. We would see who was making the most cuts. "Most surgeons fall in a certain range," Albertini told me. "But some are going to be way out there adding time and expense to the procedure and unnecessary surgery for patients."

Albertini said that the project's success would depend on the buy-in of his colleagues: the leaders of the Mohs surgery association. We made a plan for me to join the association's executive leadership team when they gathered at the American Dermatology Association conference in Washington, D.C.

A Crucial Buy-in

I was nervous walking into the hotel conference room, so I took a pass on the cantaloupe cubes. This was my first time pitching to a surgical society the idea of analyzing the practice patterns of individual doctors. I hoped they would agree that lowering health care costs can start with eliminating medical care that doesn't need to be done in the first place.

This meeting could be critical. We as a country spend more than $15 billion a year reporting quality metrics to the government and to one another.[2] Doctors tire of flavor-of-the-month quality improvement campaigns—especially those imposed on us without our input. I knew doctors on the front lines had to define which practice patterns were appropriate and which were not. I needed to see consensus from them. I needed them to tell me the best way to proceed.

Albertini welcomed me, introducing me to the titans of the field. Sitting around the conference table were Dr. Tom Stasko from Oklahoma, Dr. Allison Vidimos from Cleveland Clinic, Dr. Richard Bennett from UCLA, Dr. Victor Marks from Geisinger, Dr. Barry Leshin from Winston-Salem, and Dr. Brett Coldiron from Cincinnati. I had read about Dr. Coldiron: he alone had performed more than 50,000 of these state-of-the art Mohs operations.

I dived into my presentation. I told them about the Improving Wisely model. I explained that the first step would be to identify something that's overdone in their field, then devise a smart way to measure how often a doctor does it, and then see if there is an agreement about how much is too much. Finally, we would reach out to the doctors whose practice patterns fell outside the boundary of what they considered appropriate. That feedback would show them how they compare to their peers and allow us the opportunity to help these doctors improve. My research team had taken Albertini's idea and run with it. I provided preliminary numbers showing that most surgeons averaged one or two stages during Mohs operations. But some averaged three or four.

As I talked, the surgeons were murmuring and nodding. The vibes were good. Then they started jumping in with comments supporting what I was saying.

"Makes sense," said one of the board members. "We need to do something about surgeons out there who are operating with no accountability."

"There are practice patterns that clearly cross a threshold," another surgeon added.

"This is what a professional association is supposed to be doing," chimed in one of the other Mohs leaders.

They got it! They felt pride in their profession and a duty to act. The surgeons there were concerned that a small number of doctors in their field might be sucking a lot of money from the system. They agreed that doctors who were out of line would not like being identified as outliers in their field. They hypothesized that these doctors' competitive nature would kick in and they would probably reduce their overuse on their own. From my own observations in medicine, I couldn't have agreed more. People respond well to competition.

The Mohs surgery leaders liked Albertini's proposal, and I did, too. Our intention wasn't to penalize or even require preauthorization for a doctor to remove a cancer in three stages or more; in some cases, it might be necessary. But a pattern of doing three blocks in a large number of patients is something these experts said seemed inappropriate. Cutting through the tumor rather than around it was a lucrative temptation doctors face frequently. Skin cancer is the most common cancer in the world, and the technique is used to treat the basal cell and squamous cell subtypes and is increasingly being applied to melanoma as well.

The Improving Wisely approach sure beat the old way of measuring infection rates and readmissions to the hospital. Both are exceedingly rare with Mohs surgery, which is done as an outpatient procedure. The board enthusiastically accepted the offer to partner with me and my team at Johns Hopkins. We were ready for takeoff.

Identifying Outliers

I got to work with my research team. We obtained data from the federal government for every patient in Medicare, the government's insurance program for the disabled and patients over age 65. The data included each doctor's identification number, and it showed the number of stages billed for each operation. We used the data to graph each surgeon in the United States by the average number of tissue blocks they removed during the skin cancer operations performed. Sure enough, as the Mohs surgery leaders had predicted, most doctors were within a range of normal practice variation. The typical surgeon averaged between 1.2 and 2 blocks, or stages, per patient over the course of a year. But there were also some outliers who averaged 4 or more stages per patient.

We took our results to the Mohs surgery leaders and they said the analysis confirmed their suspicions. They even recognized the names of some of the doctors who were in the top 2% of the outliers. They had heard stories about them or seen some of their patients for follow-up care. The experts in the field said that any high-volume surgeon who averaged more than 2.2 stages per operation was beyond the threshold of what they would consider appropriate. We had consensus.

Next, we sent letters to about half of the surgeons we analyzed. We didn't reach out to all of them right away because we wanted to study whether our outreach had any effect on their performance. We needed one group with whom we intervened and another that we did not (a control group). The letters came from the American College of Mohs Surgery (ACMS) and my team at Johns Hopkins. They included a one-page report that showed each surgeon how he or she compared to the rest of the Mohs surgeons in the country. A graphic designer helped my team generate physician-specific reports showing where each doctor stood on the bell curve. Doctors who used an average of 3 and 4 stages or more per case were way out on the tail end of the chart.

We didn't chastise anyone who fell into the outlier category. We simply said "This is where you stand relative to the rest of the Mohs surgeons in the country." We also indicated in the report that the association embraced a range of normal variation in the average number of stages per operation. According to the Mohs experts who designed the reports with us, it would be obvious to the outliers that they were well outside the range of what seemed appropriate.

The letter, signed by the top leaders in the field, also offered educational resources and invited feedback on the project.

We sent out about a thousand reports and then I held my breath. Would the notification make any difference?

Surprising Response

In the days after we notified the Mohs surgeons, I kept expecting the phone to ring with complaints. But the gripes didn't come— neither to me nor to the Mohs surgery leaders who had cosigned the report's cover letter. Then the emails began to roll in:

- *Thank you for the recent report. I had no idea where I stood relative to my peers nationally and now I know. I'm above average but will take a careful look to see how I can improve.*
- *I love showing this metric to my patients.*
- *I just wanted to give you a quick word of feedback on the Individual Surgeon Data Report I just received: I absolutely love it! I have wanted to know for some time where I stand relative to my peers regarding my average number of stages versus my peers and to my chagrin it just arrived in the mail! It gives us a nice benchmark to how we are doing.*
- *Thanks for sharing this data. I'll work on my technique. Will this information be used for anything? Will it be made public? Please let me know.*
- *I'd like to learn more about the retraining offered by ACMS.*
- *When will the next report be delivered?*
- *Thank you for the report. Very important.*
- *I had heard of the reports coming out and was glad to see I'm not an outlier.*

The surgeons appreciated seeing their data! Sure, the emails were anecdotal, but none of the responses challenged the metric. My team followed up with a survey that found that 80% of all surgeons in the association believed that sharing performance data like this was important. In my opinion, the positive response to the "Dear Doctor" letters was because this program was 100% homegrown, based on the wisdom of practicing doctors who understood the proper use and misuse of their craft.

But the million-dollar question was whether our intervention would work. Would it spur outliers to change their practice patterns? Our goal wasn't merely to inform the surgeons; we wanted change. We gave it a year and checked the national Medicare data again for the doctors we notified. The results were striking. We found that 83% of notified outliers had changed their ways for the better. Moreover, the reduction in blocks per case appeared to be sustained.[3]

The long-term follow-up data revealed an additional interesting trend. In the months after we sent the letters, even the outlier surgeons in the control group, whom we did not contact, began changing their behavior. They had not even seen their data but began to reduce their average number of stages per case, albeit to a lesser extent. Our intervention appeared to have had a crossover effect. And I can see why. It created a lot of buzz when we sent out the reports, and word travels fast among doctors within a specialty. The Mohs leaders also wrote commentaries about the initiative and gave talks about the importance of the program. I heard that some surgeons who fared well in our analysis were broadcasting the fact to their friends and peers. Hey, nothing wrong with that. The program had sent a message to outliers: your national leaders are monitoring the macro trends in your practice data.

Albertini liked what he was seeing. The initiative had created a culture of accountability, and he was hearing stories confirming the improvements were real. "Moreover, no one got humiliated or penalized," Albertini said. "It's a confidential peer-to-peer way to address our outliers in a civil way."

The entire program cost $150,000 that first year, but it resulted in $11.1 million in direct savings to Medicare—that is, to U.S. taxpayers. At the time I submitted this book to the publisher, the savings had escalated to $21 million in the two years after the intervention. Not only were the findings well-received by the medical community, but the publication of the results was accompanied by a very supportive editorial entitled "Physicians Respond to Accurate, Actionable Data

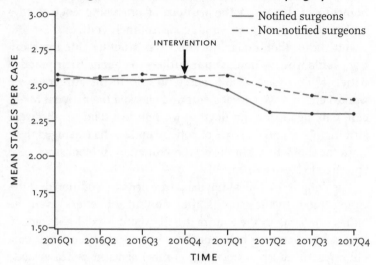

Average number of tissue blocks removed (stages)*

*analysis limited to only high-volume surgeons

on Their Performance," written by the American Medical Association board chair Dr. Jack Resneck and University of Iowa Mohs surgeon Dr. Marta Van Beek. The national conversation that followed affirmed the notion that when doctors are involved in quality improvement from the get-go, the results can be incredible. What else in health care yields a 7,430% return on investment?

But why do some performance improvement programs work so well while others struggle? I attribute part of the success to civility. By including practicing doctors early and by using a peer-to-peer method of sharing data in a way that is nonpunitive and confidential, we were highly effective. Moreover, the project focused on what doctors believe to be important. I have visited hundreds of U.S. hospitals and a consistent message I hear from their quality improvement leaders is "We collect all this data, now what do we do with it?" They're burdened with tracking all sorts of things, some of which don't matter. Ultimately, out of a sense of helplessness, the leaders dump this data on the doctors, who in turn explain it away with the claim "My patients are sicker."

The "My patients are sicker" argument has been a major barrier to improving health care. But it's code for something else. This is doctors saying "You don't understand me or what I do." It's what happens when quality improvement programs are forced on doctors without their consensus. To be effective, a method of measuring care must be developed and endorsed by the doctors and clinicians who work in that specialty. The input needs to come from a range of physicians who serve diverse patient populations. As we expanded Improving Wisely, I required that all the doctors on the expert panels spend at least 70% of their time in patient care. And I insisted on rural and community hospital representation to balance the doctors representing big academic hospitals.

Many other industries have their practice patterns measured. In 2009, the utility company Positive Energy (now Opower) was interested in reducing power use in neighborhoods. Their data showed that some households used far more electricity than their neighbors. After all, there are no standardized protocols on turning lights on or off when one vacates a room. Just ask anyone who's argued with a spouse about this issue.

The company decided to mail each household a regular feedback report that compared their electricity and natural gas usage to that of similarly sized households in their neighborhood. Playing on the benchmarking theme, the data feedback intervention resulted in an overall reduction in household energy use. When people saw they were outliers, they modified their habits so their usage fell more into line with that of their peers. In a year, this simple intervention reduced the total carbon emissions of the participating houses by the equivalent of 14.3 million gallons of gasoline, saving consumers more than $20 million.[4] Lots of utility companies now take this approach—and it works.

Metrics Matter

I've examined hundreds of quality metrics over the years and developed my own. I've come to believe many of them need context to be meaningful. The metrics must zero in on what it means for a patient's quality of life and potential disability. The criteria should focus on significant harm or waste by extreme outliers rather than small variations in practice. The metric also must be measurable and designed so it can't be tainted by bias or gaming. And finally, a sound metric should be highly actionable for the physician. Metrics such as mortality, while easy to collect, are hard to make actionable. We need more measures that provide direct insight into what the individual physicians can do right now to modify the way they practice.

After the skin cancer project with the American College of Mohs Surgery, I asked its leadership if anyone had ever proposed the measure they used for the project to Medicare or the broader health care community. Our data suggested that reining in these unwarranted practice variations has dramatic implications for lowering health care costs. "No," they said. No one in the broader medical policy world ever asked for their input, they explained. Yet again, I saw the disconnect between those making the rules in health care and those practicing it.

To try to address this gap, I set up a meeting with midlevel Medicare leaders. They liked the idea of setting boundaries of acceptable variation. They referred me to their website, which lays out their standard process for proposing a new quality measure for Medicare to consider using. I noticed that one of the requirements was that any proposed new measure be supported with multiple published articles proving that the measure was evidence-based. That's a nice idea, but a narrow way to look at quality improvement. No one would ever do a trial comparing the outcomes of surgeons who take two versus three blocks per case. For one thing, a trial subjecting people to three blocks per case would be unethical. I gave up on the website.

Medicare requires a quality measure to be based on published evidence. But in the Robert Wood Johnson Foundation project on Mohs surgery, we had a different way of looking at things. We used the wisdom of busy practicing doctors to create a specialty-specific way to measure quality.

The following year, I was invited to meet with the new batch of Medicare leaders at the highest level, Seema Verma, Paul Mango, Kim Brandt, and Adam Boehler. I explained to them that these pattern measures were very telling and that using them had broad implications for cutting waste in Medicare. Waste like the unnecessary vascular procedures Medicare was paying for, such as the ones being performed on church members down the street. The Medicare leaders I met with quickly "got it" and made further work on pattern measurement a priority. Within months, Medicare made plans to send out "Dear Doctor" letters to the country's most extreme outliers.

The peer comparison program conducted by the American College of Mohs Surgery was extremely well received. The following year, the association's leadership decided to expand the program to tackle overuse of skin flaps (a technique to move skin) and the overuse of Mohs surgery in areas of the body where it was rarely indicated, such as lesions on the trunk and legs.

The Improving Wisely project looking at skin cancer surgery rejected the conventional way that we measure performance. Instead it measured a physician's patterns to identify practices experts deemed dangerous or otherwise indefensible. We published our "appropriateness measure" for skin cancer surgery at the surgeon level, and then it was time to press forward. We would soon scale the model. Improving Wisely[5] was about to get a lot bigger.

CHAPTER 8

Scaling Improvement

The hospital cafeteria at Johns Hopkins is the Grand Central Station of new ideas in medicine. Grabbing yogurt and fruit one morning, I bumped into Dr. Ali Bydon, a very smart and jovial colleague specializing in spine surgery. I always enjoyed my conversations with Ali because he has such a pragmatic approach to medicine. We caught up quickly and I filled him in on the Improving Wisely project I was undertaking with the skin cancer surgeons. I treasure these interdisciplinary conversations with colleagues because I learn so much from them. When I asked Dr. Bydon if there was something in spine surgery that was over-done in a way that was measurable, he perked up. Some surgeons will inappropriately perform surgery for back pain in patients who have never tried physical therapy (PT), he said. In most cases, physical therapy manages the pain better than surgery. It should *always* be tried first. If PT fails, then surgery may be necessary.

His idea sounded as though it had potential for the Improving Wisely project. I asked him which specific operations he was refer-ring to, to see if I could pull the cases from the Medicare data. He rattled off a series of elective operations by name: lumbar laminec-tomy, discectomy, hardware insertion, and other elective (non-urgent) procedures. He also listed specific situations to exclude from the analysis because they could warrant emergency back surgery. For example, he told us not to include any operation that involved trauma, possible neurological injury, a spinal tumor, or paralysis.

Once I gathered the medical codes for each operation and clinical diagnosis, I swung by Ali Bydon's office and asked him the big question: "If we measured the percentage of elective back surgery operations that a surgeon does in which the patient had at least one physical therapy appointment in the preceding year, would that be a reasonable measure of appropriateness?"

"That would tell you a lot about the surgeon," said Bydon. "If there's no PT, that would probably tell you which surgeons are doing operations they shouldn't be doing."

I took the idea back to my research team and we graphed out every back surgeon in the United States by the proportion of elective back operations prior to which the patient had had at least one physical therapy visit in the preceding year. Sure enough, most surgeons were in the same range, but a small group of surgeons were doing a large proportion of their operations in patients who had never tried physical therapy even once before surgery.

Later, I went back to his office and this time brought a med student observing with me that day. I shared the findings with Dr. Bydon and he pointed out the subgroup of outlier surgeons on the graph. "Those are the surgeons doing unnecessary back surgery," he said. After a closer look, he remarked that most doctors do the right thing, but a segment of outlier surgeons had a practice pattern that was indefensible. "This is amazing data."

The med student asked, "Why can't you just require physical therapy before all back surgery?" Bydon pointed out there are rare exceptions when physical therapy does not make sense, or an occasional miscoded patient in the data. For those reasons, we wanted to create an acceptable range for a surgeon. For this measure, Bydon and other experts determined that at least half of a surgeon's elective back surgery patients should have physical therapy first, regardless of circumstances. That would be a starting point to promote best practices.

Surgeons who had none of their patients try physical therapy before back surgery were obviously outliers. Looking at their names in the national data made Bydon furious. Becoming a spine surgeon requires years of specialized training. It's a technical tour de force, an amazing specialty that can cure disability and other ailments. The outliers were playing a lucrative trick on patients and it was no secret in the spine surgery community. In the past, they had just not been identified.

Looking at the analysis again, Bydon said, "These doctors are giving spine surgeons a bad name."

In medicine, a recommended treatment guideline is rarely absolute. It could be entirely appropriate to modify procedures in an individual patient's situation. On the other hand, a recommended treatment could be modified because the doctor is profiteering, responding to our consumerist patient culture. Or perhaps the doctor is unaware of the best practice. Or it could be a mix of these reasons. In any case, it's difficult to determine whether deviating from the standards is okay or not. The approach of measuring patterns appealed to Bydon and other doctors because it factored in rare cases by creating an acceptable range. Doctors wouldn't be treated like miscreants for making an exception for a patient who needed it.

Bydon asked me if anyone had ever cut the data this way. I explained that we only recently got access to the information. Researchers, including me, had lobbied the government to give us access to the national Medicare data. We argued that since it's funded by taxpayers it should be accessible to the public. Medicare responded by providing a limited group of us access to the Medicare servers under a user agreement allowing us to look at a physician's unique national identification number. Even though it took a year to get access to the Medicare servers, we were now able to study pattern data. That's how my team was able to generate physician-specific reports for skin cancer surgeons. Prior to this unprecedented access, researchers like me were only given data that was three years old.

Measuring patterns also seems novel because it's hammered into every doctor—from medical school to residency and throughout our careers—that we cannot believe anything unless a randomized controlled trial has proved it. Of course, no one had ever done a trial in which patients were randomized to have elective back surgery without first trying physical therapy. Randomized trials done just to prove such a point would be unethical. We've all seen with our own eyes patients who avoided surgery because a physical therapist did a great job treating them. Even if someone did such a trial, it wouldn't tell you how often patients should have surgery without first doing physical therapy. The idea is ludicrous. Where I've challenged academic elites is that the randomized controlled trial design of research was developed to test medications compared to a placebo. Thankfully, others have spoken up as well. An entire issue of the journal *Social Science and Medicine* was recently devoted to it, with many articles pointing to the shortcomings of randomized trials.[1] Here's one way to think of it: randomized controlled trials are not the way one should evaluate whether a parachute is effective in saving the lives of skydivers.

Unfortunately, some physicians believe that a lack of a randomized controlled trial means there's no evidence. That sloppy and dangerous thinking gets worse when the medical community conflates "no evidence" with "not true." That's a logical fallacy. The term "no evidence to support" actually means one of two things: it's been studied and evidence does not support it, or it has not been studied and could be true. The liberal use of "no evidence to support" has conditioned us to distrust anything not supported by trial. I've taught my students and residents to do better, replacing the sloppy phrase "There is no evidence" with either "It is unknown because it has not been adequately studied" or "It has been studied adequately and has not been shown to be effective."

The concept behind Improving Wisely is to apply the wisdom of expert doctors to identify practice patterns that appear inappropriate. When I show the practice pattern data to doctors and they see outliers, they say "I get it." No trial necessary.

Engaging Doctors

Over the next year, as I had cafeteria and hallway conversations with my Johns Hopkins colleagues, I'd inquire about overuse in their particular specialty. Then I would ask whether the overuse could be measured as a pattern. Most of the time, the doctors had an immediate response. They often started with practices targeted by the Choosing Wisely project. But most of those can't be measured in big data because most national data lack the needed granularity. After more conversation, I could usually pique their interest and develop some sort of measure with them. For a time, I asked these same questions of almost every doctor I ran into, including at hospitals where I spoke as a visiting professor and at national medical conferences. My list of overused medical practices started growing. Insider insights shared with me were both fascinating and alarming.

In talking with my colleagues who do breast surgery, for instance, they told me that some surgeons have very high rates of calling patients back after a lumpectomy for a reexcision. I had Peiqi, my analyst, pull the national data, and what we found was remarkable. While most surgeons have a reexcision rate below 20% (a number that my colleagues thought was a reasonable boundary of what should be considered acceptable), nearly one in seven breast surgeons have a reexcision rate over 30%. Here's the data, a distribution of all U.S. surgeons who perform more than ten lumpectomy procedures per year on Medicare patients (see graph on next page). What was surreal was to see the actual names of the outlier doctors (see chart on next page). Tragically, they were getting paid a lot more for being outliers.

We presented this work at a leading surgical conference, the Southern Surgical Association,[2] which generated tremendous interest, along with frustration that these wide variations in quality persist.

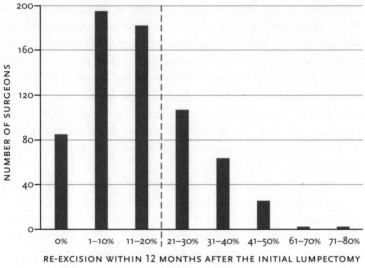

Breast re-operation (re-excision) rate, by surgeon*

Clinical consensus is that re-excision rates should never exceed 20%

RE-EXCISION WITHIN 12 MONTHS AFTER THE INITIAL LUMPECTOMY
FOR BREAST CANCER

*analysis limited to only high-volume breast surgeons

Examples of High Outlier Physicians

NAME	LOCATION	PROCEDURE VOLUME	RE-EXCISION RATE
Physician A	Gulfport, Mississippi	83	66.3%
Physician B	Northern California	155	60.0%
Physician C	Indianapolis, Indiana	509	59.5%
Physician D	Richmond, Virginia	54	57.4%
Physician E	Gainesville, Florida	84	56.0%

GI

I often work with gastroenterology (GI) doctors, so naturally I began to ask them about areas of overtreatment and waste in their specialty. They unloaded a treasure trove of areas to measure patterns of overuse. They told me of the hemorrhoid banding procedure, in which a doctor wraps a rubber band around the base of a hemorrhoid to cut off its blood supply. The bands shouldn't be applied in more than about 10% of cases. But some doctors band every hemorrhoid they can get their hands on. When I asked why they do it so often, the GI docs responded with a comment I started hearing a lot: "It pays well." Within days, I showed the GI doctors the data supporting their suspicion: a fraction of doctors performed hemorrhoid banding on nearly every patient they evaluated. And yes, it hurts to write about it.

Another GI colleague, Dr. Eun Ji Shin, told me some doctors maximize their billing by spreading out over two separate days two procedures that should be done at the same time. It's common for non-urgent patients with stomach complaints or severe heart-burn to need both an upper endoscopy and a lower colonoscopy. Whenever possible, their doctor should do both procedures in sequence while they are sedated. But Dr. Shin said there were doctors who game the system by scheduling the two procedures on different days. When the doctor owns or co-owns the procedure center, they can make much more money that way. Of course, some-times doing it in two procedures is the right thing to do, but he explained how a pattern would uncover those playing the game.

Taking this information, I went back to the database. As Dr. Shin predicted, I discovered that most doctors combine the procedures, as they should. The average doctor does the procedures over two days only about 18% of the time.[3] But that's misleading. At bigger institutions, the average is 13%. At smaller, privately owned endos-copy centers, the average is 24%. Then we found the outliers. A small group of GI doctors performed the procedures on separate days *every time!* And a bunch more did it on two different days more than half the time—a threshold GI experts called indefen-sible. This not only creates a lot of hassle and expense for patients, it's risky, because the patient must go under anesthesia a second time.

As my GI colleagues and I began to draft a research article describing our findings, we invited two GI doctors who were new to our faculty to review the study. I noticed them having a side conversation as if something was wrong. I stopped and asked them if they had additional insights. It turns out they were relieved to learn that their department chair, a coauthor of the study, did not expect them to maximize billing by doing the procedures on different days.

"We don't do that at this hospital," one of their new GI colleagues told them. "We do what's best for the patient."

"Whew," one of the new doctors said. "Where we came from, we were expected to separate all upper and lower endoscopy procedures into different days. We assumed the same was true here."

We laughed, but this was gallows humor, based on a shared recognition that our health care system was corrupt and we were all part of it.

I was shocked to hear how common it was to break up the procedures and how accepted it had become. Thankfully, that day both doctors were liberated from the different-day endoscopy game. If that was something that needed clarifying at Johns Hopkins, it could be happening anywhere.

Cardiac

Other specialists also gave me additional leads to expand the Improving Wisely project. My heart surgeon colleagues down the hallway told me about operations on the mitral valve, which allows blood to flow from one chamber of the heart, the left atrium, into another chamber, the left ventricle. When the mitral valve malfunctions, they can either replace it or repair it with scissors and stitches. Repairing the mitral valve is a much better option for patients when possible. Among other benefits, patients are spared the need to take expensive and risky blood thinners for the rest of their lives. But deciding to do a repair requires a heat-of-the-moment decision, since inspecting the valve during surgery is part of the process. The cardiac surgeons told me it's possible to repair the valve in up to half the cases. But some of their colleagues take the one-hammer approach and replace them all.

Children

In pediatric surgery, the surgeons told me about an outdated practice of routinely operating on one- and two-year-old kids who happen to have a small belly button hernia, what lay people call an "outie" and what we call an umbilical hernia. Best practices in the specialty have matured. The vast majority of these hernias close on their own as the child grows. It's recommended that surgeons wait until a kid turns six or seven. On top of that, new research has found that general anesthesia in young kids can be associated with learning disabilities. Bottom line: there are only rare cases when a surgeon needs to close an umbilical type hernia in a child under age four. (Inguinal hernias are a different matter.)

After a robust discussion with Dr. Mehul Raval and other pediatric surgeons, we created a measure to capture the inappropriate pattern of operating on kids too early. The metric was simple. We decided to look at the proportion of all elective umbilical hernia operations a surgeon performs on children under age four. It should be rare, less than 10%. But the data showed that for about one in five surgeons, doing the operation on kids under age four was the rule, not the exception. Without looking at patterns, a reviewer would not be able to discern from the patient's record whether or not it was unnecessary. Each case would have documentation of soft criteria for surgery, such as abdominal pain.

End of Life

In cancer care, the oncologists recommended measuring the proportion of cancer deaths in an oncologist's practice when the patient was receiving chemotherapy or radiation in the two weeks prior to their death. If an oncologist had 10 or 20% of their patients die while on chemo or radiation, it could mean the patients' deaths weren't anticipated. But if 80 to 100% of an oncologist's patients received chemo or radiation within two weeks of dying, the doctor may not be exercising good judgment about when to back off the aggressive treatment in a case that's past hope.

Dental Care

In dentistry, silver diamine fluoride drops were found in a large study to stop cavities. The drops can be reapplied as needed and can replace the need to drill a tooth and put in a filling. The only side effect is that it can darken the tooth, even turn it black if reapplied multiple times. That's not good for baby Zoolanders, but it might spare a child the trauma of drilling. I offered both options to my eight-year-old nephew when his dentist recommended drilling, and guess what? He chose the drops.

I asked dentists about the ethics of putting kids through drilling when the drops were effective. Most of them downplayed the silver drop therapy. Other dentists said it's highly effective, well proven, and ideal when the teeth are going to be falling out anyway. They also said it's vastly underused because it's a threat to the lucrative business of drilling. My team worked with a group of dentists to construct the measure: What proportion of children does a dentist treat with silver diamine fluoride versus drill? If a dentist drills every cavity and never applies silver diamine fluoride, that dentist is probably not presenting the drops option to patients. Dental procedures for cavities are a common Medicaid expenditure. Silver diamine fluoride costs $109, about a quarter to half the price of a filling, depending on who's doing it.

What It All Means

These appropriateness measures have implications for the overall cost of health care. Operations cost thousands of dollars, endoscopy procedures are common, and chemotherapy costs an arm and a leg. Medicare pays for a lot of it.

The more doctors I sat down with, the more I discovered that overtreatment penetrates most corners of medicine. Many procedure suggestions I got from medical professionals were not measurable. But the ones we could measure were telling. Many of the areas of overuse are tests and procedures that generate money. Our growing list of practice pattern measures largely focused on expensive items. Given the broad interest in lowering health care costs, the Improving Wisely metrics got popular fast. Health care organizations started calling me asking if I could run the algorithms on their data. I learned secondhand that some people called the algorithms "waste metrics." I prefer "appropriateness metrics," since that was the spirit of what we were trying to measure. After thousands of sit-down conversations and follow-up chats with specialists and subspecialists, I laid out and validated more than a hundred metrics (of which I have been able to publish only a few in the medical literature because of the slow pace of medical journals in reviewing and publishing articles).

Within a year, the national demand for the measures outpaced my ability to develop them. In one case, a health care organization asked my team to run the appropriateness metrics on an orthopedic group it wanted to acquire. Before sticking their brand on the practice, they wanted to know whether the group did a lot of unnecessary surgery.

A Wide Impact

I decided it was time to recruit help. My surgical practice had a great staff, but we were fielding more calls than we could handle. I remembered the two previous times in my career when the phones were ringing off the hook like this. The first was when Bryan Sexton, Peter Pronovost, and I published a hospital employee safety culture survey and demonstrated how it can be used by hospital leaders.[4] At that time, Sexton handed the survey to an entrepreneur on a silver platter to free himself of the logistics.

Pascal Metrics, a D.C.-based health care software company, took over the process and it continued to grow. I stayed financially independent so I could be free to advocate for the survey.

The other time our phones rang off the hook was when I published the first article describing a surgery checklist in the medical literature.[5,6,7,8] Similarly, I was able to hand it off to the World Health Organization, which used it as the basis for its surgery checklist.[9] The WHO had a good platform and asked me to help adapt my checklist into a formal version with the WHO stamp on it. Similarly, I remained financially independent in order to promote the checklist free of bias.

Looking for help in meeting the nationwide demand for the metrics, I called Jim Fields, a friend at the Chicago-based consulting firm Oliver Wyman. Jim had heard me speak on my early work on measuring appropriateness and saw its potential. Jim was the right guy to partner with because he was the real deal. He had two young girls with profound disabilities, one the result in part of medical care that was inappropriate. For him, reducing unnecessary medical care was personal.

Over a dinner at a Chicago steakhouse, I told Jim that I was blowing off offers from companies that wanted to monetize our efforts because I wanted to ensure that these measures remained doctor-developed, doctor-endorsed, and doctor-friendly. I knew that it worked to collaborate with experts to create and display practice patterns and then share the data with outliers. I also knew that cutting corners on the tedious process of gaining expert physician consensus could result in doctors being unfairly measured. As a pancreas surgeon who had been unfairly branded for my high readmission rate, even though it was intrinsic to pancreas surgery, I did not want to see that happen to anyone else.

The goal was to embrace practice variation, I told Jim. Medicine is an art and different doctors take care of diverse populations. But when there is consensus, practice variation should be within physician-endorsed boundaries. "The goal here is to let outliers know that they are outliers and help guide them toward best practices," I said. "The goal is improvement." Jim clearly agreed.

Will Bruhn and I created a consortium for health care organizations interested in measuring the appropriateness of care in their data. Health care organizations subscribe to the consortium, called Global Appropriateness Measures (GAMeasures.com), learn about the measures, and apply the algorithms to their data. Many organizations have now used the results to drive real improvement and address outlier physicians. The algorithms are essentially a screening tool to detect physician practice patterns that warrant a deeper clinical review—doctors who, in my mind, may need help. One patient navigation company, Accolade, uses the appropriateness measures to help patients as they seek care. These appropriateness measures represent a novel area with tremendous potential to improve quality and lower health care costs.

I attended some of the meetings with hospital leaders to review their data. At one medical center, we were looking at how often doctors did biopsies during a screening colonoscopy. Colon polyps occur only about 24% of the time in the general population.[10] Our experts determined that doctors who remove polyps in more than 50% of screening colonoscopies have a pattern that signals possible overuse. One of the doctors at this medical center did biopsies in more than 90% of the procedures. "I'm going to have his department chair talk with him," said the hospital's chief medical officer.

Over the next two years, my team and I marched out the same model through many areas of medicine, focusing on unnecessary medical care as determined by expert consensus. Between my research group and the larger effort to scale our model, we created more than 500 measures of clinical appropriateness. We identified hundreds of millions of dollars in potential savings if the overuse can be eliminated—not to mention all the harm to patients that could be avoided. For each of these measures, we defined the metric carefully using input from experts, brought the results (i.e. the distribution of doctors) back to the experts in that field, and then asked them to define the range within which doctors should fall. In other words, for each of the 500 measures, we relied on the experts to define a threshold that would clearly identify outliers in that clinical situation. The goal was not to punish outliers, but to let them know where they stand and offer help. In some instances, institutions would undertake a more focused review of outliers. In other cases, the awareness that patterns were being examined created a culture of accountability.

Metrics will need to be revisited each year based on the latest scientific research, society guidelines, and an evolving consensus among practicing specialists. The Global Appropriateness Measures project now allows leaders to see where their doctors stand in relation to local, state, and national benchmarks. These metrics also need to be updated as medical research and practice evolve. For example, as I write this book, a new study shows that women with a common type of Stage 1 breast cancer may not need chemotherapy if a certain genetic test yields a positive result.[11] Accordingly, in early 2019 we finalized a new metric: the proportion of early breast cancer patients a physician treats who have the genetic test done. If an oncologist rarely or never orders the test, it can be deduced that some of their patients are inappropriately receiving chemo.

The metrics have had a big impact in the organizations that use them. But like most innovations in health care, they are not comprehensive ways to measure quality. They are only a starting point to flag overuse in certain common clinical situations. There are many areas of medicine for which big data is too clumsy to precisely measure—for example, psychiatry. Some data can capture overuse of medications and certain medication interactions, but it's a challenging area to measure.

In the opening of the book, I described my experience observing the predatory screening practices of doctors at church health fairs. At that time, I had shared my observations with Dr. Jim Black and Dr. Caitlin Hicks, my vascular surgery colleagues. Both were markedly disturbed by what was happening in the community. They told me about a surgeon in the area who they believed was often doing unnecessary stent procedures, generating as much as $100,000 per day.

Susan Hutfless, a PhD epidemiologist on my team, hadn't forgotten about that issue. We ran our new appropriateness metric in the national Medicare data and found an alarming trend. The expected procedure rate for claudication—the leg pain resulting from poor circulation—should be less than 10%. Also, surgeons who do the procedure should not routinely separate it into stages on different days. Despite this, the data revealed that some doctors operated on more than half of the patients they evaluated with claudication and routinely strung out the procedure over multiple days. One of the top people on the list in the United States was the very doctor Dr. Black had told me about. He alone was milking millions of dollars from the system.

Susan ran the data several times, looking to see if there was any mathematical or clinical reason why this one doctor would be such an outlier. But every time she reviewed the data, it was clear that this finding was not a statistical error. Plus, it fit with what Dr. Black had heard. Months later, Susan asked to meet with me. She walked into my office, initially calm, but as she spoke, her voice cracked with emotion.

"Marty, isn't there something we should do about this doctor?"

I understood her frustration. Doing this data analysis had big implications and put the people who saw the results in an awkward position. We had tried to get the professional association involved with the vascular procedures but hit bureaucratic roadblocks. It takes time for large organizations to obtain consensus within their members.

Susan is highly professional and stoic. But as we discussed the dilemma, tears welled up in her eyes. "I just don't understand. This person is hurting a lot of people."

Susan raised a good point. She confronted me with a moral decision: Now that we can identify extreme outliers in the data, do we have a duty to let them know?

Susan knew the politics involved and the importance of engaging specialty societies rather than working around them. The societies were sometimes quick to respond, but other times they moved like molasses. In one instance, a specialty society's leadership told me that letting outliers know they were outliers was a great idea but it wasn't a priority of theirs.

Dr. Caitlin Hicks and I sent the list of outlier physicians to the Centers for Medicare & Medicaid Services (CMS) and to the Society for Vascular Surgery, who both took action.[12] It would be the beginning of a larger national effort to share data with physicians to address "low-value care." The Society for Vascular Surgery put Dr. Hicks in charge of their efforts to address unnecessary surgery and she soon emerged as a national leader in using data for quality improvement.

Susan's ethical concern had a big impact on me. Thinking about the opioid epidemic alone—another manifestation of overtreatment—makes me wish something could be done sooner. Now that data on extreme outliers is available and experts agree on which practice patterns are inappropriate and even downright wrong, what should our society do about it? I believe we have a duty to act.

CHAPTER 9

Opioids like Candy

For most of my surgical career, I gave out opioids like candy. I was unaware that about 1 in 16 patients become chronic users, according to the recent research by doctors at the University of Michigan. My colleagues and I didn't realize we were fueling a national crisis. But today opioids are the leading cause of death in America of people under 50 years of age.[1]

As a medical student and surgical resident, I spent thousands of hours learning how to diagnose breast cancer, how to cut out breast cancer, and how to recommend chemo and radiation after breast surgery. But at no point was I taught that the way we liberally prescribed opioids was creating an epidemic of addiction that would eventually kill more people in the United States than breast cancer itself.[2]

My "aha" moment came when I watched my father recover from an operation. Coincidentally, it happened to be an operation I routinely perform. I customarily prescribed 60 opioid tablets when I did it. But that night after dad's surgery, I watched him recover comfortably at home with a single tablet of ibuprofen.

Wow. It directly contradicted my residency training, in which I was taught to give every patient a boatload of opioid tablets upon discharge. The medical community at large ingrained in all of us that opioids were not addictive and urged us to prescribe generously. And that's exactly what we did.

Coming Clean

The hundreds of excessive opioid prescriptions I wrote in 2015 alone (the last year for which national data is available) were only a tiny fraction of the country's 249 million prescriptions filled that year. That means physicians gave out the equivalent of one opioid prescription for every American adult. And in that year, the U.S. pharmaceutical industry produced 14 billion opioid pills. That's about 40 pills for every American citizen. These were all funded by you, the American public, through tax dollars, health insurance premiums, and cash payments.

Now that I see headline after headline about tragedies stemming from prescription narcotics, I feel horrible about how copiously I prescribed opioid pills. Each news story makes me angry that I didn't know more about the bondage that can arise from a prescription. Each headline also makes me wish I had known then what I know now—that non-opioid alternatives can be extremely effective in managing pain.

My dad practiced hematology: the science of blood disorders, leukemia, and lymphoma. He explained to me how we got into this mess. For decades, cancer patients were undertreated for pain. But then things swung to the other extreme when pharmaceutical companies sold us on the lie that opioids were not addictive. Then pain became a vital measurement in medicine. The consumerist pain rating system elevated pain as a leading quality measure, overshadowing actual medical quality. As the race to measure quality took off, things that were easy and cheap to measure rose to the top: readmission rates, patient satisfaction, and pain scores. The question "How often did the hospital staff do everything they could to help you with your pain?" became a measuring stick by which all U.S. hospitals were rated. This created a perverse incentive to distribute excessive opioids.

When I reflect on the enormity of the opioid crisis, I'm amazed that politicians still talk about solving it almost exclusively in terms of how much money they can spend on treatment and putting naloxone, the overdose antidote, in every McDonald's and Starbucks in America. Yes, treatment is vital. But the root cause of the problem is overprescribing. Ironically, as our country debates how we can get out of the opioid crisis, we continue to flood communities with these powerfully addictive, sometimes fatal pills. The opioid crisis is another manifestation of the broader problem of overtreatment in medicine. It is essentially an issue of appropriateness.

Even now that the opioid crisis has blown up and become a top priority for many health care leaders, far too many Americans still walk out of a hospital, surgery center, or dental clinic with a prescription for opioids they don't need. Take C-section, for example, one of the most common operations paid for by Medicaid. Some doctors appropriately prescribe 5 to 10 opioid tablets to certain patients after the procedure (in combination with non-opioid medication, as recommended by the American Pain Society). Meanwhile, other doctors are still doing what I did for years: prescribing every patient a bottle of 60 highly addictive narcotic painkillers.

Perhaps the most embarrassing study that was released at the height of the opioid epidemic looked at surgical patients who stayed in the hospital after their procedure. The study showed that half of patients who did not take opioids on their last day in the hospital were still given a prescription for the potentially deadly painkillers when they went home. That was the situation for my patient Suzette Morgan.

Suzette works at Johns Hopkins in the office of research administration. She knew me because she personally helped me compile and mail several research grant applications. As I've come to know her professionally during my years at the university, she came up to me one day and asked me to perform an operation she needed: a laparoscopic gallbladder removal. I agreed and did the procedure, which went well. But weeks later she came to my office to give me an earful about the 30 opioid tablets she was prescribed after surgery.

"I didn't take them while in the hospital after surgery, so why would I need them after leaving the hospital?" she complained. Humiliated, I apologized, realizing that someone on my team had given her the opioid prescription.

I called an urgent meeting of my clinical and research teams to discuss opioid prescribing at our hospital. As a scientist of health care quality, I was perplexed. This epidemic had been going on for about a decade but I was unaware of any national best practices for what should be prescribed to a patient after a standard operation.

Building Consensus

For this urgent meeting, I invited our local expert in pain management at Johns Hopkins, and a few residents and nurses. About a dozen of us crowded around a table in my office. I asked the million-dollar question: What *should* we be prescribing when patients are discharged after a standard operation, like a gallbladder surgery, assuming the patient is an average person who does not have a preexisting pain issue? When the experts in the room began talking, instead of directly answering the question, they said, in varying ways, that it's really a matter of surgeon style or preference. I rephrased the question: What *should* a prescription read for an average adult patient going home after a laparoscopic gallbladder surgery?

I put our head of pain management on the spot. She responded by saying what is done rather than what should be done. "Some surgeons like to give a few, others like to give a lot," she said. I responded by repeating my original question. She turned it back on me: "Marty, you're a surgeon, you might know better than me what they *should* be prescribing."

"I don't know," I admitted. "That's why I called this meeting. And to be very frank, I don't actually write the prescriptions for my patients. My residents do."

I turned to my residents in the room. One of them pointed out that our electronic health record, EPIC, had an e-prescribing default that recommended a 30-day supply. An intern also explained, "Some chief residents will yell at us if we prescribe anything below 30 pills." A different resident said prescribing too few could result in calls during off hours when it's inconvenient to prescribe more.

These reasons were frustrating to hear, but they were honest. I knew these unwritten rules from my "residency survival manual."

"This is pathetic," I said. "We've been the number one hospital in the United States for 22 of the last 28 years in the *U.S. News & World Report* rankings. The experts in this room are at the mountaintop of academic medicine. But we can't even agree on what patients should go home with?"

Again, I pressed them on the number of pills we *should* be prescribing rather than what we *are* prescribing. One resident said 30, another said 50, and another said 60, then one of them got bold. "We prescribe based on what our last resident taught us," he admitted. "To be honest, we don't know because we don't follow the patients after they go home like the nurse practitioners do."

Finally, I turned to my nurse practitioner, Christi Walsh. She calls every patient at home after surgery. She knew more about this than any of us. Christi silenced the room by answering my question in her usual matter-of-fact manner: "Marty, they don't need any opioids."

We were all stunned, as well as embarrassed. "Most patients don't need the opioids we've been prescribing after a laparoscopic gallbladder operation," she explained. "Good patient education and non-opioid alternatives keep the vast majority of them comfortable."

Christi had said what no one else was willing to say. At that moment, it became clear to me. The field of surgery needed thoughtful guidelines on what we should be prescribing after surgery.

Opioid prescribing policies have been introduced since the addiction crisis took center stage. But it's mostly state governments and insurance companies setting limits that get imposed on every patient, no matter the circumstances. I knew as a surgeon that every operation carries a different level of invasiveness and a different level of pain. An open chest operation is a heck of a lot more painful than needle biopsy. An opioid prescribing guideline, in principle, needed to be procedure-specific. It also needed to exclude patients already on other pain medications, since that can change a patient's tolerance level and pain threshold.

How could one prescribing limit be applied to different types of operations? I asked the group in my office that day to move on and talk about another operation, an open hysterectomy. For that procedure, Christi again educated us. She said we should prescribe at most 15 opioid pills, based on the hundreds of conversations she had had with patients who had recovered from the procedure. Christi's estimate would be affirmed months later when a study from Dartmouth found that 70% of the opioid pills surgeons prescribe are never taken.[3]

In the absence of any published procedure-specific guidelines, it was time to do something. My colleagues and I decided to create guidelines for our own Johns Hopkins surgical group and, in the spirit of transparency, offer them for the world to see. We agreed that the best approach to creating new guidelines would be to invite a broad range of experts, including surgeons, anesthesiologists, pain specialists, residents, nurses, pharmacists, and patients to form an expert panel. That panel would issue a consensus statement on the maximum number of opioids a narcotic-naïve adult should be prescribed after each of 20 common surgical procedures. Recognizing that treating pain depends on many patient factors, we created a range rather than a number of opioids for each procedure. But the upper limit was a real ceiling—a limit that should not be exceeded, according to our panel's consensus.

To do this, we considered tapping the bureaucracy of our professional associations, but we were in a national opioid crisis and wanted to move fast. The next week, my research colleague Dr. Heidi Overton and I invited surgeons, pain specialists, nurses, residents, pharmacists and, most important, patients to an expert panel meeting.

For three hours in a large room at the center of the Johns Hopkins Hospital, we went through 20 of the most common procedures in health care. We had a patient and a clinician discuss their opinions about what the opioid prescribing guideline should be for each operation. We used a consensus-building process called the Delphi method. Everyone on the expert panel voted, then listened to one another explain their votes, then revoted. The average of the revote would become the consensus guideline.

The discussions were intense but productive. Patients described their pain after surgery in detail and doctors shared their experiences treating pain after surgery. Others in the room described their experiences caring for patients in the days after surgery. Interestingly, when it came time to vote for an opioid prescribing limit, patients always voted for fewer pills than the surgeons.

For each operation, a consensus was finally achieved. For many of the procedures, we recommended between 10 and 15 opioid pills, and we never recommended exceeding 20. Of course, this did not mean that patients who had a genuine need for more opioids would not be able to get them. It applied only to the prescriptions that patients received when they were sent home.

We didn't want to wait for a medical journal to publish our guidelines. That would take six months if we were lucky, after submitting a formal manuscript perfectly formatted according to their stringent specifications about fonts, margins, and spacing. Instead, we created a website called SolveTheCrisis.org, where the day after the expert panel concluded we posted our opioid prescribing guidelines. The site got thousands of hits a day. Months later, the *New York Times* wrote a piece about the guidelines and we started getting tens of thousands of hits each day. People were eager for guidance on what doctors should be prescribing after common operations.

Nine months later, we also published the recommendations in a formal article in the *Journal of the American College of Surgeons.*[4] It would be the first ever procedure-specific opioid prescribing guideline. We didn't stop. Working with a dentist in the school of public health, Dr. Owais Farooqi, we convened another expert panel of dentists and dental hygienists. We used the same consensus approach to create opioid prescribing guidelines for dental procedures. And in collaboration with the organization Allied Against Opioid Abuse, we created educational videos[5] for patients to watch before surgery, reminding them it's normal for surgery to cause soreness. It's pain that limits activity that we want to aggressively treat, beginning with non-opioid alternatives in most cases. Opioids are an option, if patients choose, to treat severe pain, but they should know that they carry a risk of addiction, which can be fatal. Usually when I mention that to patients, they beg me to prescribe something else when they leave the hospital—a nudge for good.

During and after our work to create procedure-specific guidelines, I watched the government and some insurance companies continue to issue draconian policies that limited opioid prescriptions to a 4-, 10- or 30-day supply. How could anyone dictate hard-and-fast limits when the amount of pain resulting from every procedure was different? Drilling bone to do a hip replacement is far more of a shock to the system than a lymph node biopsy.

Guiding Change

The opioid crisis created an obvious opportunity to use the Improving Wisely approach to look at a surgeon's prescribing patterns in the national data. We wanted to see which clinicians had a pattern of prescribing far too many pills after certain operations. Our analysis excluded patients with preexisting opioid use or pain syndromes. We wanted to include only patients who had not previously taken narcotics, which is an important factor that clinicians should take into account when prescribing opioids.

The analysis uncovered a stunning range in the way doctors prescribed opioids. Some doctors fell within our Johns Hopkins expert panel guideline of zero to 10 opioid tablets after, say, a prostate surgery. Other surgeons were still routinely prescribing a whopping 50 or 60 tablets to their narcotic-naïve patients.

We ran the analysis for the surgeons who did that laparoscopic gallbladder surgery that led to the creation of our expert panel. Our panel concluded that zero to 10 pills is the recommended opioid prescribing range for that operation, yet the data we looked at as a team revealed doctors that were still prescribing as recklessly as I had done, averaging 30 pills.

Someone on the team pointed to a dot on the graph that represented the surgeon averaging 45 opioid pills after the operation. "That surgeon is crazy."

"No," I countered. "That surgeon needs help." We have a duty to take care of each other in medicine. "That surgeon needs to be educated as I got educated a few years ago."

My research team repeated the analysis for many common procedures, including operations that can be managed with non-opioid alternatives. The doctor distribution graphs kept showing us the same thing: opioid prescribing patterns vary widely, even within an identical procedure. One analysis of lumpectomy operations revealed that some surgeons routinely prescribe more than 60 opioid pills. Our consensus panel of medical experts and patients recommended between zero and 10, advocating for non-opioid alternatives. Now that the data allowed us to see which doctors need help, we had a duty to help them.

We are working to apply the Improving Wisely approach to the opioid overprescribing problem. In addition to the many potential lives saved, imagine the cost of these unnecessary opioid pills being dispensed. Add to that the addiction treatment costs for the 1 in 16 patients who will become addicted. Prevention is still the best treatment.

In hopes of creating an honest conversation about the overprescribing culture, I published an account of my own overprescribing regrets and my "aha" moment when my dad had surgery. The story made the front page of *USA Today*[6] and hundreds of doctors reached out to me to tell me that they, too, were amazed at the way medicine had embraced a culture of opioid overprescribing, oblivious to the impact. A friend from my internship days texted me. "Good piece in *USA Today*, remember when Dr. F required us to write for 100 opioid pills for everyone?"

Even after all the efforts to reduce overprescribing, we have a long way to go. I was asked to give a speech at a medical conference in Lebanon and offered to give a talk about the opioid epidemic. The conference organizers told me, "That's a uniquely American problem. We don't have that problem here because we prescribe opioids sparingly." Most doctors worldwide reserve opioids for the classic indications—like terminal cancer, burns, and major surgery. I felt a bit ashamed, but it was true. The opioid crisis was unique to American medicine.

There are concrete things we can do to address this crisis. We can start by changing perverse financial incentives. It is difficult to find doctors interested in carefully managing a patient's pain medications because doing so pays so little. A doctor might get only $50 for a 30-minute visit. That might not even cover overhead. Our reimbursement system should value expert advice and counseling on pain management. Moreover, pain specialists should be paid not just for doing procedures, but for their time managing pain.

We also need insurance companies to change. Ironically, acetaminophen and NSAIDs (nonsteroidal anti-inflammatory drugs) are over-the-counter medicines and thus rarely covered by insurance. But the insurers do cover narcotic painkillers. As I've talked to my patients, I've come to believe that one simple solution is that all non-opioid pain meds should be fully covered after surgery with no copay or deductible. Those who think that the $10 to $20 price for a bottle of NSAIDs is a not a barrier to patients buying them should meet some of my poor patients from inner-city Baltimore. I have had patients buy heroin to manage their surgical pain because it cost less than their copay.

Finally, patients should inquire about having a nerve block when they have a painful procedure. It's well established that when nerve blocks are injected in a surgical area or nerve root, patients require fewer pain pills. Hopefully, someday, physicians will be able to manage local pain with local therapy rather than systemic therapy, which has collateral damage.

I'm shocked that no one in politics has requested to review the analyzed national Medicare data for surgeons' prescribing patterns by procedure in narcotic-naïve patients. I tried to get the attention of members of Congress who have high rates of addiction in their home districts. I told them I can show them the specific doctors who are prescribing too many of the pills. But they respond with hot air and no action. But after a lot of persistence, a breakthrough. I presented the data to Medicare leaders Kim Brandt, Kate Goodrich, Paul Mango, and others who decided to do something about it. They launched an initiative to send opioid prescribing reports to outlier high prescribers, showing surgeons where they stood on the bell curve. The reports were specific to a procedure and used data on narcotic-naive patients so there would be no reason for pushback that one surgeon's patients were "different." We had a valid way to measure where the opioid faucet is still pouring out, and finally Medicare was on top of it. At the same time, a grant from the Laura and John Arnold Foundation to my Hopkins research team allowed us to expand the project beyond what Medicare could do and also launched a national program to lower opioid prescribing defaults in electronic health records. This project, called the SOLVE collaborative (SolveTheCrisis.org), resets opioid e-prescribing defaults from sky-high legacy numbers, like a 30-day supply, to a consensus amount that is much lower and specific to the procedure performed. For many procedures, that default number is now 5, 10, or zero.

My favorite moment of the broader rollout was when a surgeon identified to be a very high prescriber of opioids after prostate surgery complained that it was not he but his nurse practitioner who was writing those opioids in the recovery room after his surgery. He said our measure was flawed, but later we watched the opioids prescribed to his patients plummet after he saw his opioid prescribing data.

If ever there was a practice pattern of overtreating patients, it is the way we prescribe opioids. Using data to identify prescribing patterns and changing incentives to reward pain management best practices are far less expensive than rehab. Engaging doctors who overprescribe, as I did, can have a broad impact. Treatment for opioid addiction is essential, but we should remember that preventing addiction is even better. To address the opioid crisis, we need to take away the matches, not just put out the fires.

CHAPTER 10

Overtreated Patients like Me

It had been a long, grueling day of surgery. After driving home and trudging through the front door, I turned on the news and flopped onto the couch. There I lay, horizontal and half asleep, until something caught my attention. I heard the anchor announce breaking news of a medical study that found some heartburn medications like Nexium increased the chance of stroke and kidney failure. *What?* I sat straight up. Not only did I frequently prescribe the heartburn medication Nexium, but I was taking it myself.

I jumped off the couch and listened carefully to the broadcast. I pulled out my computer and hunted down the study to learn more. Ironically, the research came from Johns Hopkins.[1]

My gosh, is this true? I called my friend Dr. Tony Kalloo, head of gastroenterology at Johns Hopkins, who acknowledged the new findings of the study and the risks of Nexium. I told him I'd swing by his office in the morning to talk more. I hung up the phone, walked to my medicine cabinet, and glared into the soul of my orange plastic bottle of Nexium tablets. Just a moment ago I had considered it my friend. *Et tu, Nexi?*

My love affair with Nexium began when I told my primary care doctor that I sometimes get heartburn when I perform long operations. He wrote me a prescription for Nexium, a medication I had known personally for years and prescribed to thousands of patients after surgery. I told patients it was safe and would perfectly cure their heartburn the majority of the time.

When I started taking Nexium myself, it did exactly that—
it cured me, affirming my belief that it worked wonders. I didn't
like the $40 copay I had each month, but luckily, my insurance
company paid the bulk of the expense. It shelled out $120 each
month for the medication. Life seemed good. Until this new study
came out.

The day after the study hit the nightly news, I walked into
Dr. Kalloo's office. He's a good friend, a jovial man from Trinidad.
"It's over between me and Nexium," I told him. "Now what do I
take instead?"

He laughed hard and long, then gained enough composure to
look at me. "Marty, there's this thing called lifestyle modification."
He paused with a big smile, then asked sarcastically, "Maybe you've
heard of it?"

Oh, gee, I thought, there *is* a natural way to cure heartburn that
I learned in medical school and then stored deep in the attic of my
brain. Let me see if I can remember what it involves: (1) No eating
before bedtime, (2) No eating between meals, and (3) No processed
foods.

The thought of monitoring and changing my eating habits
was already making me tired. I felt betrayed by those who taught
me Nexium was perfectly safe. I reluctantly agreed to try the lifestyle modification protocol. I stopped eating a bowl of cereal
before going to bed. I removed the jar of peppermint patties I had
been dipping into at my front office desk. And I stopped buying
processed foods altogether in favor of whole foods.

It worked perfectly. My heartburn was cured, this time without
medication. With little effort, I had successfully avoided the risks
of a drug, cut out the daily routine of popping a pill, and saved a
lot of money for me and all the people paying premiums to my
health insurance plan. In total, I saved myself $480 a year, and I
saved my insurance plan $1,440. Sure, the nonprocessed foods cost
more, but net-net I came out on top. And I felt great. My own experience was a powerful lesson—getting off lifestyle medications
can improve health and lower medical costs.

But was my story a one-off anecdote or a viable step in solving
our health care cost crisis?

Consider this simple fact: Last year, physicians prescribed a record 4.5 billion medications.[2] That's about double the number we prescribed just a decade ago. Did the incidence of disease double in the last ten years? Of course not. Most of the doubling represents pills that could be avoided with lifestyle changes or more judicious prescribing. More than half of Americans are now on four or more medications, according to *Consumer Reports*.[3] As if that's not shocking enough, my research team published a study showing the average person on Medicare is on twelve medications.[4]

I learned many things in medical school, but overtreatment was not on the syllabus. Both the doctors prescribing and the patients demanding these medications have a role to play in reversing the dangerous and costly trend. A quick message to all people who walk into a doctor's office demanding an antibiotic for a viral infection or Nexium for heartburn: please stop putting pressure on doctors to prescribe something.

My experience taking Nexium reminded me how ingrained in our culture pill popping has become. The medicalization of ordinary life is so widespread it's hard to avoid. As a physician, my experience writing prescriptions for too many opioids after surgery reminds me how doctors can also do better with our prescribing.

In medical school, a practical topic like the hazards of too much medical care took a back seat to all the rote memorization and regurgitation of facts. We learned Latin just for the sake of knowledge, but the traditionalists who designed my extensive medical education left out some of the most important parts of being a good doctor: effective communication and self-awareness. Moreover, they did not teach an important caveat to everything in our medical textbooks and journal articles: the risks of medications and procedures are understated because of publication bias (a tendency to publish only good results) and the lack of studies evaluating long-term consequences.

Second Tour of Duty

As if lightning never strikes twice, I went in for my next routine annual checkup with my primary care doctor. (If I can be honest, as a doctor it feels weird to be a patient. Doctors tend to be skeptical and explore extreme alternatives to what *our* own doctors recommend.) During this visit, my doctor told me I have high cholesterol and that I should start taking a statin, a common drug used for lowering cholesterol numbers. With the trashed Nexium bottle still fresh in my mind, I was reluctant to take a statin.

To be honest, I didn't like the idea of taking any medication, let alone one with well-known side effects. But every cardiologist I grabbed in the hospital hallways told me "Statins save lives." I read the leading studies myself and couldn't deny the survival benefit. But one cardiologist I respect thought the survival benefit was limited to a subgroup of people who took them and that it was due to the anti-inflammatory effect of statins rather than their cholesterol-lowering effect. That made sense, but regardless, the data made it clear that statins save lives. I reluctantly took the medication daily for three months.

But then the multicultural part of me came out. I realized that all the studies were done predominantly with Anglo subjects, not people like me.

I recalled that everyone in my family lives long and that family history was the biggest determinant of heart disease. I also realized that no one in my family had heart disease or had ever had a heart attack. My grandma Fifi, back in Egypt, was almost 100 years old and had never had a heart issue. I called an uncle, a Cairo cardiologist and the go-to doctor for my extended family, and asked for Fifi's cholesterol numbers. He took my numbers and said they were the same as those of my grandma and grandpa and everyone else in the family.

When I started to tell him my doctor recommended I start a statin, he interrupted. "No, you don't need to take it." He also took the opportunity to say that U.S. doctors are well known in the international cardiology community to overmedicate, overstent, and overtreat. He pointed out that one popular statin medication in the United States was banned in the UK because of its side effects, and he commented that Americans are on way too many meds.

I went back to my personal primary care doctor and explained to him that my family history contains zero heart disease and that everyone in my family lives into their nineties with the same cholesterol profile as mine. I told him if my cholesterol numbers were good enough for Fifi, they were good enough for me. His humble response impressed me. He thanked me for doing the research and said based on my family history, he wouldn't recommend the statin medication.

My doctor had also checked several new science markers of heart disease risk: my LP(a) level, ApoB level, and my hs-CRP, all of which were good. Finally, we agreed that if my calcium score was zero, I would not take any meds. It was. My wallet and I were off the hook.

For the three months I took statins every day, who was paying for them? It wasn't just me, it was everyone else insured by my health insurance company. The insurance company sets premiums based on what they pay out each year. If I had not stopped my unnecessary Nexium and statin medications, the total cost passed along to everyone paying insurance premiums would have been approximately $30,000 over the next ten years. For people wondering why insurance premiums are going up, one of the leading drivers is the doubling of prescription medications our country has witnessed over the last decade.

One Last Round

By the time I went back to my doctor the following year, the fact that I had been on two unnecessary medications over the last few years was water under the bridge. This time I went to him for something that was real. I had developed back pain from standing in the operation room doing pancreas islet transplant operations for six to ten hours at a stretch. I had two spine surgeons evaluate me for the pain. One told me to do physical therapy, and the other offered to do surgery.

Around that time, Steve Kerr, coach of the Golden State Warriors basketball team, missed most of his team's playoff games for health reasons. *Oh my*, I thought. *He must have something serious*. Well, he did, but it was not a virus or heart attack—it was the endemic problem of too much medical care.

He had been disabled by one of his back operations for chronic pain. His words sent chills down my spine. "I can tell you, if you're listening out there, stay away from back surgery," Kerr said. "I can say that from the bottom of my heart. Rehab, rehab, rehab. Don't let anyone get in there." Stanford spine surgeon Dr. Robert Aptekar called what Kerr said "good advice."[5]

After talking to more spine surgeons about my back problem, I was amazed by how many of them told me the same thing Coach Kerr had said. My physical therapist worked wonders and I never had spine surgery. I didn't need it.

In this chapter, I've discussed only my personal experience. But overtreatment is pervasive in health care. A detailed report released by 21 Washington State physicians who are part of the nonprofit Washington Health Alliance found that 45% of Washington State health care services were unnecessary. In total, they found that 600,000 patients in Washington underwent medical services they didn't need, costing an estimated $282 million in one year.[6] Topping the list were frequent screenings and tests deemed irrelevant to care, such as unnecessary lab tests routinely performed before minor surgery.

In recent years, a plethora of studies have shown that doctors have been overtesting, overmedicating, and overoperating. If there's one theme I've observed in medical journals over the last few years, it's a massive rollback of broad recommendations. Studies in the *New England Journal of Medicine* have challenged surgical dogma on when we should be doing knee replacement, appendicitis, and thyroid surgeries. Many of these surgeon-authors point out that we have been overdoing them.[7]

There's also the psychological harm to patients who get spooked by a screening test that simply captures normal variants of the human body. I've seen patients tormented with anxiety thinking that they are carrying a time bomb inside them and doing everything to avoid living with regret if they develop cancer. A needless scare can consume people with emotional trauma, affecting mental health.

Don't Forget the Bill

Who paid for Coach Steve Kerr's back operations? We all did. His most recent operation probably cost more than $200,000, if you include the complications. In contrast, my physical therapy sessions cost $85 each. Just like the medications I was taking that I didn't need, his surgery was paid for by his insurance company, which then sets premiums based on what they pay out each year.

What we need is a grassroots change to put the patient back at the center of health care. We need to tackle the problem of inappropriate medical care. These are self-inflicted wounds.

Medicine has a tremendous heritage of solving problems. Medical science and clinical wisdom are now addressing the issue of what we call low-value care: medical care with little to no benefit and significant risks of harm. One of the leading medical journals, *JAMA Internal Medicine*, now has a regular section titled "Less Is More." An alliance of 90 medical centers has just formed the High Value Practice Academic Alliance, started by my colleague Pam Johnson, a radiologist at Johns Hopkins who decided to do something about all the unnecessary CT scans, ultrasounds, and MRIs she saw being ordered.[8] Finally, after decades downplaying the magnitude of the problem, conversations to address unnecessary care are more common at our national medical conferences. I believe a solution is in sight.

To get at these drivers of cost, hospitals and insurers need to partner with the grassroots groundswell of doctors who are writing, speaking, and fighting for more appropriate medical care in the United States. Together, they need to call for a reversal of payment models that incentivize quantity over quality.

For years, health care reform in Washington, D.C., has asked the question: How do we *pay for* health care? But the real question is: How do we *fix* the health care system? Addressing the epidemic of *too much* medical care (which doctors believe represents 21% of all medical care delivered) is a practical solution.[9] My own medical experiences have reminded me that the problem is not just administrative waste, it's clinical waste as well that's driving up health care costs for everyone.

Overtreatment is not just a side issue in medicine. It is the root cause of some of our greatest public health crises. Consider the antibiotic resistance problem, a leading public health concern of the World Health Organization. Consider the opioid crisis. It's essentially a public health crisis stemming from overprescribing. Consider the health care cost crisis. It is fueled by the 21% of medical care that doctors believe is unnecessary. Consider the antimicrobial resistance crisis. It is essentially a result of the overuse of antibiotics both in medicine and in animal food production.[10] These public health crises are all manifestations of the problem of too much medical care.

Korea's Thyroid Cancer Epidemic

A few years ago, South Korea found itself in the middle of a thyroid cancer epidemic. Starting around 2000, Korean doctors were finding an alarming number of cancerous tumors on the thyroid, a gland in the neck that makes hormones to regulate the body. The rate of thyroid cancer rose at an alarming rate, with yearly increases. Between 1992 and 2011, the Korean thyroid cancer rate increased by a factor of 15, making it the worst in the world for the disease.[11]

Thyroid cancer is easy to treat if caught early. And the Korean medical industry responded to the crisis with full force. Hospitals expanded thyroid clinics, hired surgeons, and invested in surgical robots to perform operations to remove tumors. The rate of thyroid surgery skyrocketed more than tenfold. About 4,000 Korean patients underwent surgery for thyroid cancer in 2001. By 2012, about 44,000 Koreans had undergone the same operation. Thyroid cancer cases consumed valuable resources, and the economic burden of thyroid cancer in South Korea increased sevenfold, from $257 million in 2000 to $1.7 billion in 2010. Korean surgeons got very good at the operation. I remember watching teaching videos from Korea showing elegant and creative ways to remove the thyroid gland, or parts of it, through an incision in the armpit. We often joked that the reason Korean surgeons were the slickest in the world at minimally invasive thyroid surgery was that there were no obese people in Korea.

When you look back a few years later, you would think everyone would celebrate the Korean medical community's response to the crisis. But instead, medical journals recount it as a tragic cautionary tale. About 90% of the cancer cases identified during the "epidemic" were actually overdiagnoses. Research published in the *New England Journal of Medicine* found that a third of all adults normally harbor small papillary thyroid cancers, and the vast majority won't ever produce symptoms. The tumors are so common, and often so harmless, that most would be better considered a "variant" of normal rather than a deadly disease.

What caused the Korean epidemic wasn't an increase in cases of dangerous thyroid cancer. The rate grew so fast because the medical community started widespread screening of patients who had nothing wrong with them. The screening identified a lot of cases that probably wouldn't have caused any problems. And identifying those cases led to treatment.

Looking back, we can see several telltale signs that the Korean cancer epidemic was not real. During the spike in thyroid cancer cases there was no corresponding increase in mortality. In 2011, more than 40,000 Koreans were diagnosed with thyroid cancer, but fewer than 400 died—a similar figure to previous years. In addition, the median tumor size of the tumors that were surgically removed got much smaller over time: from 20 millimeters in 1999 to 9 millimeters in 2008.[12] Tumors of 9 millimeters are too small for patients or doctors to notice at high rates, a study in the *BMJ* said. "It is not possible that so many tumors of less than 20 mm were detected clinically."

A group of Korean doctors first raised the alarm that overdiagnosis may be to blame for the apparent outbreak of thyroid cancer.[13] In 2014, eight Korean doctors formed the Physician Coalition for Prevention of Overdiagnosis of Thyroid Cancer. The coalition wrote an open letter to the public that flagged screening with ultrasonography as the possible culprit for the spike in diagnoses. That led to media coverage, and in the next year, thyroid cancer operations dropped by 35% in South Korea.[14]

Korea isn't the only country that's had a thyroid cancer "epidemic." It's estimated that 50 to 90% of thyroid cancers in women in high-income countries could be overdiagnoses, according to a 2016 report by the International Agency for Research on Cancer in collaboration with the Aviano National Cancer Institute in Italy.[15] Korea was the most extreme example. An estimated 70 to 80% of women in Australia, France, Italy, and the United States with the diagnosis were misdiagnosed, according to the report. "More than half a million people are estimated to have been overdiagnosed with thyroid cancer in the 12 countries studied," the IARC director said in a press release. He called the overdiagnosis problem a "serious public health concern."

Global Public Health

The overuse of medical services represents one of the greatest public health issues of the modern world. We don't often think of the appropriateness issue in health care the way we think of Ebola or Zika. Yet new research, and my own personal conversations with many physicians overseas, seems to indicate that more people are harmed from unnecessary care or poor-quality care than from Ebola and Zika combined. In 2017, the *Lancet* produced a special issue on overuse called "Right Care." It defined overuse as "the provision of medical services that are more likely to cause harm than good."[16]

There's a continuum of overuse. At one end are tests and treatments that are beneficial when used on the right patient. At the other end of the continuum are services that are entirely futile or even so risky they should never be delivered. Some examples of overtreatment around the world cited in the *Lancet* series were unnecessary procedures performed at a rate of 26% of knee replacements in Spain, 49% of upper endoscopies in Switzerland, 55% of cardiac interventions and one third of hysterectomies performed in women younger than 35 performed in India, and 20% of hysterectomies performed in Taiwan. Fifty-five percent of Thai children with acute diarrhea inappropriately received antibiotics.

On medical travels throughout the world, I've asked physicians to tell me about the burden of unnecessary medical care. They don't hold back. A general surgeon from Sudan told me of a patient who was told by another surgeon that she needed a mastectomy of both her breasts for a small lump in one breast that was never biopsied. Not only that, the woman was told she needed to have the surgery within 24 hours to prevent the cancer from spreading. Of course, the recommendation was bogus, and the tight time frame was nothing more than a technique to manipulate patients into having surgery and not getting another opinion so the surgeon doesn't lose business.

A pediatrician in North Africa told me a child was taken for heart surgery and only had the skin cut open, then immediately sewn shut at the time of surgery. The parents were told by the surgeon that a heart operation had been performed. Another surgeon told me of a doctor who, while doing a colon operation, removed a kidney to transplant into another patient without asking the patient. The scandal of inappropriate medical care can sometimes be criminal.

One of the surgeons I became fond of in Egypt, Dr. Sami, demonstrated to me how he takes the surgical specimen out to the waiting room and shows it to the family. I couldn't believe what he was doing. My patients back home would probably vomit and give me one star in all the online reviews. In the Middle East, he explained, some families ask to see the specimen with their own eyes to be sure that the operation was actually performed.

Adam Elshaug, professor of health policy at the University of Sydney in Australia, was a contributor to the *Lancet* special issue on overuse. When he was asked in a Q&A with the Commonwealth Fund whether the problem of overuse is as bad as we've been led to believe, he said, "It might be worse. Evidence suggests that the world's various health care systems are becoming even less efficient. We're moving in the wrong direction."

As we address the challenges of global public health, we should remember that it's not just too little care that is the problem. In some areas, the problem is also too much medical care. If overtreatment were a disease, it would rank as one of the leading public health threats across the world. The appropriateness in medicine problem exists in the United States but may be many times worse in some of the poor countries I visited. The crisis of appropriateness in medicine is a global public health issue.

PART III
Redesigning Health Care

CHAPTER 11

Starting from Scratch

Walking into a car dealership puts a knot in the pit of my stomach. I feel cheapened by the whole experience. I know that I will have to haggle with the salesperson, as the sticker price is never the *real* price. I will endure the silly playacting ("Let me see what my manager can do"). Even if I walk out with a good deal, I leave feeling ambushed, frazzled.

But one day, while walking through a mall, I stumbled upon a Tesla showroom and took notice. Maybe it was the sight of a beautiful electric car glistening under LED lighting. Or perhaps it was the music coming from its powerful sound system serenading me through the vehicle's open doors that drew me in. I was hypnotized. I strolled around a car and sat in the driver's seat. A few young Tesla reps were on hand, fielding questions from prospective customers. But there was no pressure, no games. The experience was completely different than visiting the average car dealership.

I asked a few basic questions about how fast the car charges and how many miles it would go on a single charge. Blown away by this modern showroom concept, I asked the sales rep if he was paid on a commission. He said "no." I liked that—the pressure was off. Maybe his incentives might actually be aligned with mine.

A few months later, walking around San Diego, I saw another Tesla on display. This car wasn't in a mall; it was on a street corner downtown that had a lot of foot traffic. A Tesla representative had

parked the car there, opened all the doors, blasted some great
tunes, and encouraged people to sit inside. Again, I took a look, sat
in the driver's seat, and asked questions, all while feeling zero pressure to purchase the vehicle. I learned I could schedule a test drive
in which a Tesla rep would drive a car to my house and let me take
it for a spin. That's great service.

I did the test drive and fell in love with the smooth ride, the
safety features, and the fact that it had essentially no maintenance to worry about. A Tesla has few parts. No engine, hence no
spark plugs, no belts, no oil to change, no emissions inspection.
I researched it for a couple more weeks and then returned to the
Tesla store in the mall where I first saw the car. I walked up to the
sales rep who had helped me the first time.

"I've done my research and I'd like to go ahead and buy one," I
told him.

"That's great!" He stood there, looking at me with a big smile.

The pause continued long enough to become awkward. Finally I
asked, "Well, how do I order the car?" I had allotted two hours that
day to be at the store doing paperwork and didn't want to waste time.

"Just go to Tesla.com," the rep relied. "You can buy it there."

I went home, logged on to the site, clicked on the model I wanted,
and selected a few options. I entered my credit card information
for the deposit. Within five minutes, I had purchased the car. It
was as easy as buying an airline ticket. The experience represented
a milestone, a complete change from how I'd bought cars in the
past. Gone were the days of haggling. I had just enjoyed the most
streamlined, honest, and consumer-centered car buying experience I could imagine.

Now I understood how Tesla is disrupting the century-old
system of going to a car dealership and playing hardball in the
negotiation spin cycle. When I picked up my Tesla, I got a one-hour
orientation on how to use it. The Tesla rep gave me a 24-hour
customer service number to call anytime. I learned that in the
event of a repair, a service technician will come to my house if the
job is small enough. Tesla has created an experience centered on
the customer, rather than sticking with a system entrenched in
outmoded practices.

It's no wonder that when Tesla announced their all-electric mass market car, the $35,000 Model 3, they instantly got half a million preorders. People nationwide lined up outside Tesla stores early the morning before they opened, all to order a car that didn't yet exist. It made automotive history.

Do you see long lines of people waiting outside other car dealerships early in the morning before they open to buy a car they've never seen? I don't. In fact, locally, I witnessed one of the most generous political donors in state politics, the Virginia Automotive Dealers Association, sue Tesla to keep them from opening a store in Richmond,[1] which was one fight in an ongoing battle against Tesla in the state capitol.[2]

Tesla's market cap surpassed that of Ford. All the while, do you know how much money Tesla has spent on advertising? Nothing. Zero dollars. Tesla has won people over with their intense focus on the consumer—a strategy common to disrupters of entrenched billion-dollar industries.

What would happen if someone redesigned medical care so that it was laser-focused on the patient?

That's precisely what Iora Health is doing. Iora's founder and CEO, Dr. Rushika Fernandopulle, a Harvard-trained primary care doctor, didn't like what he was seeing in the health care industry: the assembly line method of seeing complex patients, rushing them through the exam rooms, ordering large swaths of tests, then chasing down insurance companies for payment. I met up with Dr. Fernandopulle at a conference to learn more about his new model. Hearing him describe the problems of modern primary care struck a chord with me. I told him that's why I had gone into surgery. He chuckled. We agreed that the current model exasperates patients and burns out doctors. After doing it for years, he finally said "No, thanks." He left a distinguished career as executive director of the Harvard Interfaculty Program for Health Systems Improvement to take a chance on a completely redesigned model of primary care.

Fernandopulle and his colleagues began with the mission of restoring humanity to medicine through what they call "relationship-based" care. Together with nurses, social workers,

nutritionists, and other experts, they sought to find the most effective way to engage patients on a deep level. At the core of the model
is time. Iora carves out a lot of time for each patient. They want to
see you, talk to your other doctors on your behalf, and teach lifestyle
changes to avoid unnecessary dependence on medication. Rejecting
the high-throughput, high-billing model of health care, they try to
understand a patient's social and economic conditions—what we
call the "social determinants of health." They coordinate care and
strive to achieve the best health outcomes. Depending on the situation, they'll make house calls, send a Lyft car to take a patient to
a cooking class for diabetics, or do whatever they determine is
needed to get and stay healthy. And they do all this at no out-of-
pocket cost to the patient.

It's a reimagined way of taking care of a population. When
Dr. Fernandopulle opened the first clinic in 2010, little did he and
his team know that starting with a clean slate would allow them
to create one of the most exciting disruptions in health care today.

"We had the advantage of starting completely from scratch,"
Fernandopulle said, describing their approach. Fernandopulle,
born in Sri Lanka, named the clinic after the iora, a small bird
native to Sri Lanka known for its bright colors and loud whistle.

As Fernandopulle explained the Iora model, I thought it made
perfect sense, but seemed too good to be true. Iora is based in
Boston, Massachusetts, but has locations in about a half dozen
states. I asked Dr. Fernandopulle if I could travel to Phoenix to visit
one of their health centers.

Days later, I walked into an immaculate facility, the Iora clinic
on Indian School Road, and was greeted by the local clinic supervisor, Sarah Cabou.

Good People Attract Good People

It was 7:00 A.M., but Sarah Cabou, who is also a nurse, began to
give me a quick tour of the facility before the daily morning
"huddle." Cabou came to work at Iora because she was frustrated
with jobs she had in the traditional fee-for-service health care

system. In her previous jobs, she saw patients on medications they didn't need because no one took the time to fully explain things to them. She saw patients fail to get the care they needed because they couldn't navigate the system. She also saw how corporate medicine was all too often penny wise and pound foolish, failing to address underlying problems that actually made people sick. Cabou has an MBA and an MHA (master's in hospital administration), but it didn't take an advanced education to see that the fast throughput and billing model of primary care was badly broken. She saw patients fall through the cracks and incur high costs because the system was too fragmented, too rigid, and too hard to navigate.

In Phoenix, I learned more about how Iora works. They are hired by an employer or insurance company to take care of a population of people, such as a group of 10,000 seniors. Each person in that population is assigned an Iora doctor and an Iora health coach.

The coach joins each patient for their doctor appointments. After the doctor leaves, the coach stays with the patient to go over next steps. Health coaches call patients to check in with them and help coordinate the other specialist doctors the patient may need to see. They get to know their patient's situation well and facilitate good communication between doctors. Iora doctors and nurses are free to take care of people in whatever way they see fit, ranging from home visits, to giving a ride to see a specialist, to enrolling their patients in one of their classes. They pride themselves in spending a lot of time with patients so they can understand the individual's goals, struggles, and barriers. The Iora health coaches make everyone's job a lot easier.

Sarah Cabou told me about her previous job before coming to Iora. She was the nurse supervisor of an outpatient bone marrow transplant center where patients would routinely fall through the cracks. While I personally don't do that procedure, I know that bone marrow transplants are a care coordination challenge—perhaps even the hardest care coordination challenge in medicine. Here's why: Patients are hit hard with chemo for weeks or months until their bone marrow counts hit an all-time low, then they are given a bone marrow transplant, perfectly timed and perfectly matched with a donor. To be cleared for the transplant, these patients require a slew of consults with nephrologists, cardiologists, infectious disease doctors, and other specialists, due to the toxic effects of the chemo. Cabou told me that she often watched patients have their cancer recur simply because the coordination was too much for any one patient to manage.

She also previously worked with Medicaid patients. She routinely saw patients missing appointments because of confusion, complicated insurance procedures, not having a ride, being in the hospital at the time of their appointment, or avoiding care because they never wanted it in the first place. She saw enormous waste in the system and felt compelled to be a part of something better. The final straw was when she watched a doctor seeing patients for 15-minute visits with an egg timer on his desk. "We'll talk until the timer goes off," Cabou recalled his telling patients. "Fee-for-service medicine values quantity, not quality," she said.

She showed me around the clinic, which included a community room for cooking classes and game nights for lonely seniors. We walked to a modern conference room where every member of the ten-person staff had set up a small workstation. The open office design looked more like a tech start-up than a clinic. Impromptu conversations about patients filled the room.

I had seen the whole operation when it hit me: "Where is the billing office? Where is the business area where insurance claims are processed?"

The clinic staff who heard my question began to laugh. They had no billing people. The clinic is paid a lump sum annually to care for a population of patients, so there isn't a lot of paper to push, or time to spend cajoling anyone to pay up. *Gosh*, I thought, *back in Baltimore, my office staff and nurse practitioner spend hours on the phone with insurance companies.* Iora spends almost no time on that stuff.

"We don't need a back room for billing, so we use it for health activities," Cabou explained. The extra space allowed them to hold sessions on yoga or fitness or how to manage your lifestyle if you have a chronic disease.

I couldn't believe what I was seeing. A true *health* center.

It was now 8 A.M., time for the daily staff huddle in the open workroom. Around the table with the big screens on the walls, the room was set up to talk about each patient who had an appointment that day while reviewing their data on the screens. Present at the huddle was the entire clinic staff: health coaches, nurse practitioners, a doctor, and two receptionists who handled the phone lines. A different team member leads the huddle each day, instead of just having a doctor do it. Sara said it was designed that way to promote a more egalitarian culture, so everyone feels free to speak up about any patient. On the clinic schedule, most patients were allotted an hour. Evidently that's common. Iora staff want to ensure they have plenty of time with each patient.

For the next hour, I watched the Iora team perform like an orchestra. Almost everyone in the room knew every patient being discussed and had something to contribute. When someone announced good news about a patient, everyone cheered. When a difficult case was discussed, they put their heads together and came up with a creative way to handle it. Everyone seemed invested. As they ran through the list of patients, I heard people in the group say things like "I'll give her a call to remind her," "I'll go visit her to make sure she's doing okay," "I'll call her hematologist to make sure we're on the same page," or "I'll see how she's doing since we stopped her medication."

The group also reviewed outstanding issues from patients they saw the day before. Sarah Cabou would assign follow-up tasks to health coaches to close the loop on next steps. The group took time to discuss patients in their practice who had been admitted to a hospital or gone to an ER. When they learned of a patient's admission, they called the hospital doctor to provide the patient's medical and social background. While I was there, a patient of theirs showed up at Mayo Scottsdale with a high INR level—a test indicating the blood is too thin from blood-thinning medication. A health coach quickly followed up with the patient to review how to properly take their blood-thinning meds. The receptionists had extensive insight on each patient coming in. They routinely called each patient to remind them of their appointment and to make sure they had a ride. If they didn't have a ride, they offered to send

a car to pick them up. At one point during the huddle, a receptionist told the group that a patient was apprehensive, and at risk
of not showing up. For another patient, a receptionist mentioned
she thought a patient might be trying to game the system.

Including front office staff on morning rounds was brilliant.
I learn a lot about my patients from my office manager, Trish
McGinty. She knows which patients are doing well, which are
leaning against having surgery, and which are also coping with
other social problems. The inside information that Trish gleans
from talking to my patients is invaluable. Once she even warned
me about a patient's angry husband. Even though the woman was
cheerful and thankful when I saw her in clinic, I was grateful for
the heads-up!

As patients began to come in that morning, each one was
ushered into a spacious examination room with a round table and
three chairs: one for the doctor, one for the patient, and one for
the patient's health coach. Extra chairs were nearby for family or
friends. The health coach sat in on every doctor appointment, took
notes, and followed up with the patient to coach them toward the
goals the doctor recommended. As patients were being seen in the
examination rooms, the staff conference room turned into a busy
command center; each staff person sat at the table like an open
office and tossed questions or concerns about patients to Sarah
Cabou, who would make decisions or delegate them to the doctor.

Sitting in the conference room for a few hours, I watched health
coaches pop in and give detailed information on patients to the
doctor and clinic supervisor. They would work through problems,
make calls, and coordinate care.

"What I love about this job is that everything is at my disposal to
help patients," one of the clinicians told me. "I can bring someone
in with a car service, set up a video chat, or send a health coach to
their house."

At one point, a phlebotomist (a health care professional trained
to draw blood) walked in and told Cabou, "This patient's cardiologist ordered a lab test that we already did two weeks ago. Do we
really need to repeat it?" Instead of sticking the patient with a

needle again, the team submitted a copy of the prior results to the cardiologist, who then agreed not to repeat the test.

One patient was a 73-year-old bus driver for kids with disabilities. He kept getting readmitted to the hospital for congestive heart failure (CHF), a condition treated with a medication called a diuretic, which addresses fluid buildup by making a person urinate. The Iora team got alerted about his hospitalization for CHF-related fluid overload at the huddle, and someone asked, "Why is this patient not taking his meds and why is he getting readmitted so frequently?" They probed further and learned that he did not want to urinate often because he feared leaving the kids alone on his bus. The patient insisted he'd rather suffer heart failure than abandon the kids even for one minute.

After discussing his case, the Iora team compromised by switching the patient to a more moderate medication. It would treat his CHF without causing such frequent urination. They were also able to change his medication schedule so he didn't have to make so many bathroom stops when he was with the kids. It worked. The patient was able to do what he loved doing—driving kids—while getting a reasonable treatment for his heart disease and avoiding frequent hospitalizations. Sarah Cabou attributed the success to their strong rapport with the patient, which allowed them to understand his unique situation.

At another point in the day, there was an elderly new patient who had been feeling light-headed. Without doing a litany of brain MRIs and other tests, the doctor, Sara Peña, realized he was on medication that was lowering his blood pressure. After spending a lot of time with the patient, she learned he had a lifetime history of high blood pressure. His body had adjusted to that high pressure to supply blood to his brain and other organs. Given his history, Dr. Peña adjusted his medications so that his blood pressure would be on the high-normal side rather than the low-normal side. His light-headedness went away. No pricey brain scans were necessary.

"I think there is so much overtreatment because doctors don't have time to explore what patients are capable of doing,"

Dr. Peña explained. "What they want to do, and what they feel is important."

Patients love the care they receive from Iora. Most say they would highly recommend the clinic to a friend, according to the company's net promoter score, which gauges customer satisfaction.[3] Iora's score is over 90, meaning that 90% of customers would recommend Iora to a friend. A score that high is rare in health care. By comparison, United Airlines has a net promoter score of 10, and most primary care doctors have net promoter scores around 30.

The patients may love Iora partly because the culture is so friendly. Increasingly, when I talk to patients I meet in my clinic or on the road, I'm convinced we are living in an age of rampant loneliness. It's reached endemic levels. I see more patients coming to appointments alone than I ever have in my career. When I ask who will be with them during surgery, or whom I should call afterward to confirm they are okay, they often answer "No one." I see it in the gym, too. Back in college, we would all socialize and talk between lifting weights. Now everyone wears earphones and walks around like a zombie. Loneliness is a leading public health problem. At Iora, they hold game nights and cooking classes designed to provide community. "We see people make friends," Cabou told me. "We need that, because many of our seniors are lonely."

After my visit to the Iora Health clinic in Phoenix, I asked Dr. Fernandopulle how he created such a great organizational culture.

"We hire for empathy and teach for skill," he said. Iora's hiring process begins with running applicants through something akin to speed dating, to identify those that have the needed people skills. "Unfortunately, so much of what is done in health care is transactional," said Fernandopulle. "But transactions don't treat people, relationships do." As a doctor, I found Iora's teamwork approach to their patients refreshing. Team-based care frees up doctors to be more efficient. As a result, they care for more patients. At Iora, nurses and health coaches do as much as they can, including following up on treatment plans set by the doctor. As a busy doc myself, I'm convinced there are so many aspects of a physician's job that can be done by a highly motivated helper. With the right attitude, a reliable assistant can make all the difference in the world, regardless of their level of formal schooling. For example, I could train a highly dedicated college graduate to manage medication compliance, do nutrition teaching, and follow up on tasks. This kind of trained help allows doctors to concentrate on the critical decision making at the heart of the practice of medicine. It's no surprise that Iora staff have high rates of job satisfaction at a time when about a third of doctors nationwide are burning out. The enthusiasm at Iora was palpable.

Sara Peña said she loved working with colleagues who believe in medicine that is patient-centered rather than business-centered. She also said she loved having resources to help—from the coaches to the rides and video chats. She enjoyed the autonomy to do whatever she believed was best for the patient. You may be surprised by how many people who work in medicine want to be a part of something this holistic. Iora draws these types of health care providers, or clinicians, who believe in treating the root causes of medical conditions and are keenly aware of the risks of overtreatment.

At the same time, it's important to note that Iora staff are not playing in an amusement park without accountability. Their performance is measured using standard metrics of health care quality and utilization—such as how many people in their population go to the ER or are hospitalized, among other outcomes. They have a lot of data on the "frequent flyer" patients in their practice—that is, patients who keep bouncing back to the hospital.

Iora is not cherry-picking, taking care of only healthy patients. Most of their patients are on Medicare. Two thirds of Medicare beneficiaries have three or more chronic conditions, 27% report fair or poor health, and 31% have cognitive or mental impairment.[4] These patients are extremely expensive to the health care system. Moreover, they are particularly vulnerable to health complications.

Dr. Peña pointed out that while their team cares for "a population," they are held to metrics for the entire group. They do outreach to patients who have never come to clinic or who miss appointments. The receptionists call them and report back on what's keeping them from getting medical care. Every staff member in the clinic could quote to me one of Dr. Fernando-pulle's goals: "We need to talk about the patients that don't see us as much as we talk about the patients that do see us."

Meeting with the clinic's staff, I learned how Iora's model helps overcome barriers to good health. After all, do we really think doctors can manage overlapping chronic diseases with a couple of 15-minute visits per year? The current health care system is like a game of whack-a-mole. Iora shows that good health care is best achieved by a team of doctors and nondoctors who can dive deep into their patients' work, social, eating, sleeping, stress, and exercise life. By using a relationship-based approach, Iora is getting ahead of the underlying drivers of chronic conditions. In addition to restoring humanity to medicine, Iora is lowering health care costs.

After at least three months of engagement with an Iora care team, the number of patients whose hypertension was controlled increased from 59% to 74%. Results from a cohort of 1,176 Iora Medicare enrollees over an 18-month period showed hospital admissions cut in half and emergency department visits reduced by 20%. The total medical spending by the insurer declined 12%. Since that study, Iora has now reduced health care spending for the populations they care for by 15%. Imagine what a 15% reduction in Medicare's roughly $1 trillion budget would mean for the country. "The goal is not to save money, but if you do the right thing, it does save money," Fernandopulle told me.

The Iora model offers a novel model of delivering patient-centered health care that actually saves money. An investment in relationship-based, holistic medical care has paid off with bigger savings in the form of patients taking fewer medications, and fewer trips to the hospital. Given the high cost of an ER visit or hospitalization, it's no surprise that well-designed care has a strong value proposition. The model works, and other primary care groups like ChenMed, a Florida-based group, and Oak Street Health, an Illinois-based group, are having great success using it as well. ChenMed not only delivers holistic primary care, but they also take on the financial responsibility for each patient's downstream medical costs, whatever they might be. Accordingly, ChenMed refers their patients to highly screened specialists who believe strongly in the appropriateness of care. ChenMed's success is a testament that great medical care is often less costly medical care. Together these companies are disrupting health care.

My optimism about the future of health care stems from the many committed, smart people, like Iora founder Fernandopulle, with big ideas on how to challenge the status quo to restore medicine to its sacred mission. Iora and other disrupters that are laser-focused on putting the patients at the center of their efforts are becoming the Tesla of health care.

CHAPTER 12

Disruption

My friend Dina came to town to visit me for a weekend. During her stay, Dina began to feel sick. I took her to the local emergency room, and in doing so, I saw firsthand what patients go through.

"You are out-of-network," barked the receptionist. She acted as if Dina was a junior high student caught stealing chocolate milk.

The law is clear in the United States. Hospitals are required to treat patients during an emergency, regardless of insurance status.[1] I stepped into the conversation to talk to the receptionist. "Is this hospital still going to take care of her as the law requires?" I asked.

The receptionist gave me a look of disgust. Then she prepared us for billing Armageddon. "Your insurance may not pay, in which case you will be responsible for the bill," she warned.

Why does our health care system treat ordinary people like criminals when they are out-of-network? Dina was in pain and trying to survive a scary situation. Out-of-network patients are ordinary, hardworking, insured Americans who are terrified that their medical condition might be serious. They are not cheaters.

Soon after checking in to the emergency room, I warned Dina, she would be given a famous form to sign. The single document was really two contracts blended together for a reason. It would get her to agree to two things with one signature. First, that she agrees to be treated. No problem there. Second, it would say she agrees to pay 100% of whatever is charged. That could be a problem. Federal law requires a hospital to care for urgent and emergent patients whether they agree to pay or not (the EMTALA law). Patients should obviously pay a fair price for their treatment, but too often this is a rigged game. The hospital charges don't have to be reality-based. The amounts they accept from insurance companies don't have to be disclosed. The price the patient will pay is not shared before treatment takes place. This isn't like other consumer transactions in which people pay for services.

Sure enough, within 15 minutes a hospital representative came by her room in the emergency department and asked her to sign the form I predicted would rear its head. But this one was on an iPad, which made it impossible to modify. I told the hospital representative they needed to find a paper form for her to sign. And in the meantime, I had her write on a piece of paper I pulled off the copy machine that she consented to be treated and sign the paper, what we surgeons call a battlefield consent form.

After a lot of commotion, they printed the form. Sure enough, it included a clause that said she would sign away her financial life before seeing any of the bills. She crossed out the clause and then signed. She had a minor operation, recovered quickly, and went home a few days later.

Weeks after Dina left the hospital, the bills started pouring in. When you added them up, Dina's out-of-network bill came in at $60,000. Dina called the billing office and asked for help understanding her bill. She spoke to someone in a call center that wasn't even located in the same state as the hospital. Per the typical routine, the call center representative couldn't provide any insight. But she did manage to pile on the guilt for Dina's out-of-network status.

Dina signed an authorization form so I could step in and negotiate for her. As was the case when I had intervened on behalf of my sister's friend Heather, the hospital would accept the form only via fax. I had to drive to a UPS store to send it. After jumping through hoops, including paying a $25 fee to get an itemized bill (again, payable only by a paper check sent in the mail), I finally got someone on the phone. Time to play the game.

What they didn't realize is that I had been able to find out how much the hospital would have taken from an insurance company for the same procedure. I used a website called HealthcareBlue-book.com, which shows the typical rates hospitals get paid for various common operations. The site showed me that the fair price, the one the hospital actually takes from in-network patients, is about $12,000.

The hospital had charged Dina a 500% markup. Her crime was being out-of-network. Did it cost them more to do her operation? Absolutely not. I steeled my nerves and got ready to haggle as if I was back in the Egyptian bazaar in the heart of my beloved Cairo.

The hospital had charged $60,000 and demanded the full price. That wasn't reasonable.

"Would your hospital be willing to accept $12,000 for the same service for an insured patient who is in-network?" I asked the representative on the phone.

The woman got upset. "We can charge someone out-of-network as much as we want," she told me. "The law says we can."

Testy. That's to be expected. The Egyptian vendors at the bazaar always make a show out of being offended, too. It's how the game is played.

I asked to speak to the director of revenue cycle for the hospital. At first, they said I could not. I had to talk to a supervisor and explain that I was a doctor. The director called me back a week later.

I told him that Dina didn't have a contractual obligation to pay, which she didn't, because she had struck out the clause saying she'd pay whatever they charged. I added that the law prohibited collections agencies from hurting her credit if they did not have a contract for services.

The hospital director then made a big show of offering Dina financial aid. But mind you, this wasn't an act of generosity. The Affordable Care Act requires hospitals to have financial assistance policies, and sets parameters for what a hospital can do. The rules say hospitals are not allowed to discourage patients from receiving emergency care by such stratagems as requiring up-front payments. They're also not allowed to charge patients who qualify for finan-cial aid more than they would charge a typical insured patient.[2] There are various ways this can be interpreted, according to the consumer advocacy organization Community Catalyst. Hospitals are required to publicize the policies far and wide—online and in print copies that are on display for patients and visitors.

The hospital director acted as if he was doing Dina a favor by offering financial assistance. He built the gesture up as an act of kindness, then proposed a 10% discount. Never mind that the bill had been marked up 500%. That's like a merchant at the bazaar telling a tourist she can pay $90 for the trinket that's priced at $100 but worth a buck.

He also said they could put her on a monthly payment plan. How generous.

I told him it would be only fair for Dina to pay the hospital the same amount it accepts for other patients: $12,000.

"I can do $30,000," he said. With five words, he slashed the bill in half.

I asked the director what an in-network insurance company would have paid for Dina's bill. As I expected, he said he wasn't allowed to disclose his discounted rate with any insurance company.

"Look, if Dina can pay $30,000, I'll write off the difference," he said, trying to close the deal.

"She can do $12,000," I replied.

"How about $25,000?" Surround him with camels and pyramids and he'd be right at home in the bazaar.

"She can do $12,000."

"How about $20,000?"

"She can do $12,000"

"How about $19,000?"

I said no, thank you, and have a nice day.

Sure enough, Dina's bill got sent to collections. When the collections agency called, I had prepped her to ask the agent to send her a written record of her obligation to pay the bill. Dina had deleted the portion of the agreement that said she had to pay whatever they charged. The bill collectors never called back.

My friend, who had no legal obligation to pay anything, instead made a $5,000 donation to the hospital as a part of its fundraising drive. That's enough to get her name on the facility's wall of generous donors. I went back to the surgeon who did her operation and it turns out he had no idea what the markup was and how the patient was shaken down. Dina paid the surgeon's part of the bill, but he sounded embarrassed by it all.

And, frankly, it *is* embarrassing. Health care doesn't have to be so different from any other business in America. Imagine you see an orange in the supermarket with no price on it. You take it to the register to get a price check.

"How much for the orange?"

"You have to buy it to find out," the cashier says.

You're hungry, so you buy the orange. But you recoil when you see the cashier has charged your credit card $500. And there are no returns.

If that happened at the grocery store, you would be outraged. But that's how our current health care system operates. You can't see the price until after you've had the service or operation or test. That's understandable if you come in to a hospital with trauma or sepsis in the ICU. But most health care services delivered in the United States are predictable, that is, "shoppable." That is, you come in for a knee replacement and you leave with a knee replacement. So why can't people get a price quote for medical services?

What if hospitals published a menu of prices for the common nonemergency procedures they offered? Dina could have been diagnosed and given a price for the procedure she needed. She could have accepted the price and agreed to pay it. Or perhaps, because she did have time, she could have checked nearby facilities to see what they charged for the same operation. She could have shopped for the best deal, just as she does in other aspects of her life. It would have been a fair transaction that helped her understand health care costs. And the openness would also spur hospitals to compete with one another based on cost and quality. It would bring down the prices.

Dina's experience is repeated every day across the country. It happened to Jeffrey Rice, too. He decided to do something about it.

Healthcare Bluebook

Jeffrey founded Healthcare Bluebook after he became a victim of the game. I could see the power of his company's work after my experience with Dina. I traveled to Nashville and met him at a diner that oozed Southern charm and hospitality.

Jeffrey's story began when his 12-year-old son hurt his ankle and needed elective surgery to lengthen his Achilles tendon. Jeffrey is not your average Nashville dad. He's a doctor who practiced medicine and worked in hospital administration. In addition to his MD, he also has a law degree from Duke University.

His son needed a standard procedure. Jeffrey looked up the billing code and called the hospital to ask how much it would cost. The first place he called said it would be $37,000, but not to worry, his insurance would pay most of it.

That didn't sit right with Jeffrey. He had to pay the first $5,000 himself because of his deductible. He became curious about the system and asked how they came to their price. He knew of other, much more invasive procedures that didn't cost as much. Since he had the billing code, he wondered if they could cut through the fluff and explain why it cost so much.

The hospital representative got flustered and said she would call him back. When he got the return call, the price had dropped to $15,000 once she factored in a possible network discount. Again, the hospital employee assured him his insurance would pay everything above his $5,000 deductible.

Jeffrey said "Thank you" and called the surgeon who would be doing the operation. "Do you do this same operation at any other facility?"

Surgeons often work at multiple hospitals. And sure enough, this surgeon said yes. The surgeon directed him to a different facility and assured him that the operation would be the same quality at either place. Jeffrey called the new facility for a quote and they told him $1,500. His son had the surgery at that facility and everyone left happy.

Jeffrey mulled over the experience in the following months. He couldn't let it go. The first price quote had been almost

25 times as much as he eventually paid for the same procedure. He had medical and legal degrees and had worked in both hospital and health plan administration, and he had barely managed to navigate the system to get a fair price. How would anyone else have a chance? When you buy a car, you can check the Kelley Blue Book to see the fair price. But nothing like that existed in health care.

Jeffrey decided to start his own company showing the "fair price" for common medical procedures and tests. Healthcare Bluebook collects pricing data from partnering employers who self-fund their health care, reviews all the prices that different patients pay, and uses them to establish a fair price amount.

Employers that partner with Healthcare Bluebook are able to flag the price gougers in the market to their employees and point them to a fair-priced provider. Jeffrey and his team categorize every medical center and doctor in an employer's area based on their markups. Each medical facility gets a rank of green, yellow, or red, rated on prices and a composite quality score.

Bluebook has an incentive program that rewards employees with a bonus check of $50 if they choose a facility with a green rating. If patients choose an MRI test at a facility where it costs $400 instead of another imaging center where it costs $1,500, the patient gets a check. Patients still have total freedom of choice but get rewarded for shopping wisely. The business model is genius: If an employer saves $20,000 as a result of a patient's choosing a fair-priced hospital over an overpriced hospital, why not share the savings? Using this model, patients and the employers paying for their medical care are aligned in a way that doesn't discourage patients from seeing any provider they want. Healthcare Bluebook cracks the code on aligning the patient with an incentive to choose fair-priced care without compromising quality.

Getting patients to shop wisely is a milestone in health care. A large study by the group RAND found that when patients who are not paying for their medical care can choose between lower-cost and higher-cost care, they choose the more expensive care. They assume the more expensive, the better, a correlation that may work in other industries. But that's not the case for many types of treatment in American health care.

Employers love Healthcare Bluebook and pay for the service because they may be saving the difference between $37,000 and $1,500, just as Jeffrey did when he shopped for a hospital for his son's operation. More than 4,500 employers have now signed on to the service, and the number is growing. Healthcare Bluebook makes it easy for your employees to both know the fair price for medical procedures and find the nearest health care providers that offer fair prices. Patients shopping for care will seriously disrupt the business of medicine in America.

A Legislative Beam of Hope

One day I received a call from a Florida legislator who read my last book, which is about accountability in medicine. He asked me to talk to their legislators about the potential impact of transparency to transform medicine. They were interested in making health care prices public. That phone call led to three trips to the state capitol in Tallahassee, where I met Representative José Oliva, as well as Speaker of the House Richard Corcoran, Senator Rob Bradley, and a host of bipartisan members. Unlike other political leaders I had encountered, these legislators were serious about using sunlight as a disinfectant. They wanted to disrupt the money games of health care with transparency. "We heard from people whose lives were radically changed by high bills," Representative Chris Sprowls told me.

Ultimately, with strong support from Governor Rick Scott, the elected leaders passed a milestone law. It requires hospitals to show the average amount they are being paid for procedures, not just how much they charge. This is game-changing, because other attempts at price transparency have required hospitals to show only sticker prices, not the discounted amounts they have been secretly accepting. The prices are now viewable at FloridaHealthPrice-Finder.com. So, for example, if you need a knee replacement, you can go to the site and see that the average cost in Florida and nationwide is about $35,000. The site doesn't have facility data published yet, but it's coming. Florida is doing something big.

During one of the hearings for the bill, Florida health care lobbyists urged the legislators to publish only charges—the sticker price, which is much higher than what they'd accept from an insurance company. They didn't want to publish what they actually got paid.

That would be "comparing apples and automobiles—they are radically different things," Sprowls said. "They're not even in the same genre. Chargemaster prices are imaginary numbers that rarely get paid." I was impressed that he and his colleagues had a command of this distinction—one at the dark heart of health care's cost crisis. We spend enough money on health care in the United States that we should be able to cover every citizen. "It's the waste that strains the system," Sprowls added.

Price transparency alone will not solve all the problems of predatory screening and unnecessary medical care. But it could save the health care system hundreds of billions of dollars currently being wasted on the game. In the words of senator and physician Tom Coburn, getting price transparency right is the first step in fixing health care because it ushers in quality transparency. We need to see prices, so patients and health plans can determine which facilities are operating in a way that's efficient, and which are just trying to maximize their profit. It's common sense.

Those who want to do their part to solve our health care crisis should work with their state representative to pass the same price transparency law that's now taking effect in Florida. New Hampshire has done the same, seeing the futility of requiring sticker prices to be public and instead requiring what is actually paid to hospitals to be information that is available. FAIR Health is one New York–based nonprofit also advancing transparent pricing for health care.

From all my experience traveling to Washington, D.C., Oklahoma, Wyoming, and Florida and visiting with people on the front lines of health care, I've become convinced that American businesses and households want honest medical care at an honest price. Doctors have earned the trust of patients over centuries, but now that trust is threatened. Dr. Jeffrey Rice, and current Speaker of the Florida House José Oliva, make me optimistic about American health care. It's my hope that these disrupters and others will make markets rational and efficient rather than secretive and predatory.

CHAPTER 13

Buying Health Insurance

The limo driver pulled the shiny black Audi A8L up to the office of a small lumber manufacturer in North Carolina. He put the car in park and walked around to open the back door. David Contorno stepped out, dressed to the nines. Contorno was not a Wall Street banker or high-powered attorney. He was the company's health insurance broker.

Contorno left his chauffeur to wait by the car. Upon entering the office, he strode confidently toward the meeting room, flashing his perfect smile and shaking hands along the way.

Contorno was there to do what he did so well: explain why the price of health insurance was going up—and get his clients to renew their health insurance contract. Though Contorno had the title of independent broker, he, like most brokers, got paid tens of thousands of dollars in kickbacks from health insurance carriers for every renewal or new client he secured. Perhaps as a result, he adapted his sales pitch to subtly guide the lumber manufacturer to renew at the higher rates. He had mastered the art of steering employers to the insurance options that brought him the highest return. He failed to mention other insurance options, including buying insurance plans or the popular option for an employer to self-insure their employees' health care expenses. For Contorno, getting businesses to renew was relatively easy, and his bank account reflected that.

During the meeting, one woman at the lumber company began to fret about the rising health insurance costs. She asked a few questions and complained a bit. It was a reaction with which Contorno was very familiar. He knew how to manage "sticker shock," redirecting her anger toward hospital costs, technology, drug companies, and even people who don't exercise enough. It was a routine. Contorno, an empathetic listener, was a pro at rotating cannons to ensure they were aiming off the ship.

But as Contorno blamed external factors and assured them that renewing with their present health insurance carrier was their best option, an older man sat silently in the corner of the room. With his worn work clothes and weathered skin, he exuded the authority of a lumberyard manager. At the end of the meeting, when Contorno offered to answer any questions, the old man spoke up. "Don't blow smoke up my ass," he erupted. "My wife can't even afford her multiple sclerosis medication and you come up here in your limo! We're struggling, and all you people are getting rich off of us."

Despite the old man's protest, the company signed the renewal contract, and Contorno left. But as he stepped back into his limo he felt a sense of shame. He knew his kickback for getting the contract renewed would be hefty. And on top of that he would get paid a handsome 4% of whatever the lumber company spent on health insurance premiums each month, as has become standard in the industry. Contorno just made a lot of money, but he left feeling deeply conflicted. He couldn't stop thinking about the scolding he'd received from the old man or about the man's struggling wife. The experience gave Contorno a crisis of conscience, and he changed. That next day, he committed his brokerage firm to a new way of selling health insurance, one that liberated him and his colleagues from the perverse incentives of insurance company commissions and kickbacks.

In subsequent meetings with clients, Contorno spoke freely, no longer beholden to insurance companies. He began recommending health insurance options based on what was the best value for employers, rather than the ones that paid him the most. Contorno felt uninhibited. "It was a great feeling," he told me as we discussed his experiences, adding that he saw clients save millions by being put into the best health plan for them.

One of those businesses was the Gerry Wood Auto Group. Gerry began selling cars in 1994 and grew his North Carolina small business from one to three dealerships: Honda, Kia, and Chrysler. The company now employs 175 full-time workers. I called Gerry to ask him about his experience buying health insurance for his business.

"My business was constantly getting hammered with health care costs," Gerry told me. "It's our single biggest line item."

Gerry had bought insurance in the past through a random broker who claimed to be an "independent benefits consultant." Later Gerry learned that, like most brokers, the insurance companies he sold for paid him.

"He wasn't straight with me," Gerry explained. "I had no idea what was going on. Nor did my friend that used the broker for his flower business. I'm in the car business, not in the health care business."

What triggered Gerry's call to Contorno was a letter he received from the health insurance company about another big rate hike. Contorno, now on a crusade to be honest with clients, had switched from commission and kickbacks to a performance-based consulting model of compensation. Contorno sat down with Gerry and gave him every option, free of bias, and recommended the best one for his employees.

Gerry had been spending $650,000 a year to United Healthcare to cover his employees. Contorno advised him to cut off that contract and instead set up a $475,000 fund to self-insure the health care of his employees. Contorno added catastrophic insurance coverage to protect Gerry against any individual costs over $100,000. Contorno offered him catastrophic insurance from one of 20 "stop-loss" carriers who sold these policies across state lines. Unlike the very limited options for traditional health insurance carriers, stop-loss insurance was sold in a robust market, where competition kept prices low.

Gerry explained to me how the new benefits structure did not limit choice of doctors and saved his business more than half a million dollars over three years, money he used to reinvest in the business, renovate his mechanic shops, and give his employees better retirement benefits.

But Contorno's commitment to do the best for clients came at a price. A few months after he began recommending that employers switch to better value plans, he received a nasty letter from Blue Cross Blue Shield of North Carolina. They essentially blackballed him. They wrote that they were deappointing him and would no longer do business with him or pay him commissions.

Contorno is a particularly bold and talented man. He was able to attract enough business to stay afloat, and today his company, EPowered Benefits, has expanded across the country. With a business model of charging a consulting fee and not accepting commissions or kickbacks, EPowered Benefits is now thriving, saving employers across the country millions of dollars.

Contorno's story was enlightening, but I wanted to learn more about the people who buy, sell, and rent access to medical care. I decided to fly to Orlando to attend a health insurance broker conference.

I seemed to be the only doctor at the conference, and I was surprised by how easy it was to talk to people. I simply told some of the brokers I met that I'm a doctor trying to learn more about how health insurance gets sold to employers in America. One broker, Phil, offered to talk with me over drinks one night. There at the hotel bar, Phil and his broker friends laid it all out.

"Marty, the dirty little secret in health care that no one is talking about is the way we brokers get paid," Phil said. He was about to retire so he wasn't worried about breaking the code of silence. He said he simply couldn't stand it anymore. "I went into this business because I thought it was noble to advise employers on the right health insurance coverage for their employees. But this business is not what I thought it was."

That night, I learned things they don't teach in health policy textbooks or graduate schools. I learned, in vivid detail, exactly how insurance brokers get kickbacks for selling health insurance and pharmacy benefit manager plans to employers, just as Contorno had explained to me. I realized that brokers are often the shepherds leading the sheep. They can convince an employer to buy an over-priced plan or a great value plan. They can convince an employer to switch insurance carriers, stick with their current carrier, go to the mat for a better price, or bypass health insurance and simply self-insure. Brokers have a lot of power. Employers grow to trust them. But what employers don't know is how insurance companies use cash to control the brokers. At the Orlando conference, I heard story after story of companies calling brokers to dangle a big bonus in front of them if they kept an employer on the hook.

I barely knew what a health insurance broker did before I attended that conference. Phil and his colleagues got me up to speed fast as we sipped piña coladas in the Florida heat. Slouching back in cozy chairs at the terrace bar, they spoke candidly about the business. I was leaning forward, taking notes, my eyes popping out of my head.

"The way brokers are paid is one reason people are paying too much for health insurance, and I can't believe no one is talking about it." Phil said. Throughout his career, he had regularly been offered hundreds of kickbacks from insurance companies, ranging from $30,000 to $100,000 (often referred to in the industry as "bonuses," "overrides," "persistency bonuses," or "contingent income").

"Sometimes that money pushed me to put employers into plans that were way too expensive for them," Phil admitted.

But as I learned from Contorno's experience of getting black-balled by Blue Cross Blue Shield of North Carolina, health insurance companies don't just use carrots, they also use sticks. Brokers told me if they lost a key employer, an insurance company might "fire" them from their entire book of business. That means the broker would be cut off from the gravy train—the 1 to 5% commission on every premium dollar the broker had brought to that company. That's a few hundred dollars *per employee* going to the commission payout every year! And as the employers' costs rise, so, too, does the broker's revenue. One broker, who switched an employer to a different health insurance plan, told me how he got blackballed, then trash-talked by the carrier who was telling other employers to avoid him simply because he was fired from working with them. The bad-mouthing was not merely to get revenge on that one broker. It sent a signal, loud and clear, to other brokers who might want to encourage employers to switch to a different plan.

The Fog of Benefits

Brokers do provide an important service. They help explain the insurance benefits and sort through the options for people.

I enjoyed my candid conversations with insurance brokers in Orlando. They were not bad people. They are just responding rationally to market forces. Some told me how they would do what's best for their client even if it meant a lower commission for them or forgoing a bonus, but that was not the norm. Many brokers unloaded the dirty way insurance companies paid them because they dislike the system. Some hated the commission and kickback structure. They had gone into health insurance sales to help businesses make good choices, not to be pushed to overcharge employers. As one broker explained, "people think we're independent, I even think that sometimes, but I often feel like a hired salesman for one insurance company. You wouldn't ask a Ford salesperson if you should buy a Honda."

Most of us would respond to similar market forces the same way. Think about it in a different context. Imagine you're an elementary school student and you told every kid in your school that you could get an ice cream vending machine in the school cafeteria, and by golly, one day there it is. They might hesitate when they see that you are getting 5% of every ice cream cone sale. But hey, you got them their ice cream, so they can't complain. What they don't know is that on top of that steady revenue stream, the ice cream supplier, every now and then, hands you a $100 bill.

Everyone loves the ice cream, and you like the cash flow. You introduce the ice cream supplier to four other schools in your town and quintuple your monthly commissions. All this for brokering a one-time agreement between each school and the vending machine company. You become known as the ice cream vending machine industry expert. But now a few students at the first school start to complain because the ice cream supplier doubled the prices. They think they might be able to pay less for ice cream if they went to a competitor. But you're the ice cream expert, so they come to you and ask about changing suppliers.

You tell your supplier the other kids aren't happy, but they won't work with you. They say if you go to a competing company they will cut your commission at all five schools. They'll fire you as the broker. What would be a rational economic response?

You would probably urge the unhappy kids to stick with the current supplier. You might resort to some trusted sales retention tactics. You might tell people they're getting higher quality ice cream from the current supplier, so it's worth the price. You might tell them a nightmare salmonella story about a person who ate a competitor's ice cream. You might explain that it costs more to start over with a new supplier than it does to stick with what they're paying. Your willingness to float such rumors would likely roughly correspond to the amount of money on the table. If it's just $1, you might say goodbye to the pricey supplier. If it's $1,000, that's a lot of bubble gum at stake. And if it's $10,000, you're in the money for a car when you turn 16. You might do whatever it takes to maintain the status quo.

This make-believe ice cream broker is analogous to a health insurance broker, but in health care there's a ton of money on the table. I met brokers who made hundreds of thousands of dollars a year for simply ensuring that their "ice cream vending machines" stayed in the "schools" despite surging prices. Where does the health insurance company get the money to pay the brokers so well for so long? They build it into the price of health insurance. In other words, that money comes from you.

The brokers told me they have as many as 17 different revenue streams from health insurance companies or pharmacy benefits managers. Some are never disclosed to the employer. This lack of disclosure is more common the smaller the employer. Sometimes the kickbacks go to a brokerage firm that employs brokers. That creates intense internal pressure at the firm to keep a book of business. Some brokerages spend their entire base commission on their business expenses and rely on bonuses as their sole source of profit.

This system is akin to the days when stockbrokers were told to sell 10,000 shares of a particular stock no matter what it took, with major repercussions for not meeting the target. The "I don't care how you do it, just do it" approach from supervisors leads to mischief and deception. Just ask Wells Fargo, where internal corporate pressure resulted in bankers' crossing the line and opening empty accounts in clients' names without their consent. That scam led to a $142 million settlement and a huge loss of credibility for the bank. The executives claimed they did not know. "I do want to make very clear that there was no orchestrated effort, or scheme as some have called it, by the company," said the Wells Fargo CEO. But bank employees said they were pressured to meet unrealistic sales goals,[1] that they opened bogus accounts so they wouldn't lose their jobs.[2] Turns out they lost their jobs anyway. Wells Fargo fired 5,300 employees for opening sham accounts to meet sales targets. When I talk to captains of the health insurance establishment, they make the same arguments, telling me that they do not put pressure on brokers. But the brokers on the ground tell a different story.

As I spoke with more brokers I realized how stressful their job is, with the bullying and bonus lures from health insurance companies. Sure, scoring three large employers could mean $100,000 to $200,000 in bonuses each year, along with a hefty commission on the premiums. But there's midlife-crisis-level stress when an employer calls to say "Hey, I want to reevaluate our health insurance options."

Why don't employers get educated and demand full transparency for what they are buying? Well, some do, but it's hard. It's challenging to compare health insurance benefits. It's ten times harder to interpret the pharmacy benefits—which are a whole 'nother shell game altogether.

As a physician, I was shocked at the business of how health insurance is sold to businesses in America; I couldn't believe what I was hearing. This is the way health care is sold in America? I didn't even know there was such a thing as a broker who sold health care to employers. What they were really selling was access to physicians like me. And this is how the business was conducted?

We suffered the financial crisis of 2007 in part because people were buying and selling products they didn't understand. Retirement plans were buying collateralized debt obligations (CDOs) even though no one had any idea what assets they contained. The market was too complicated for anyone to deconstruct. Employers have similar problems understanding the health insurance products they purchase. They are designed to be complicated so employers won't try to figure out where their money is going.

The similarities to the subprime mortgage crisis are striking. Back then, mortgage brokers were paid bonuses for putting people into subprime mortgages they couldn't afford. Both mortgage brokers and health insurance brokers were selling their clients products they didn't understand. The main difference was that after the global recession, the government cleaned up the mortgage broker business. The health insurance broker business, on the other hand, has never faced a reckoning.

I flew back to Johns Hopkins from the Orlando health insurance broker conference and asked doctors on our staff whether they knew how our services were sold. None did. I asked ten doctors: Have you ever heard of a health insurance broker? All said "no." Nor did any of them know how health insurance was sold in the United States. I was struck by the disconnect between those who deliver health care and those who sell it. It reminded me of what Senator Bill Frist, who is also a surgeon, said to me the day we met. Frist said doctors are educated in medicine but not in health care. I was seeing afresh how right he was.

Brandon Luckett

As I got to know insurance brokers around the country and started to get my head around their business, it was hard to believe how big a business it was. Nearly half of the nation's businesses buy insurance from brokers. In the Baltimore area alone, there are nearly a thousand brokers. Of the many I met, I noticed they often had strong sales skills, some were great golfers, and all were super friendly.

I realized that one of my friends, Brandon Luckett, is in the business. He's executive vice president of the benefits advising company Employee One.

I drove to Columbia, Maryland, to meet him for lunch at a famous Indian restaurant. I told Brandon what I had learned: the good, the bad, and the ugly side of the business. As I spoke, he appeared to agree. At one point, he interrupted.

"We took no bonuses last year," Brandon said about his company's relationship with insurance carriers.

"But don't most brokers get paid with bonuses?" I asked him.

"Yes, but we want to be different."

Whenever possible, Brandon gets paid a flat fee for his services based on the number of employees in a particular plan. The traditional commissions lead to higher health insurance costs, he said. They don't allow the broker to be a strong advocate for the employer, he added.

"We don't play the kickback game," he told me.

Over tandoori chicken and naan, Brandon told me he generally recommends that employers self-fund (self-insure) their benefits. That means the employer is the one who pays the health care bills, not an insurance company. Instead of paying premiums, the employer and employees pay into an escrow account that funds the plan. The employer hires a company called a third party administrator to manage the plans. Many traditional insurance companies offer administrative services. Brandon then makes sure that an employer has catastrophic insurance to cover any massive bills, maybe anything over $80,000 or $100,000. It depends on how much cost risk the employer can afford. Brandon shows the options and prices to the employer and lets them pick. It's not complicated. Overall, Brandon saves businesses millions of dollars a year just by restructuring the way they pay for health care.

In most cases, bypassing traditional health insurance and self-funding is the best value for employers. It saves so much it's like giving every employee an instant pay raise. But employers often don't make the changes, he said. That morning he met with an employer who was hesitant about self-funding, even though it would save a lot of money without reducing benefits.

I asked Brandon if eliminating undisclosed insurance company kickbacks would be a simple reform that would have a big impact. "Bingo," he said.

Brandon said that a small but growing number of brokers have gone to the flat fee model. I did some research on my own to find other broker firms that use a flat fee commission and found Bernard Health in Nashville, Tennessee. After one trip I had to Nashville, I swung by their offices and met Alex Tolbert and Ryan McCostlin. They affirmed what Contorno and Luckett had both told me: the broken commission-based model was increasing demand for brokers like them, whose payments are aligned with what's best for employers.

Creating a Brand of Trust—Health Rosetta

American business owners have a tremendous opportunity to lower their health care costs. Dave Chase is trying to arm them with information while establishing standards for the broker industry. Chase created a credentialing process called Health Rosetta. His standards are principles for fair trade for the industry. One of the fundamental commitments of his standards is to complete transparency. Employers should be able to see how brokers, insurance companies, pharmacy benefit managers, and providers are being paid.

When I met Chase at a restaurant in Washington, D.C., a few blocks from the White House, he struck me as a man of deep passion and moral conviction. He had made a fortune as a successful technology executive, leading the health care business for Microsoft for a dozen years. Chase also worked at the firm now called Accenture, consulting for hospitals. From his broad business experience in health care, he quickly learned about the business of buying health insurance through brokers and benefits consultants. In due time, Chase became an expert on the administrative waste in health care. He knew the money games and the middlemen as well as anyone.

Chase founded Health Rosetta to disrupt this business of employer-sponsored benefits. His mission is to educate employers on how to buy health insurance products based on value rather than broker kickbacks. Health Rosetta is a certification process for health insurance brokers and benefits consultants that uses principles of full transparency. Chase has brokers sign a code of conduct and agree to use a standard disclosure form that shows all the different ways they are being paid. Contorno was one of those brokers attracted to Chase's effort early on, and Contorno's firm, EPowered Benefits, became one of the first Health Rosetta–certified brokerage firms out of the hundreds certified today.

Using the "open source" concept he had espoused in his past technology work, Chase decided to make everything freely accessible, including the code of conduct and disclosure forms. You can find it all at HealthRosetta.org.

The Big Picture

Some have called for legislation to shine light on the health insurance broker industry. Consumer protections are one approach. After all, after the crash of 2008, the mortgage industry benefited from tighter legislation. But market forces can also be a powerful change agent. Next time your business buys health insurance, ask if the broker is "Health Rosetta–certified" or if it follows the principles of full disclosure and fair trade that Health Rosetta outlines on their website. At a minimum, download the Health Rosetta disclosure form and ask your broker or health benefits consultant to fill it out. And consider giving your business to brokers that charge a flat fee, or make their commission based on how much is *saved* instead of how much is spent.

Some individuals and employers are leaving the insurance industry behind altogether. In recent years, faith-based sharing ministries have become more popular. Samaritan Ministries in Illinois and others are taking the Christian concept of sharing one another's burdens quite literally. They pool the resources of their members to pay one another's bills. Samaritan says its 250,000 members share more than $27 million per month in medical costs. Their growth shows they're meeting a need, and also that the same old way of doing health insurance is not working. The plans are typically less expensive than insurance. But don't rely on your health insurance broker to tell you about this low-cost option. Samaritan Ministries and other health insurance co-ops don't pay kickbacks to brokers.

American employers spent an estimated $738 billion on health benefits in 2018, a figure that has been rising about 5% annually in recent years.[3] The average premiums for a family reached almost $20,000, according to the Kaiser Family Foundation.[4] If employers could provide their excellent benefits for less, it would save billions.

One myth of employer-based health care is that the employers are paying for it. Company owners, executives, and HR people love to say the organization pays for the health benefits—or for most of them. That's not the most accurate way to describe what's happening. The employers pay for health benefits out of the pool of money they use for worker compensation. Therefore, that compensation allocated to rising health care costs is not going toward increasing an employee's wages. In other words, it's coming right out of the employee's pocket. It's one of the main reasons wages have been stagnant in recent years.

It's time to clean up the business of buying health insurance, with transparency and competition. It's time we gave American workers a raise.

CHAPTER 14

Pharmacy Hieroglyphics

After finishing my speech at an employee benefits conference for Michigan business leaders, I handed the microphone to Danny Toth, the next speaker. Toth is a gracious, somewhat frail man from LaGrange, Georgia. I hadn't met him before, but his cowboy boots, modest appearance, and matter-of-fact manner sent a strong message: *I don't care what you think, I'm going to do some straight talk.*

And that's exactly what he did. When Toth stood before the audience, he described what sounded like a cartel. Most people are familiar with a few bad actors in the pharmaceutical industry. The media had a field day when the infamous "pharma bro" Martin Shkreli jacked up the price of his company's drugs—and then smirked his way through subsequent court proceedings. But the underworld described by Toth was much larger than a few high-profile cases of executives inflating prices. What Toth revealed was the inner workings of a drug pricing game that's a million times bigger—and more expensive—than the games of the pharma bad actors.

Toth detailed how a giant industry of middlemen called pharmacy benefit managers—PBMs for short—are systematically gouging American businesses. Employers, directly or through their health insurance company, hire a PBM to manage the pharmacy benefits for their employees. But Toth explained how PBMs, who collectively manage pharmacy benefits for 266 million

Americans, routinely fleece American businesses using clever shell games.

As I learned more about PBMs, I recalled the research advice many pharmacists have whispered to me over the years: "You should take a look at PBMs. Their margins are sick."

"The Spread"

One of the most important terms to understand the PBM world is "the spread." "The spread" is the difference between what the PBM pays a pharmacy for a medication and what they invoice an employer or health plan for that same medication. You would think it's a simple transaction: the pharmacy charges $10 for a medication, so the employer pays $10. But it's not so simple. The PBM is the middleman, so if the pharmacy charges $10 for the medication, the PBM might bill the employer $50 and pocket the extra $40—that's "the spread."

Wanting to get into the weeds, I asked Toth if we could meet. There in Grand Rapids, we found a time that worked and met in the café, where we pulled two chairs up to a small table. He had a thick briefcase and I had a notepad and pen. I started by asking him if it was common for PBMs to have giant spreads. He grabbed a stash of documents out of his briefcase and showed me jaw-dropping numbers. He had data examples in which employers were paying their PBM 5 to 20 times more than what the PBM was paying a pharmacy for the medication. That's the spread, and it's where PBMs cash in.

In the weeks that followed, I talked to industry insiders and obtained a confidential document that showed the "spreads" between what one PBM paid a pharmacy for a drug and what it charged one employer for the same drug. I've withheld the names of the employer and PBM, but I assure you, this is a real-life example.

I couldn't believe this breakdown when I saw it. I have personally prescribed some of these medications for my patients. I had no idea what happened behind the scenes. I had even taken a

"THE SPREAD"

*Difference between what a PBM charged one employer and
what they paid out to a pharmacy*

DRUG NAME (brand name example)	STRENGTH	QUANTITY	AMOUNT PBM CHARGED THE EMPLOYER	AMOUNT PBM PAID TO PHARMACY*	"THE SPREAD"
Omeprazole (Prilosec)	40 mg	30	$70.85	$0.00	$70.85
Bupropion XL (Zyban)	300 mg	30	$188.88	$0.00	$188.88
Escitalopram (Lexapro)	10 mg	30	$103.47	$0.00	$103.47
Losartan (Cozaar)	50 mg	90	$204.00	$25.22	$178.78
Azithromycin (Zithromax Z-pack)	250 mg	6	$46.70	$0.00	$46.70
Fluoxetine (Prozac)	20 mg	30	$126.03	$59.50	$66.53
Ketorolac (Acular)	10 mg	20	$43.14	$14.00	$29.14
Pantoprazole (Protonix)	40 mg	30	$159.85	$0.00	$159.85
Meloxicam (Mobic)	15 mg	30	$145.33	$0.00	$145.33
Lisinopril (Zestril)	30 mg	30	$45.21	$2.75	$42.46
Paroxetine (Paxil)	30 mg	90	$253.35	$35.63	$217.72
Simvastatin (Zocor)	40 mg	90	$442.85	$34.94	$407.91
Baclofen (Gablofen)	10 mg	270	$667.17	$126.49	$549.68
Quetiapine (Seroquel)	200 mg	10	$129.37	$5.07	$124.30
Fluocinonide Cream (Vanos)	0.1 %	240gm	$3,174.47	$997.00	$2,177.74
Atorvastatin (Lipitor)	20 mg	30	$173.02	$0.00	$173.02

*$0.00 indicates the patient's copay covered the entire cost of the medication, thus
the PBM charged the employer for the medication but paid the pharmacy nothing.

heartburn medication like the first one listed. Seeing these spreads almost reactivated my heartburn.

A PBM can charge an employer almost any price for a drug, and it gets paid. In the above table, a PBM billed an employer $188 for bupropion but paid the pharmacy nothing. In that case, the employee copay covered the entire cost of the medication, but the employer got charged an arm and a leg anyway.

Similarly, a PBM can set any copay for patients regardless of the medication or the true cost. One patient paid a $285 copay for a $40 medication.[1] This is not an extreme case of criminal fraud, it's perfectly legal. It's the business model of most of today's PBMs.

But why would any business or government health plan paying for these meds tolerate this? Well, imagine that you are an employer reading this list, and it's thousands of lines long and does not have the "Amount Paid to Pharmacy" column. You would not see the spread. That's what businesses see in the real world.

The above list—minus the spread—is typical of what's sent to most businesses and health plans by their PBMs when itemizing medications used by their employees. For a typical midsized company, this list is thousands of medications long. For a human resources (HR) person handling health care benefits at a company receiving this list, it might as well be written in ancient Egyptian hieroglyphics.

At the bottom of a typical report is some big sum of money the employer owes the PBM. It has the appearance of transparency because each pill is itemized in detail with a price. But "the spread is nowhere to be seen." The PBMs have gone to great lengths to keep the real prices secret, using a fog of fees, rebates, and discounts that make a true value too complicated for anyone to determine. Even if an employer figured out the spread on a few medications, there are thousands of these meds and they go by different names, have different comparables, different generics, different schedules and different dosages—and each combination of these variables is priced differently.

As one employer said, "I got a 100-page printout of all the medications my employees take and the price of each. I wouldn't know where to start." He's right. It's daunting. Health care is typically the second largest expenditure for most businesses after wages. I began to realize why so many of them were getting taken for a ride when I started asking CEOs how they picked the PBM to manage their employees' pharmacy benefits. They often responded saying that it just came with their health insurance plan, or that their broker recommended it, or that the PBM they chose was one of the big three so they went with them. CEOs would sometimes boast that their PBM gives them a 10 or 20% discount on the meds. But most CEOs were simply fed up with the high cost of it all and the fact that it goes up year after year.

Getting Information

Unfortunately, even going directly to the pharmacy and comparing what their business's PBM was paying for a certain medication probably wouldn't accomplish anything. A curious CEO would likely hit a wall because pharmacists are gagged under their PBM contract to not disclose what they are paid by the PBM.

When I learned that many pharmacists were contractually gagged, I couldn't believe it. I had heard of hospitals encouraging doctors to use their own MRI machines but never contractual gagging—restricting what a clinician can tell a patient. Gagging a health professional violates everything that sets medicine apart as a noble profession. It compromises our heritage of trust, a craft rooted in compassion, and undermines our commitment to do what's best for the patient.

My grandfather was a pharmacist. In his day, pharmacists dispensed medications without a prescription, as a physician would. Grandpa would be sad to see how corporate medicine has gagged today's pharmacists. As I talked to other pharmacists, I saw the scope of the problem—and became convinced something needs to be done. We need to stand against gagging of all health professionals everywhere. Their conversations with patients must never be restricted by outside forces. It's just wrong.

Some pharmacists told me they put patients over corporate interests and break the rules by telling patients what's best for them.

These honorable pharmacists risk getting fired from their pharmacy. At independent pharmacies, they risk losing their large PBM contracts altogether, which could put them out of business. In my opinion, they are heroes. Thankfully, a new federal law passed in 2018 ended the common practice of prohibiting pharmacists from helping patients find less expensive options.

Cookie Benefit Manager

Think about how this PBM game might look if it happened with another important commodity: Girl Scout cookies. Let's say a dad approaches the CEO of a small company and offers to provide discounted Girl Scout cookies services to the company's 100 employees. The busy CEO has no idea how much the different boxes of Girl Scout cookies normally cost (who does?), but he likes the simplicity of getting all his cookies from one guy. And he's intrigued by the promise of a bulk discount the dad claims he can pass along to the company. The CEO agrees to make the dad the exclusive Girl Scout cookie manager for his employees.

A week later, the dad arranges for a few young Girl Scouts to set up a stand at the company office. One employee walks up and asks for a box of Thin Mints—everybody's favorite. The girl asks if he's an employee of the company, and he says "yes." She says it will cost him only $2. He pays the $2 "copay" for his box and gobbles them up. The girls go on to sell a hundred boxes. The CEO is glad to see his employees enjoying the cookies.

A month later, the dad bills the company's CEO a whopping $50 per box and subtracts a "20% discount," bringing the bill to roughly $40 per box. The busy CEO can't decipher the bill but pays it anyway, comforted by the 20% discount reflected on the bill.

The dad then gives the Girl Scouts $1 for each box that they sold, so the girls collect a total of $3 per box ($2 copay from the employee + $1 from the cookie manager). Their wholesale cost is $2.50, so the girls make 50 cents per box. The dad makes $39 per box, or $3,900 for the day, for "managing the employee cookie benefit."

Eventually, someone tells the CEO that a box of Girl Scout cookies normally sells for $5. When he finds out the real price, his smile disappears. He's been played.

Crazy, right? No one would put up with the scheme of that profiteering dad. But that's how it works in health care. The dad is the PBM and the Girl Scouts are the pharmacies.

Of course, this is where the analogy breaks down, because in the PBM world, finding out the street price for thousands of medications is very difficult for a CEO. For one thing, the prices vary by substitute drug name, dose, capsules versus tablets, etc.

Today, approximately 80% of Americans get their medications through a PBM.[2] American businesses financing the coverage and the employees paying for their medications are usually oblivious to the price gouging. When people get frustrated that drug prices keep going up, they often point the finger at pharma bad boys like Martin Shkreli. More often, though, the price spikes are taking place right under their noses.

Very disturbed by what I was learning, I decided to walk over to the office of Dr. Gerard Anderson, a colleague of mine at the Johns Hopkins School of Public Health and one of the nation's leading authorities on drug pricing. Jerry is a terrific colleague who has mentored thousands of students, and some faculty like me, and he is always happy to talk. He greeted me with his characteristic big smile. I told him what I was learning and how bothered I was by it. I asked him were people—the public, business owners, policy makers—aware of the secretive practices of PBMs jacking up the price of health care?

"Marty, of course not. Secrecy is how everyone in the drug supply chain makes so much money. The sad part is that patients are being asked to pay more and more of the higher and higher prices," Jerry explained.

Rebates and Mail Order Meds

If "the spread" is the leading shenanigan of PBMs, rebates are a close second. Rebates are the smoke bomb of the PBM world.

Pharmaceutical companies offer rebates for medications, but the employer paying for medication doesn't know the amount of the rebate, or that it even exists. The PBM keeps all or part of the pharma rebate for itself, for "administrative work." This could also be called a "kickback."

In his presentation, Danny Toth enumerated so many schemes that I couldn't keep up. There are so many that they add up to a lot of money. A 2018 study in the *Journal of the American Medical Association* showed that customers overpaid for one quarter of their prescriptions, with an average overpayment of $7.69 per prescription. Overpayments totaled $135 million during a six-month period.[3]

Justin Simon is a respected health care analyst and investor. I met Justin for lunch in Washington, D.C., and he confirmed everything Toth had said. It's a burden to health plans all over America, he said. Simon said one of the biggest problems he's seeing with PBMs is that they now often own the pharmacies filling the prescriptions.

"PBMs claim they are saving you money by managing your medication costs," Simon said. "But the more the pharmacies sell, the more they make. It's a conflict of interest."

The fundamental conflict is that the PBM claims to reduce what you spend on drugs while owning a pharmacy that profits when you spend more. This leads to yet another PBM shenanigan: signing up patients for mail order drug delivery.

It goes like this: A PBM figures out in their data that you, the patient, had a medication refilled. The PBM then calls you incessantly trying to get you to sign up for their mail order program, enticing you with a lower copay. But once you get on the mail order train, it's hard to get off. All of a sudden, you're getting stockpiles of medications you don't want or need because the PBM is getting your doctor to sign a refill request even though you never asked for one. When the doctor's office receives a refill request they often just sign it. I've done it myself.

The PBM has a different spin. They report that they are increasing patient compliance. But then I have to ask: Does sending a medication to a patient's house mean the patient actually took it?

Toth's Transparency

Can business leaders who suspect that they are paying too much for pharmacy benefits do anything about it?

That's where Danny Toth comes in. He has a way of making things transparent. I had dinner with Toth and learned the recipe for his secret sauce. As a former pharmacist and someone who ran an honest PBM for years, Toth has great relationships with many pharmacists. He takes the medication list PBMs send to employers and does undercover work to find out exactly how much the PBMs are paying pharmacies. He then shows employers "the spread."

After Toth sends employers through all five stages of grief, he offers them a solution. Toth helps them renegotiate their contract so the PBM is paid a reasonable flat fee—say, $3 per prescription. Toth calls it an administration fee. According to Toth, that more than covers their management costs and yields a healthy profit for the PBM. When employers say $4 is too much to pay a middleman for each prescription, Toth reminds them that PBMs often make more than $50 per prescription in the markup-discount system.

If we could slash the spread, it would make a tremendous difference for thousands of businesses. According to a recent analysis in the journal *Health Affairs*, reducing generic reimbursement by $1 per prescription would lower health spending by $5.6 billion annually.[4]

Toth and his colleagues at Timber Ridge Consultants have saved employers millions of dollars by renegotiating PBM contracts. For one employer, a city government in Georgia, Toth saved over $1 million. The savings came at a critical time because the city government had been faced with a growing deficit that threatened their bond rating. The savings Toth got them on a better PBM contract meant their city bond rating stayed strong.

With this seemingly simple recipe for saving millions, I asked Toth why all the businesses in America aren't negotiating better PBM rates. "Because the health insurance companies that cover the same employers are in cahoots with the PBMs," he said. "In fact, many times they are co-owned." Health insurance companies direct their business to their own PBMs, which increases their margins.

For example, OptumRx, one of the big three PBMs, is owned by America's largest health insurance company, UnitedHealth Group. Insurers may offer less expensive health insurance premiums. But then they use their PBM to achieve a greater profit margin.

The PBM Express Scripts is now owned by the insurance company Cigna, and as I write this book, a merger between the PBM CVS Caremark and the insurer Aetna is being finalized. Together, the big three PBMs—OptumRx, Express Scripts, and CVS Caremark—control approximately 85% of the U.S. market and manage medication benefits for most people in the United States.

But what about the free market? Can't employers just say enough is enough and switch to a better-value PBM? For many employers, it's not that easy. The PBMs are so integrated with insurance companies today that carving out a PBM so you can switch carriers is hard.

Toth went on to explain to me why he's fighting the system. When he worked as a community pharmacist he saw patients so poor they had to sift through their pocket change to pay for their meds. He believes that if doctors, patients, and employers could understand the business of PBM spreads and kickbacks, they would take issue with it.

Scamming the Government

Just as Toth uses insider expertise to expose PBM spreads to employers, governments can use their clout to get this information for their own government-sponsored health plans that use PBMs. That's what the state auditor of Ohio did in 2018. The auditor uncovered the spreads of the PBM being paid with taxpayer money and found that in a single year, the spread had cost the state's Medicaid program $224 million. That's about 10% of the total amount of money the Medicaid plan spent on drugs during that time period.[5]

Unbound by gag rules, the Ohio Pharmacy Association spoke up. "What we see in this report are the truly unfathomable lengths that these massive corporate middlemen will go to manipulate the prescription drug marketplace and hide their litany of revenue streams," said the association's government affairs director. "It is now overwhelmingly apparent that PBMs are operating the biggest shell game in modern history, and we are all paying for it."[6]

The pharmacy association pointed out something especially nefarious about the spread schemes. The spread increased over the course of the year and appeared to hit its peak right when the PBMs made cuts to the pharmacists. In other words, the PBMs were not just overcharging the Medicaid plan. They were also reducing what they paid to the pharmacies. They were increasing their take on both ends.

Other states have also begun to protect themselves from predatory PBMs. In Texas, the state Medicaid program is no longer allowed to contract with a PBM that uses the spread pricing model. Texas also requires periodic audits of the pharmacy middlemen.

In Montana, a tough negotiator named Marilyn Bartlett took over the state employee benefits plan and scrutinized its pharmacy benefit contracts, among other aspects. The health plan was projected to go broke when she took over in 2014. Bartlett, an accountant with an eye for detail, dug into the PBM contracts. She discovered that the plan, which had 30,000 members, was losing money to both the spread and rebate schemes. She ditched her old PBM and found a new one, Navitus Health Solutions, that would play fair with the employer. In the next year, the Montana plan had a similar mix and volume of drugs, but it saved almost $16 per prescription. The savings included $2 million on the spread and an additional $3.5 million in rebates. Bartlett's work saved the health plan and showed how employers have power to bring about change. She says they have to push back against the industry to ensure PBMs don't sneak away with their money.[7]

The Ohio auditor report stunned the industry, but it merely scratched the surface because it solely examined the spread. The PBMs have lots of other devious stratagems. The auditor said further study is needed to examine the other schemes—including some of the ones Toth mentioned.

As PBM money games are exposed to daylight, it's important for all of us, health professionals, business leaders, and consumers, to speak up and end the games, returning to a fair and transparent market.

The National Community Pharmacists Association has said the current lack of transparency is bad for patients. "If you want to reduce prescription drug costs, policymakers must demand greater transparency from PBMs," said the pharmacists' association.[8]

Tips for Your Next Pharmacy Encounter

The next time you need to buy a medication, consider shopping for it outside your insurance. Examine your copay for your current medications, too, and see if you could get them for less without going through a PBM.

Consumer Reports sent more than 150 "secret shoppers" to buy common medications at pharmacies in six metropolitan areas around the United States. They found that pharmacies offered the same drugs at a wide range of prices, up to a tenfold difference. And the prices you'd pay without insurance are often lower than what you would pay with insurance.[9]

In one example, the secret shoppers called each pharmacy asking their combined retail cash price for five common drugs. The batch of five drugs was just $66 online at HealthWarehouse .com. But the national retailers CVS and Rite Aid priced them at almost $900. The big national chains said their price is before discounts get applied. But when the secret shoppers tried to get the discounts, they found they weren't applied consistently. Some pharmacies marked down the prices a lot. Others didn't discount them at all. In Dallas alone, the price of generic Cymbalta, an antidepressant, ranged from $22 at an independent pharmacy to $251 at a Walgreens.

Consumer Reports recommends three steps to shop around:

- *Use online discounts.*
  Consumer Reports recommends websites like GoodRx, Blink Health, and WeRx.org. The sites show what you can

expect to pay for various drugs at different locations. They also have discount coupons or vouchers you can use.

- *Don't always shop at the same old places.*
HealthWarehouse.com is an online pharmacy and had some of the lowest prices. Costco and Sam's Club also consistently had good prices in the *Consumer Reports* analysis. Independent pharmacies and grocery store pharmacies also had some of the best prices.

- *Push the pharmacy to honor online discount coupons.*
The *Consumer Reports* shoppers found they almost always honor them, but the shopper had to be persistent. Also, pharmacies will almost always run the prescriptions through a patient's insurance, even when the discount would result in a lower price. In-store discounts may also exist but won't be applied unless the patient asks for them directly. "Ask for 'all available' discounts," *Consumer Reports* wrote in its report. "And then make sure to get the best option."

What Businesses Can Do

For business leaders, get a second opinion on your pharmacy benefits contract from an independent consultant like Danny Toth, who is not being paid a kickback from a PBM or health insurance company. Ask them if they subscribe to the Health Rosetta code of ethics. Insist on a PBM contract where you, the business, are paying a $2.75 to $4.00 administrative fee per prescription above the price paid by the PBM. And demand full transparency in rebates and discounts. It's not a circus; it's health care. And it should be a fair marketplace.

Employers can also disrupt the PBM industry by refusing to sign up for PBMs that gag pharmacists or have mail order requirements. Employers should refuse to be a part of any PBM that sends auto-refill requests to doctors' offices without a request from the patient. Greater awareness about the shenanigans of unscrupulous PBMs can empower employers to reward good PBMs.

If you are a patient, you should use an app like GoodRx before filling any prescription to make sure you are not being gouged. Avoid mail order medications unless you are disabled, unable to go to a pharmacy, or are positive that you are medically dependent on a particular medication for the long term. Support independent pharmacies whenever possible, tell your representatives in Congress and your state legislature to make PBM spreads transparent, and ask that state governments audit the PBMs of government health plans regularly. Pharmacies may be gagged, but you can speak up.

CHAPTER 15

4K Screens

The electrocautery is one of the most common devices used in surgery. It both dissects and seals off blood vessels, managing bleeding during surgery. Holding it like a pen, my residents and I use it for hours each day when we operate.

One day I read about an important new feature added to this important device. The innovation, created by a leading manufacturer, added a small vacuum hole to suck out the toxic smoke created from cauterizing tissue. *What a great idea!* I thought. There is a growing recognition that surgical smoke is dangerous, maybe as dangerous as secondhand cigarette smoke. I was reminded of this risk when I learned that the young surgeon who wrote the book *When Breath Becomes Air* had died of lung cancer even though he never smoked. "Let's get it," I told one of my colleagues. Months later, we were using it.

At a national surgeons meeting, I was talking to a surgeon about my positive experiences with the device and encouraged him to get it. But his hospital had a new process for getting devices approved. "It's not that easy," he said, rolling his eyes. He went on to detail a massive administrative process for all new OR purchases at his hospital. Not only did he have to convince his administrators, but a formal trial of any new product had to be conducted. He was frustrated. He knew there was no way to do a short trial to see whether surgical smoke caused lung cancer, not to mention transmitting aerosolized viruses that can become airborne in surgical smoke.

As I researched the process further, it became evident to me that on a national scale, the people buying stuff for hospitals are not only outside the operating room, they may not even live in the same city. Most medical centers today acquire devices, supplies, and medications through group purchasing organizations (GPOs) rather than directly from a manufacturer. GPOs are middlemen that catalog medical supplies for medical centers to purchase from manufacturers.

Since their inception in 1910, GPOs have simplified the way hospitals buy supplies—from toilet paper to epinephrine vials. GPOs have notable benefits. They spare hospitals the work and expense of negotiating and contracting with hundreds of different manufacturers. GPOs offer hospitals a catalog of thousands of products and sometimes provide product training and support services to hospitals. GPOs also have volume purchasing leverage to negotiate lower prices and can list multiple comparable products in their catalogs to promote competition and reward innovators. However, these benefits are based on economic assumptions that are being undermined by the modern GPO business model.

Today, GPOs ask manufacturers to pay them pay-to-play fees for product placement in their catalogs. Neither patients, researchers like me, or the public can see these fees. One GPO told me that these fees are completely transparent, but when I proceeded to ask to see them, I was denied. These fees are particularly problematic when GPOs invite a manufacturer to pay a premium fee to become a sole supplier, allowing a manufacturer to essentially purchase market share, rendering hospitals and patients dependent on a single manufacturer's supply chain. Sole supplier contracting creates a perverse financial incentive for manufacturers to use a fragile supply chain because of this lack of competition. When factory production problems occur, the result can be higher demand and higher prices.

Seeing Better

To better understand the growth of this middle layer of health care, I traveled to Boston to meet William, an executive at a medical device company. He walked me into a demonstration center where they had surgical videos playing on state-of-the-art 4K monitors. The picture was stunning. I couldn't believe it; I could see tiny details of human anatomy I'd never seen before in surgery. I thought the current high-definition (HD) monitors I used were impressive, but this was the most incredible thing I'd seen in my surgical career. I saw beautiful, wide, bright images of tiny blood vessels that were invisible landmines on the older-resolution equipment. At the risk of stating the obvious, I want the best possible view of a patient's anatomy when I'm cutting into them. "How would a surgeon get this in their operating room?" I asked.

"I used to travel the country and talk to surgeons about our new stuff," he told me. "Now I never interact with surgeons." In recent years, the decision makers at hospitals switched from surgeons to administrators. In many instances today, he told me, the surgeons say "yes" but the hospital purchasing committee says "no."

"But a surgeon can see so much better with the 4K optics!" I protested. Surely what we surgeons say should matter.

He explained that the only question many value-driven purchasing committees ask is "Is the older version 'clinically acceptable'?"

"Clinically acceptable?" I was stumped. Are we shooting for acceptable or excellent? I can see so much better with the 4K screens. Doesn't that matter? If you were going in for a surgery, wouldn't you want your surgeon to have the best possible view? Launching a formal study seemed like a waste. After all, it would take a lot of research to demonstrate what any surgeon could tell you on the spot—these screens make surgery safer.

Increasingly, the purchasing committees aren't even located in the same city as the surgeons who use the equipment, William explained. Everything goes through GPOs. The purchasing decision makers are not even administrators who roam the operating rooms and see how surgery is done. Their offices are often in separate buildings, far away. When he went to pitch one health system on the new 4K monitors, he traveled to Philadelphia to meet with a purchasing committee deciding which resolution screens to have surgeons use in Phoenix.

Personally, I haven't ever met the purchasing decision makers. How would they decide whether a surgeon can have the same 4K technology in the operating room that I already had at home to watch *Madagascar 2*?

Purchasing only equipment that is "clinically acceptable" is far too low a bar. If the patients could see the difference in resolution, I'm sure they would have something to say about it. It was certainly clear to me: we should have what's best for our patients.

Imagine you are a professional tennis player, and your agent hires an assistant to determine which tennis racket is "clinically acceptable." You might end up with a Wilson T-2000 with a tiny head. Sure, you can win with it, but you can play better with the racket that makes you play better.

The idea of group purchasing makes sense for toilet paper, but on the front lines of patient care, doctors need to be an integral part of the decision making. Group purchasing is not the problem. It's the risk that in the corporate hustle, decision makers don't work hard to get the clinical input from practicing doctors and nurses.

Market Force

GPOs are behind-the-scenes organizations, yet they dominate health care. If you are treated in any American hospital or outpatient center today, chances are you have been treated with supplies or medications purchased through a GPO. According to the American Hospital Association, the percent of U.S. hospitals that purchase through a GPO went from 68% in 2000 to 98% by 2014. The nation's largest GPO, Vizient Inc., claims to own 30% of the national market for all supplies, and collectively the four largest GPOs in the United States dominate 90% of the market.[1,2]

GPOs are like PBMs in how they operate in a fog of transactions, making value difficult for any buyer to ascertain. In the case of GPOs, hospitals may simply pass on high costs to patients in the form of a hospital bill.

Manufacturers are desperate to have GPOs list, and even favorably list, their products—just as a candy bar company is eager to have a convenience store put their products at eye level on their shelves. And GPOs are happy to offer manufacturers more favorable placement in their catalogs for a fee. As a result, manufacturers pay the GPOs to get access to the purchasers. For a much larger fee, the manufacturer can even be the sole supplier listed in the catalog. It's a simple pay-to-play setup. What's hard to believe is that it's legal.

In 1972, Congress enacted the Anti-Kickback Statute as part of the Social Security Act amendments. Designed to protect patients and federal health programs from obvious conflicts of interest, it banned kickbacks, bribes, or rebates for furnishing products or services.

But in 1987, after intense lobbying by the industry, group purchasers were granted an exception to the antikickback law, known as a safe harbor exemption. It's the same exemption that allows PBMs to receive kickbacks from the pharma companies they buy from. In the GPO world, that exemption opened the floodgates for creative strategies to increase their profits. Many GPOs began requiring manufacturers to pay them fees to be listed in their catalog. Over time, these fees kept going up, especially as competition among manufacturers increased and the number of dominant GPOs decreased. In 2018 alone, manufacturers and pharma companies paid GPOs billions of dollars in pay-to-play fees. Manufacturers and pharma companies then built those expenses into the price of the products they sold to hospitals.

Fees collected by GPOs are directly shared with GPO member hospitals. One of the nation's largest GPOs, Premier Inc., was paid $557 million in these "administration" (pay-to-play) fees in 2017— 35% of that got passed on to their member hospitals, according to its annual report.[3] The rising cost of this web of kickbacks is all borne by America's taxpayers, businesses, and patients.

As GPOs grow and gain more market share, they are in a stronger position to demand that manufacturers and pharmaceutical companies pay whatever fee the market will allow them to charge. In some instances, manufacturers have been shown to pay up to 94% of a product sale back to the GPO.[4] That would mean that if a medical product costs a hospital $100, the manufacturer paid the GPO $94 to get it listed so prominently in the catalog. To create a more transparent supply chain and to address avoidable drivers of price inflation, pay-to-play payments should be ended, or, at a minimum, disclosed to hospitals and the public. Hospitals can play a lead role in changing the business model of medical supplies by refusing to work with GPOs that charge pay-to-play fees to manufacturers. For starters, hospitals should avoid exclusive contracts with GPOs so they can purchase products outside the GPO directly from manufacturers.

Shortages

I sat at my desk a few months ago and caught up on my backlog of 58,465 unread emails. I replied to an FYI email from about two years ago with a "thanks," then noticed a new email warning me about a critical shortage of saline bags. Saline bags were in reportedly short supply because Hurricane Maria had damaged a factory that made them in Puerto Rico.[5] I wondered how our country became so dependent on this one factory. Salt and water are the two most common elements on planet Earth. And now we had a shortage?

This was not the first critical supply shortage I've had come across my email. It happens dozens of times a year. Epinephrine, propofol, heparin, and other drugs that have been around for more than 50 years are suddenly rare-earth materials. In the case of heparin, a blood thinner given to almost every patient who has surgery, the drug had been adulterated from a source in China and led to the death of more than 100 Americans.

There are indications that the market power of GPOs could be associated with the shortages. Often, only one or two manufacturers are responsible for an entire regional or national supply chain. If a factory has production problems, this reliance on a narrow supply chain can have an adverse effect on hospital inventories.

A 2016 GAO study concluded that there was a strong association between critical drug shortages and a decline in the number of drug suppliers.[6] Furthermore, GPOs were a significant focus in a U.S. House of Representatives report on drug shortages that stated, "The GPO structure reduces the number of manufacturers producing each generic drug."[7]

As I spoke with more and more people in the field, it became clear to me that GPOs can make it difficult for manufacturers to enter the market. They may reward fewer, larger manufacturers, which increases health care's dependence on a smaller number of drug producers. Conversely, I also found that there are "better" GPOs that do not demand kickbacks and choose to list as many options as possible in their catalogs. By doing so, they are eliminating barriers to entry for new products and promoting a healthy competitive marketplace.

Whenever we have a critical shortage, we blame a factory or a storm. But the real question is how we became so dependent on so few factories.

Dependence on foreign factories threatens our national security, especially during a health emergency. Having domestic manufacturing of medications, ventilators, and personal protective equipment (PPE) is an underappreciated yet critical part of our nation's health security.

Raising Costs

Independent studies have suggested hospitals could find better deals when working around their group purchasers. A 2011 study of 8,100 hospital purchases not mediated by GPOs found hospitals saved money in three out of four transactions compared to GPO purchases, with an average savings of 10%.[8] The authors of the study concluded that GPO kickbacks inflated health care costs up to $37.5 billion annually, including $17.3 billion in government payments for Medicare and Medicaid.[9] These inflated costs ultimately fell upon patients and taxpayers.[10]

As hospitals merge into even larger systems, they increasingly use their purchasing power to negotiate around the GPOs. In most instances, the GPO price is the starting point for negotiation.

Trying to rein in runaway costs associated with some drugs sold through GPOs, Intermountain Health and a group of partnering hospitals are seeking to bypass GPOs altogether for select drugs by directly acquiring generic drugs from manufacturers and vertically integrating their supply chain.[11] These endeavors aim to cut the waste associated with pay-to-play fees and kickback schemes. They also have the potential to reduce both prices and critical drug shortages. This direct purchasing model represents a prime opportunity for Amazon and other big retail sellers to disrupt the hospital supply market, including drugs.

Implications for Inventors

In some instances, a GPO's sole supplier contracting arrangements stifle innovations in medicine. The technology company Masimo discovered this firsthand when they developed a new type of pulse oximeter but it was excluded from GPOs. Tyco International, the industry giant that had a lock on the pulse oximeter market at the time, was paying pay-to-play fees to GPOs to ensure market dominance. The GPOs stayed loyal to Tyco and would not include Masimo's product. Masimo eventually sued the GPOs for violating antitrust laws and won.

Despite multiple lawsuits and several hearings from the Senate Antitrust Subcommittee, little has been done to shine light on GPO practices. The conflicts of interest inherent in the modern GPO business model continue to limit innovation, drive up prices, and cause unacceptable shortages for the most basic drugs and medical supplies.[12]

In learning about GPOs, the one thing that blew me away the most is that GPOs are not selling anything. They are simply providing a catalog for hospitals to buy directly from a supplier. In a sense, GPOs are just writing contracts.

After all my research, I concluded that GPOs can serve a valuable role in the free market of medical drugs and supplies; however, several important reforms are needed to protect free market rules of engagement.

First, Congress should repeal the 1987 safe harbor law that exempts GPOs and PBMs from antikickback laws. This reform will end opaque drivers of price distortion.

Second, hospitals should avoid GPOs that use sole supplier contracting and pay-to-play games that give manufacturers market dominance. Hospitals should also avoid GPOs that prevent them from purchasing outside their catalog. More choices with honest prices will ensure an open marketplace, so that the high cost of these money games will stop getting passed on to patients. The problem is not GPOs. The problem is that GPOs are dominated by insider payments and kickbacks, the cost of which gets passed on to ordinary Americans.[13]

It's time we banned all kickbacks in medicine.

CHAPTER 16

Diagnosis: Overwellnessed

Most workers across America have been introduced to the workplace wellness industry. Sometimes it can be a little awkward, as when employees arrive at their office and find the breakroom filled with strangers in quasimedical garb. They wear white jackets, brandish blood pressure cuffs, carry clipboards, and have stethoscopes dangling from their necks. In most cases, employees are there to meet this small army of wellness workers because their boss has warned them that if they *don't* join the program they'll pay higher insurance premiums—hundreds of dollars higher.

What's an employee supposed to do? Besides, it doesn't seem like much trouble. It's just a trip to the breakroom. They usually go to the breakroom for coffee and a doughnut. This time it's to give the company some blood and answer personal questions to be screened for mental health.

My friend Tina got lured into her company's wellness day because of her love for animals. The company poster featured adorable puppies and promised free food at the meeting. Tina showed up to a bowl of apples and two adult Doberman Pinschers. That was too much, even for a dog lover like Tina. She ran from the people holding clipboards and tried to pretend the whole thing never happened. The meeting had promised "wellness," but Tina said the experience made her feel "less well." The bait and switch made her anxious and upset.

The "wellness" industry is in full swing. Isn't more health care always a good idea? Unfortunately, too often these programs throw aside the best practices of medicine in favor of pseudoscience. When your boss decides to don a white doctor's jacket, it's time to step back and ask questions.

"Wellness" sounds like the type of thing everyone favors, like education. But America's love affair with workplace "wellness" is costly and dangerous. Employers want to lower health care costs by helping their employees stay healthy—a good thing. We all should eat sensibly, exercise, stop smoking, moderate our alcohol consumption, drop excess weight—you know, take care of ourselves. This common sense is affirmed over and over by science.

That's not what I'm talking about. Today's wellness movement is a $6 billion industry run amok. More than half of small employers and 85% of large employers offer health and wellness programs, according to a 2017 survey by the Kaiser Family Foundation.[1] There's an army of companies and consultants who can't wait to get their hands on American workers. Their paydays depend on it. But these so-called experts offer health advice that isn't always accurate. They're screening healthy people for diseases they likely don't have, which often leads to false positives and harmful medical procedures. They're forcing employees to answer extensive questionnaires that invade their privacy. Does your employer have a right to know how much alcohol you consume, or whether you're depressed, or if you are thinking about getting pregnant? In many cases, they're even selling the data they gather.

Bad Science

A friend invited me to sit in on a company's wellness class. I can sum up the instructor's message in three words: "Avoid fatty foods." There are a few problems with that message. First, it was about the only thing the health "coach" said to the 20 or so bored people in the room. But second, I cringed because it has absolutely no scientific basis.[2] This class risked making people *less* healthy; it was loaded with misinformation.

As the wellness coach hammered us to eat low-fat food, I couldn't help but wonder how much money the employer was spending for this class. It's usually a few hundred dollars per employee per year. That sounds like a generous company benefit until you realize it's ineffective and the boss pays for it out of the money earmarked for employee compensation. That's a few hundred dollars that could instead be added to workers' paychecks.

At one point, the wellness coach randomly called on me during an exercise to tabulate calories. I couldn't help myself. I responded with a detailed explanation of how sugar acts as a hormone, activating the pancreas to produce insulin levels that quickly direct fat into storage. I finished my mini-physiology lecture by recommending the book *Good Calories, Bad Calories* by Gary Taubes, which explains why calories are the wrong thing to measure. She smiled, said "Thank you," and moved on.

I love the concept of wellness—who wouldn't?—but this program was akin to requiring people to click the "I understand the terms and conditions" box before purchasing a song on iTunes. The attendees were going through the motions, merely executing a required task.

With her repeated calls to "avoid fatty foods," the wellness coach seemed blind to the new science of nutrition and deaf to its leaders, like Dr. Dariush Mozaffarian, dean of Tufts University's Friedman School of Nutrition—the nation's leading nutrition school. He recently wrote in the *Journal of the American Medical Association*, "We really need to sing it from the rooftops that the low-fat diet concept is dead, there are no health benefits to it."[3]

As a gastrointestinal surgeon and advocate for healthful foods, I'm well aware how this low-fat teaching is based on the medical establishment's embarrassing, outdated theory that saturated fat causes heart disease. A landmark 2016 article in the *Journal of the American Medical Association* found that the true science was actually being suppressed by the food industry.[4]

Highly respected medical experts like my former Johns Hopkins colleague Dr. Peter Attia are now correcting the medical establishment's sloppy teachings. He and many other lipidologists know that the low-fat bandwagon has damaged public health. It was driven by an unscientific agenda advanced by the American Heart Association and the food industry, which sponsored the misleading food pyramid. These establishment forces spent decades promoting addictive, high-carbohydrate processed foods because the low-fat foods they endorsed require more carbohydrates to retain flavor. That 40-year trend perfectly parallels our obesity epidemic.

Medical leaders like Dr. Attia have been trying to turn this aircraft carrier around, but it's been a challenge. Despite the science, the dogma remains pervasive. In hospitals today, the first thing we do to patients when they come out of surgery, exhausted and bleary-eyed, is to hand them a can of high-sugar soda. Menus given to hospitalized patients promote low-fat options with a heart next to those menu items. And when physicians order food for patients in electronic health records, there's a checkbox for us to order the "cardiac diet," which hospitals define as a low-fat diet.

Despite science showing that natural fats pose no increased risk of heart disease and that excess sugar is the real dietary threat to health, my hospital still hands every patient a pamphlet recommending the "low-fat diet" when they're discharged from the cardiac surgery unit, just as we have been doing for nearly a half century. But nowhere is that now debunked low-fat recommendation propagated as much as in wellness programs.

The Hunt for Disease

At the J.P. Morgan Healthcare Conference in San Francisco, I met Susan, whose company pitches employers on the health benefits of gene-testing their workers. For only $100 per person, Susan told me excitedly, 23andMe offers a battery of genetic tests that can estimate your risk of contracting certain diseases.

"What's the most useful piece of information this test could tell me about my health?" I asked.

"Well, it could estimate your chances of developing Alzheimer's."

"But there's no preventive treatment for Alzheimer's, so I'd rather not know," I replied.

"But don't you want to know?"

I again affirmed that I did not.

Susan did not mention that her company, 23andMe, was planning to sell this genetic data to a Big Pharma company, which they did several months after our conversation. The company clarified that their sold data is deidentified so as not to reveal the identity of the individual tested, but I'm still concerned by such deals. From there, it's not a stretch to sell personal information, as many wellness companies already do. As *The Atlantic* reported in 2018, 23andMe's $300 million deal with GlaxoSmithKline, a large British pharmaceutical company, may be just a sign of things to come.[5]

Months later, I had a similar interaction when attending a health benefits conference in Montana. A young wellness coordinator responsible for government county employees boasted to me that the state's benefits plan now covers full "biometric screening."

Biometric screening is a mainstay of workplace wellness programs. These tests measure blood pressure, height, and weight and use blood samples to hunt for disease. More than half of large employers offer biometric screening to their employees, according to the Kaiser Family Foundation.

"What is biometric screening?" I asked, playing dumb.

She explained that it was a panel of tests yielding a cornucopia of personal health information.

"At what age do you recommend doing this test?" I asked.

She looked puzzled, as if no one had ever asked this question before. But medical guidelines often stipulate that screening tests should not be done until a certain age. Younger people aren't at risk for many diseases, so screening can do more harm than good.

It's important for patients to understand the screening-industrial complex. Some medical providers see it as a way to bring in business, just like in the D.C. churches.

We don't have to guess which screening is useful and which may be bad for us. For common tests, we can rely on the work of the U.S. Preventive Services Task Force. The task force is a national group of volunteer physicians and academics from top universities who study the best available evidence on screening and see what's supported by sound research. They consult experts in each specialty but remain independent, so their guidelines are trustworthy. When we wonder whether wellness companies are leading us down the right road, we can use the task force's recommendations as a map. Wellness companies often make recommendations that go against task force guidelines.

Genetic screening sounds enticing. Same with biometric screening. But beware of tests that go fishing for diseases. At times in my medical training, I'd hear a doctor justify ordering a broad set of tests with the remark that one time, one of the tests revealed a rare medical condition. The real question is: Are these conditions treatable? Because if not, it can create tremendous angst. One patient of mine taught me just how dangerous it can be to go fishing for disease.

Tim didn't have symptoms, but he had a CT scan for the sake of screening—a fishing expedition. The scan showed a cyst on his pancreas. Three percent of all people have these cysts, and they are rarely problematic. Based on his cyst's size and features, it wasn't clear what to do about it. Tim was given options. He could just watch it and wait to see if it became a problem. Or he could undergo an operation to have it removed.

Every night, Tim tossed and turned, agonizing over stories of people who didn't do anything in the early stages of their pancreatic cancer. He felt tormented by the idea that he might be harboring a "precancerous" time bomb. The dilemma of whether to risk surgery or leave it alone consumed him. It strained his marriage and distracted him from his work.

Eventually, against my advice, he decided to put an end to the misery of not knowing. He underwent an operation to remove the cyst. The operation cost $25,000 and resulted in his missing eight weeks of work. Turns out Tim's cyst was harmless. As a surgeon, I'm trained to crush cancer. For many years, every tumor I laid my eyes on fired me up, like looking an enemy straight in the eye. My experiences made me want to hunt and destroy the disease with every tool modern medicine has to offer. But these hunts to destroy cancer can have collateral damage.

Tim's case is an excellent example of why a healthy person shouldn't have a full-body CT scan just for the sake of fishing. Screening made Tim sick.

Wishful Thinking

Like many fields that go awry, the wellness industry began with good intentions. In 1990, the Centers for Disease Control and Prevention released a famous report entitled *Healthy People 2000*. It specifically recommended "worksite health promotion programs" to combat diabetes, obesity, smoking and more—a noble goal. A decade later, the number of workplace wellness programs had more than doubled, according to the agency's subsequent *Healthy People 2010* report. The report added growth goals for workplace wellness programs, and they continued to proliferate.

The wellness industry got a boost from a questionable number cited in a puff piece written by Harvard experts in *Health Affairs*.[6] The article claimed that wellness programs have a 3.27-fold return on investment. The number had little scientific basis, but its timing was impeccable. The study came out just as the Affordable Care Act was being crafted, and the article quickly became a highly cited source as the legislation was being debated. As it turns out, the study's coauthor was a political adviser to those drafting the ACA.

Many times in my medical career, I have witnessed one person's opinion or estimate become "evidence" simply because their estimate gets published as a pretty PDF in a medical journal. That was the case for the *Health Affairs* piece. As soon as the Harvard researchers published their 3.27-fold return on investment, it got cited as "published science." I call it the pseudoscience bandwagon effect. The same journals that advanced the low-fat diet and told us opioids were safe had now, in the case of the *Health Affairs* piece, increased health care costs by publishing a misleading ROI statistic.

Then, during the debate that led to the ACA law, the grocery store Safeway was held up as the model of wellness success amid a sea of confusion about health care. Safeway's CEO had declared in a 2009 *Wall Street Journal* editorial, "How Safeway Is Cutting Health-Care Costs," that wellness saved his company big money. Soon after, the wellness story had worked its way into the president's speech before Congress, where he said, "It's a program that has helped Safeway cut health care spending by 13% and workers save over 20% on their premiums." It was a great story. There was just one problem: it wasn't true.

The *Washington Post*[7] exposed the truth months after the CEO's editorial and before the passing of the law. The supposed savings cited by the Safeway CEO was caused by an overhaul of their benefits that passed more of the costs on to employees. In truth, the *Post* reported, the company's health care costs had risen.

But truth couldn't overcome legend. Americans trying to understand health care were so hungry for a simple solution that everyone could agree on that they latched on to the Safeway story. The medical establishment and health care industry's powerful stakeholders conveniently piled on their support. I attended so many health care conferences where "experts" from the medical establishment proclaimed how the Safeway story was a big part of how to fix health care. It was a bandwagon that distracted from the real issues of price gouging, middlemen, and overtreatment. In fact, the Safeway story made victory laps around Capitol Hill. The new ACA health care law had inserted in it the "Safeway Amendment," which allowed employers to use up to 30% of the cost of an employee's health coverage as a "reward" to induce the employee to take part in the program. If you don't participate, you pay a lot more for your health insurance. That's how wellness programs proliferated in America.

I've seen this blind faith in good stories before. At Hopkins, when we described a program to lower large IV (central line) infections in hospitals, we saw policy leaders latch on as if the program were the salvation of health care. This program was important, but not a silver bullet. Similarly, when my colleagues and I published the first surgery checklist in the medical literature,[8,9,10] and a few years later, when Dr. Atul Gawande and I worked with the World Health Organization to expand it,[11] people were quick to sing its praises. I heard numerous speakers start their speeches on how to fix health care with a description of the surgery checklist as if it were the silver bullet of health care. It was a great story. But here was the problem in all the bombast: checklists address less than 1% of the preventable harm in medicine today. I wholeheartedly believe in checklists, but I know they're just one small step in fixing health care.

So why do people want to focus on things like lowering central line infections by using the surgery checklist and Safeway model? I think it's because the real drivers of health care costs are legacy stakeholders, like hospitals, insurance companies, or drug companies, or all the middlemen I'm exposing in this book. There are so many hands taking money out of the system that there's no silver bullet solution to save money. To lower costs, we must take on the powerful stakeholders. It's easy to blame bacteria for our health care woes, but infections are not the reason your premiums went up 15% last year.

Workplace wellness advocates hailed the support provided by the Affordable Care Act as a public health victory. Soon there were promises of lower rates of chronic disease and lower health care costs. Wellness companies began to pop up all over. Wellness programs began to require people to answer extensive questionnaires that delved into their privacy. Wellness programs provide only a modest profit, so companies began to sell their employees' collected personal health data to third parties. That was a good business model. On the open market, health data is coveted.

Where is the science to show that the enormous societal investment in wellness programs makes people healthier? It's nowhere to be found. The evidence we do have does not show that these programs are effective.

A Tufts Medical Center research team assessed the economic impact of the programs. They analyzed more than 2,000 peer-reviewed studies that used experimental or quasiexperimental study methods to look at medical, pharmacy and work productivity costs and indirect costs. The team's conclusion was hardly encouraging. They concluded that any evidence of a positive economic impact of workplace wellness programs was limited and inconsistent.[12]

In 2017, four members of the team behind the *Incidental Economist* blog published an extensive assessment of wellness programs and the evidence of their effectiveness. The title of the paper speaks for itself: "The Dubious Empirical and Legal Foundations of Workplace Wellness Programs."[13] They declared that most studies on the efficacy of the programs suffered "serious methodological shortcomings. Some are little more than thinly veiled promotional materials pulled together at the wellness industry's behest."

The evidence doesn't support the "unbridled enthusiasm" for wellness programs found by the team. They also revealed that certain programs appear to violate the Americans with Disabilities Act, which prohibits employers from conducting medical exams and collecting histories of their employees unless they are voluntary. Some financial incentives don't give employees a real choice about "volunteering" to share their medical information, the study said. "The evidence on wellness programs is discomfiting," the authors wrote. "Most programs do not work; some raise serious legal concerns. It is time for employers and policymakers to rethink their enthusiasm for the wellness movement."

In 2018, researchers from the Illinois Workplace Wellness Study published a large randomized controlled trial of a wellness program conducted at the University of Illinois at Urbana-Champaign. The study included nearly 5,000 employees who agreed to participate; some employees were invited to receive a biometric health screening and an online health risk assessment and offered a number of wellness activities. Employees were paid for completing screenings and participating in activities. The researchers followed the employees to see how the program affected their activities, their health, their productivity, and their medical spending. In the final analysis, there was no difference between those who did the wellness program and those who didn't. In the words of the *New York Times*, "The results were disappointing. There seemed to be no causal effects."[14] Most recently a *JAMA* study of 32,974 employees randomized to participate in a wellness program found "no significant differences in clinical markers of health; health care utilization, absenteeism, or job performance."[15]

When I first heard of them, I liked the idea of wellness programs. The idea seemed to make good sense. But after I attended the wellness class with my friend, I realized the industry had again sold America a bill of goods. It's yet another example of money earmarked for American workers getting diverted into the hands of corporations.

A Wellness Disrupter

Al Lewis went from a wellness industry advocate to its foremost critic. He spent years in the industry but came to see its futility. He left and started his own company, Quizzify. The Boston-based company educates employees about overtreatment and dispels myths about healthy living. I traveled to meet with Lewis, and he didn't hold back.

"Most of it is fluff. And I might add expensive fluff," Lewis, a tall man beaming with a smile, explained to me over a snack after he had just finished speaking to a large audience. Quizzify uses an interactive game show approach to teach people about common medical pitfalls, including the risks of overscreening. It also alerts employees to the most common unnecessary tests and procedures in medicine today, according to the Choosing Wisely campaign.[16]

I was able to attend one of his workshops and take the quiz. With his comedic, engaging style, Lewis informed participants about how long a knee replacement lasts, the latest research on heart stents, the radiation risks posed by a CT, and the role of sugar in disease. He even covered the risks of Nexium, my old heartburn medication. In that room, I witnessed Lewis educate a large group of people with highly relevant techniques they can use to make everyday decisions—from how to read a nutrition label to how to ask questions about common medical procedures.

Quizzify offers a health risk assessment. But it doesn't ask for personal information about drug, alcohol, and tobacco use. The Quizzify survey asks about diet and exercise, as well as educates people about the potential hazards of common medical tests and treatments. The idea is to help employees become wise stewards of their health and their health care spending.

Quizzify produces entertaining, interactive online quizzes to educate anyone wanting to learn more about health. The quizzes feature Lewis's offbeat humor while offering information patients can use. Lewis calls their tone "*Jeopardy!* meets Comedy Central."

Other wellness programs have value. Some employers provide fitness club memberships, regular yoga classes, medical second opinion services (I advise one called Veza Health[17]), or on-call clinicians to answer health questions. Warren Buffett's nonprofit wellness company Welcoa teaches accurate nutrition science and promote lifestyle treatments for illness. When I asked Welcoa's CEO, Ryan Picarella, why his company is so different, he said it was because they were focused on what actually makes people healthier instead of soft stuff that doesn't work.

The solution isn't to throw out all workplace wellness programs, but to choose a wellness program that is based on science and results in wiser health care choices. I like Quizzify's approach because it educates people using a fun style. For example, one quiz question asks how the radiation from a CT scan compares to the radiation from an X-ray. The answer: Most CT scans emit between 100 and 1,000 times as much radiation as X-rays. The point is not to avoid CT scans; it's to help people understand they should only be performed when necessary. CT scans are not for fishing for problems.

Lewis is part of a broader effort working to certify individuals and organizations in the wellness industry. The Validation Institute—a joint venture between Intel Corporation and GE Healthcare—certifies organizations in the wellness arena by evaluating results. The effort educates brokers and benefits consultants on how to evaluate vendors, since they are intermediaries for many in the employer marketplace.

Florida-based U.S. Preventive Medicine (USPM) is one such company that has been validated by the Validation Institute for sustained reduction in health care costs.[18] The Validation Institute says USPM reduced asthma, cardiac events, COPD, diabetes, and more across its entire book of business. USPM is a shining example of what's possible when companies do wellness right.

CHAPTER 17

The Words We Use

In junior high school, I was told I needed to take a foreign language. I had three options: French, Spanish, and Latin. I asked my guidance counselor, "Which one do I pick?"

"Well, son, what do you want to do when you grow up?"

"I think I want to be a doctor, but I'm not sure."

"Then Latin." He ruled like a judge quickly resolving a dispute.

I had never even heard of Latin. Furthermore, I didn't know what population group in the world spoke it. I quizzed my mentors around the school for their opinions, and they had the same response: "If you want to be a doctor, Latin will help you in medical school."

Even after I found out that Latin is spoken nowhere in the world, I obeyed the unanimous recommendation that it would someday help me in medical school. To be honest, I got excited at the idea of having a head start in med school. I took Latin for four years in high school, memorizing 20 new words for every Friday exam.

Four years after high school I sat in the lecture hall in medical school, ready for my first anatomy class to be taught in Latin. But med school was not taught in Latin. It was taught in English. Within months, I realized my Latin was not helping at all. Then one day in my second year of medical school, the professor said that a necrotic lymph node is a lymph node with dead tissue in it. *Yes!* I perked up. I recognized that *"necro"* meant "dead" in Latin. Even though I recalled that derivation quicker than anyone else, I felt depressed when I realized I spent four years studying Latin for the benefit of recognizing one word in medical school. I could just have memorized that one word! To this day, that one word comes a bit quicker to my mind. Say it with me: "necrosis." Meanwhile, I cannot communicate well with the 10% of my patients who are Spanish-speaking. Latin was a bad deal.

Whenever a colleague mentions that a patient has a necrosis, I flash back to those four years of Latin. That's followed by a sense of anger that I spent so much time learning stuff that doesn't matter at the expense of not learning more important stuff that does.

Today's medical education is dominated by a similar disconnect. About a dozen times in my extensive medical education I had to memorize things that I can simply look up—like the genetic conditions multiple endocrine neoplasia (MEN) type 1 and 2, conditions the majority of doctors will never see. I've seen the condition twice, and each time I quickly looked it up to refresh my memory. Yet all doctors must memorize these rare, non-urgent conditions and their specific gene mutations over and again on the road to becoming a board-certified physician.

Our medical education system is skewed toward things that don't matter. It's focused on rote memorization instead of treating the whole person. For example, it indoctrinates medical students that every adult woman needs a screening pap smear at regular intervals. But it fails to tell them that doing a screening pap smear in a 90-year-old woman is just wrong. The medical system teaches operative technique but does not prioritize care coordination. It gives students a passion to stamp out disease but fails to teach the importance of humility.

Moreover, medical school barely touches on the business of medicine. Nowhere in my training was I taught about pricing failures, overtreatment, or middlemen. The problems are staring us right in the face and the solutions are begging to be implemented. But instead of discussing them, we focus students on memorization—just as we did 50 years ago, before the Internet brought information to our fingertips nearly instantly.

Patients are crying out about care being too fragmented, too rushed, and about billing practices that are ruining their lives. Doctors must lead the charge to restore medicine to its mission. The most logical solutions have been largely absent from curricula.

Perhaps the greatest omission of medical education today has to do with the fact that most of our problems in public health are self-inflicted. Despite best intentions, medicine's limited view of healing has resulted in some of our greatest health care challenges, including the opioid crisis, antibiotic resistance, medical errors, and medicine's trail of financial toxicity. It's time to focus on what matters most to our patients.

Individualism

One entrenched problem in health care is that medical education has traditionally espoused individualism. Doctors are attracted to medicine by a deeply felt mission to help others, yet if a hospital has only two doctors in any one specialty, chances are they are at each other's throats. Exceptions abound, but if a random U.S. hospital has, say, a couple of thoracic surgeons, the odds are high that one resents the other.

I've traveled to hundreds of U.S. hospitals and met with countless doctors. I'm always amazed by the maverick phenomenon, even within small groups of physicians. Let's say there's a group of three physicians. Often, one will criticize the others for not practicing up-to-date medicine; another will feel that she deserves to take fewer calls; and the third finds a creative way to hoard the good cases.

Don't get me wrong, many doctors get along as swimmingly as my partners and I do in my surgical faculty group. We are personal friends, we don't keep score, and we help with one another's patients. But many groups wrestle with dynamics that can put internal politics above the needs of patients.

How is it that doctors can start off so altruistic and end up so cannibalistic? The answer lies in how we educate and shape young physicians. We credit individuals over teams and promote empire building. We teach technical skills, but not behavioral skills. I learned a lot in my 15 years of medical education. That's four years of premed, five years of med school and public health graduate school, five years of surgical residency, and a one-year specialty fellowship—a typical length of training for a surgical specialist. About 10% of what I learned has since been disproved and 80% is as irrelevant to how I practice medicine as the use of Botox on a furry dog.

That leaves approximately 10% of what I learned in med school that's relevant to my job. Of course, if I were a cancer research scientist, the biochemistry is something I might use every day, but that was never my path. I always knew I wanted to be a practicing surgeon, taking care of people.

I have no problem learning stuff I will never use simply for the sake of knowledge—though I prefer not to do any more Latin. Noticeably absent from that 15 years of study were the behavior skills that enable doctors to perform well. Yes, some people are naturally good at teamwork, communication, and humility. But most of us enter the profession fresh off a 20-to-30-year sprint of competing against one another academically—in a culture that promotes independence.

During my medical education, a dozen different times I had to memorize the Krebs cycle, a series of names of changing molecules inside a cell. I took a written exam almost every year to see if I could quickly recall the names of the intermediate molecules in the Krebs cycle. Of course, I could have used my brain space for things relevant to my patients, and if not, I can always look up the names of these molecules. The Krebs cycle has not come up once in my years of clinical medicine in any way, shape, or form. I would have been better off studying Latin. *Necrosis*.

There was a good reason medicine promoted memorization. Before Google and iPads, the doctor who could memorize the most differential diagnoses had a valued skill set. But now we can look things up. However, things haven't changed much on campuses because medical education is controlled by an establishment guard of accrediting boards and institutionalists.

Medical education needs lipo. Instead of teaching every medical student how to refract people's eyes to fit them for eyeglasses, how about teaching teamwork and communication skills? I learned the Krebs cycle, but not how to communicate effectively with nurses. I learned the microscopic stages of prostate cancer, but not how to deal with an underperforming person on my surgical team. I learned subatomic particles for the MCAT, but never learned how to explain diabetes at a sixth-grade reading level. To address the serious gaps in education, the traditional 15-year track to becoming a specialist doctor needs one giant enema.

Thankfully, we are getting started at Johns Hopkins. We have added teamwork and communication training to our medical curriculum and residency programs.

Humility

If you ask patients what makes a great doctor, they will tell you it's a doctor's judgment, skill, and humility. I tell my medical students that it's vitally important that they know their limits—even more than knowing your Krebs cycle. More than knowing subatomic particles, we need to know when to summon another doctor for advice. We must recognize when a patient is not understanding us, or when something causes a patient to lose trust.

When getting medical care, patients ask: Do I need this prescription? Do I need this test? Do I need this operation? They are concerned about the appropriateness of medical care. They want to get the care they need. And the number one mark of a quality doctor is how well the doctor discerns when medical care is appropriate and when it is not.

I was operating with one of our best surgeons-in-training one day when I saw him get extremely discouraged after placing a stitch a bit too far from the last one he placed. As soon as he placed the needle in the tissue, he recognized the mistake and backed it out, then placed it perfectly. "That's terrible! I should know better," he said, beating himself up. I had to stop him to remind him he was a great surgeon technically and that placing one stitch a hair off was not a problem because he immediately recognized and corrected it.

Disrupting Medical Education

Unfortunately, most medical schools still haze students by making them commit to memory thousands of details that do not need to be rapidly recalled in the real world of doctoring. Some medical schools blame the accrediting boards for requiring all the memorization. Well, here's an open invitation to the old guard of medical school accreditation: come spend a day with me in the hospital. Medical students don't need to learn facts only to forget them weeks after an exam. No patient ever died because their doctor couldn't rapidly recall the Krebs cycle. Swap out the Krebs cycle with a patient testimonial about routine medical care gone awry. Or replace the Krebs cycle with a teenager's testimonial about going to one MRI center that overcharged her so much she lost her college savings.

Medical schools should take a lesson from the innovators in medical education today, like Dr. Stephen Klasko, CEO of Thomas Jefferson University and Jefferson Health. Dr. Klasko is restructuring medical education to teach humility and compassion. His curriculum educates future physicians in effective communication and empathy and includes a strong set of courses by Dr. David Nash about the money games of medicine. Klasko believes in making medical education highly relevant to the medical, social, and financial needs of patients—the whole person.

I reached out to Klasko to find out how his school is disrupting medical education. We talked about the culture of training doctors. He shared with me the results of a simple series of interviews his team conducted with past graduates who have been in practice for years. They asked how well their medical education prepared them to practice medicine. Graduates consistently felt that their education did not prepare them well at all. When they got into practice, they didn't have the basic skills they needed, like effective communication skills, how to run a meeting, or how to recognize burnout.

Klasko based his new curriculum in part on a $1.5 million grant he received to study what makes doctors different from everybody else. He learned that the way we select and educate physicians is akin to joining a cult. He identified four fundamental traits that get ingrained early: a competitive bias, an autonomy bias, a hierarchy bias, and a noncreativity bias. He learned that the profession attracts highly creative team players but that we ingrain in them the qualities of focus, discipline, and rigidity. Other professions generally promote those who are the most creative, but medicine often rewards people who are the most focused. "We select people based on GPA, MCAT score, and organic chemistry and somehow we're amazed they're not more empathetic," said Klasko. He decided to rethink how the medical school selects students. "We decided to choose students based on self-awareness and empathy."

Klasko partnered with two nonmedical companies to learn how to select better. The medical school partnered with Southwest Airlines to see how they chose pilots to deal with crisis. They also partnered with Telios, a company that does the interviewing for Google. Once a candidate meets a certain academic standard, the criteria for certain behavioral traits that are set by the companies come into play. The difference between a great pilot and a good pilot is not scoring 99% versus 96% on their exams. It's teamwork and communication skills. Similarly, Google is far more interested in creative talent than in test scores.

Under Klasko's leadership, Jefferson selects students based on their emotional intelligence and trains them to be highly effective communicators with sound clinical judgment. Boston University is also now using a holistic admission process, and other schools are beginning to see the benefits as well.

People like Klasko are changing the culture of medicine for the better by putting the focus back on the patient.

Speaking the Right Language

My Latin didn't prepare me for medical school. My medical school didn't prepare me for doctoring. In a similar way, our approach toward fixing what's wrong with our medical system has skipped over key points.

One of our biggest problems is vocabulary. We use code words for the problems we see around us instead of calling things what they are. We should be using patient-centered terms. Instead, health care has adopted business-centered terms.

In his book *Catastrophic Care: How Healthcare Killed My Father*, David Goldhill has written eloquently how health care's vocabulary fosters a false reality. He cites the difference in impact between experts saying "Petroleum costs are increasing" and a consumer saying "Gas prices are going up." The first term creates distance between you and the problem; the latter hits home.

The official medical dictionary is full of terms that depersonalize problems by being technical when they should be visceral. We've seen this before. The banking industry told us that markets were so complex that we should leave it to the experts. They supported this notion with a lexicon that was so technical that people outside Wall Street were left out of the dialogue. But the complex terms got decoded after the financial collapse of 2008. What the experts called a "credit default swap" was really borrowed money that bypassed insurance requirements. What experts called a "collateralized debt obligation" was just a group of bad loans. In health care, we do something similar all the time. We need to start fixing health care by switching to a more honest lexicon.

Health care experts use the term "costs." We should talk about "prices."

Health care experts use the term "preventable adverse event" when we should call it "medical care gone wrong," or an "error" when appropriate. "Preventable adverse event" is a term that washes everyone clean of responsibility, while the plainer terms express the truth a patient experiences.

Heath care experts talk about variation in a hospital's "charge-to-cost ratio." That's what you and I might call a "markup." I'm not judging the principle of charging more for a medical service at Hospital A versus Hospital B. The service might be better at one place than the other. But call it what it is: a markup.

Health care experts use the term "financial aid" to describe the meager discount they might offer on marked-up charges if they agree to pay in installments. They should be calling it "predatory lending." If a bill is 1,000% higher than what Medicare would pay for the same service, a 10% discount is still taking advantage of the patient. Allowing a patient to pay that bill in monthly installments over a lifetime is manipulation.

In that same spirit, "charity care" should refer only to medical care that is entirely free. It's not the difference between what a hospital charges and what they get after shaking down the patient.

Health care experts say "employers" pay for health care for most Americans. But it's actually employees who are paying, since the money used to pay for health care comes from an allocation of funds set aside for employee compensation and benefits. We are told that payers, like insurance companies, foot the bill for medical care, but that money comes from beneficiaries like you who pay monthly premiums.

Similarly, we are often told that Medicare paid for a medical procedure, but actually U.S. taxpayers paid for it. Check your paystub and you will most likely see that you are paying a Medicare "excise" tax with every paycheck, in addition to your health care contribution. That contribution is in addition to what our employer is paying for your health care—money that could otherwise be paid to you in wages.

Using the more accurate terminology in plain English would help change the conversation about health care. People could better understand what's really happening. It can also more effectively engage people with these important issues.

My research colleagues and I are trying to change the terms we use in our public conversations. It's not easy. Several times, medical journal editors slap my wrist and insist that I use the wonky term instead of the plain English term. But to change health care, we need to alter the words we use to talk about it.

When people ask what they can do to get involved, I encourage them to discuss these topics with their local hospital board members, governors, and state and national legislative representatives. As someone who serves on a hospital board myself, I know board members are people from the community and highly accessible. Talk to them about these issues. Ask them how their hospital addresses charity care, and if the hospital sues patients.

Employers should take a hard look at their health insurance and PBM contracts and consider self-insurance or self-insurance pools. They should include pricing and quality tools to guide employees to high-value medical care. Employers are leading the redesign of health benefits in ways that are poised to disrupt the entire medical establishment, such as General Motors engaging in a direct contract with Henry Ford Health System, bypassing layers of costly middlemen.

In another example, the H-E-B grocery chain, the largest private company in Texas and an entirely self-insured business of 105,000-plus employees, is redesigning health care with new clinics, called Magenta Clinics. These clinics create a path to disrupting the medical marketplace by how they choose doctors for patient referrals; that is, how they pick specialists for the patients. Value is defined by quality and price. Using new metrics of quality and appropriateness and information on price, a large business like H-E-B could reward high-value physicians by sending them patients. At scale, this could have a powerful impact in reshaping competition for high-quality, fair-priced specialty care. Currently, we have competition in health care, but that competition has been at the wrong level. Medical centers have been competing on parking, billboards, and appointment scheduling ease. Medical centers should be competing on value (quality and price), not just on conveniences. Large businesses like H-E-B are the bright spot in health care, poised to change the way health care does its business.

The next time someone says that your insurance company, your employer, or Medicare is paying for something, you might want to remind that person that it's really all of us who are paying.

CHAPTER 18

What We Can Do

You wouldn't believe the things people tell me.

When you're a doctor, people tell you a lot about their physical problems—and not just when they're sitting in your office. It could be a social gathering, dinner party, school event, kids' soccer game, country music concert—pretty much anywhere. When some people discover I'm a doctor, it's as though we're suddenly transported into my examination room. The next thing I know they're sharing their medical and dental history: telling me about a sports injury they got in high school, whether they have vaccinations, showing me a curious rash, perhaps soliciting my opinion about an intimate health issue experienced by a family member. As a result, I have thousands of loosely bound mental medical charts floating around in my brain from cocktail reception consults. It is a little embarrassing when I later remember someone because of their spleen issue. Every now and then I'll see a guy at a social event and think, *I know that person. Oh, yes, he's the diarrhea guy.*

One evening, I was attending a Washington, D.C., cancer fundraising event, and someone at our table mentioned I was a surgeon. With those magic words, the woman sitting next to me at the table perked up. "Oh, you're a doctor?" Karen asked eagerly. "I wanted to be a doctor when I was in school." She proceeded to list all the doctors she knew in town. Then the waiter came to pour wine in her glass.

"Oh, no, thank you," she told him.

Karen turned to me and leaned in close, as though she were going to tell me a secret. Her voice dropped an octave as she explained she couldn't drink because she was taking antibiotics for a chronic sinus problem. Next, she complained about how much her medications cost and everything she'd tried to treat her chronic sinusitis. I'll admit that as Karen droned on about herself, a few times I zoned out. But then she said something that made me snap to attention: "I had the balloon done and everything."

"Wait, wait, hold on," I interrupted. "You had the balloon sinuplasty procedure? Tell me about that."

While working on the Improving Wisely project, our research group and Ear, Nose, and Throat (ENT) specialists criticized the balloon procedure. The widespread use of the procedure evoked negative reactions from the experts.

Based on these reactions, I decided to study the issue further. I led a focus group with ENTs and asked how a balloon sinuplasty works. An expert showed how a balloon at the end of a small tube is inserted into the patient's sinus and inflated to open the sinus opening. It rarely works, said the ENT doctor, and is widely overused. The other ENTs in attendance had smiled at the obvious reason everyone does them: they pay well. Intense frustration with doctors who balloon nearly every patient was palpable.

I asked if there was a group of patients the procedure did help. They shook their heads. Not really. "It's necessary for less than 5% of patients who are getting the balloon done," said one doctor. After the meeting, one of the Hopkins ENTs pulled me aside. "Doctors are taking patients for a ride," he said.

Given the widespread abuse of this procedure, you can see why Karen had my attention. Now I leaned toward her, and *my* voice dropped an octave as I asked her to share all the details. "Please, tell me everything."

She explained how the doctor placed a small tube in her nose and then inflated a balloon to open up her sinuses. She made a point of mentioning that the doctor is a very good, highly recommended doctor with gorgeous offices. The clinic even had palm trees in the lobby, she said.

"Did the balloon help with your sinus problem?"

"Umm, not really," she confessed. That's what the experts would have predicted.

"How long did the whole procedure take?"

"About 45 minutes."

"Was it done in an operating room or in the doctor's office?"

"The office."

"How much did it cost?" I asked

"Oh, my, the bill was $21,000," she said. "Thank God I only had to pay $2,500, and my insurance covered the remaining $18,500."

A $21,000 bill for a procedure taking less than an hour with no operating room costs? And it didn't even work. I was shocked.

Karen seemed content that the bill was resolved and her portion was only a fraction of the total cost.

"Do you know what an open heart surgery costs at Johns Hopkins?" I asked. She didn't. I told her it was about the same cost.

Whether the balloon procedure was indicated for in Karen's chronic sinusitis, I can't say for sure. But a few things were clear. One, my Hopkins colleagues believe the procedure is vastly overused. Two, Karen reported no benefit. And three, Karen and her insurance company were victims of price gouging.

Many people assume that insurance companies have safeguards against price gouging, but not so in Karen's case. The same is true for millions of cases like hers where the medical billing is too complicated and unclear to figure out. Insurance companies pass on the expense to everyone in the form of next year's premiums.

Karen's story captured everything wrong with health care today—and many of the things I've detailed in this book. She was price-gouged for a procedure she didn't need after taking medications that were marked up by her pharmacy benefits manager (PBM). All the while, she was oblivious to the many ways she'd been taken advantage of.

Karen's experience reminded me of a woman named Rhonda who brought her son to their doctor for a sports injury. The doctor ordered an MRI of the kid's brain, even though there was no head injury and no loss of consciousness. Following the doctor's orders, her son had the MRI, and she was charged 12 times more than she would have been at the other MRI center about a mile down the street. A single working mom with a $9,000 insurance deductible, she paid the uber-inflated MRI bill using the money she had saved up for her son to go to community college. For the first several months after she got the bill, she, like many Americans, did not have the cash on hand to pay it, and the bill was sent to collections before ultimately she paid it in full. Her FICA score was hit and, buying a small home around that time, she ended up having to pay more for her mortgage.

Physicians and hospital leaders who had no knowledge of how ugly their billing procedures had become are now becoming aware and are doing something about it. Some are talking to their hospital executives and board members to take a pledge to never sue low-income patients and to bill fairly. My team, in partnership with BrokenHealthcare.org, continues to travel to U.S. hospitals, politely asking them to make their billing procedures consistent with their hospital's charter and mission statement. The grassroots movement has also spread on a local level, to students, medical professionals, and concerned citizens who are demanding that hospitals examine their fairness in billing and do more to restore the public trust.

How did medicine transform from a charitable profession to one that has put one in five Americans into collections for medical debt? How did we get to the point where hospitals are scientifically advanced bastions of academic genius, but can't even tell you what an operation will cost? How did the noble profession of healing allow billing practices to become so predatory that some hospitals sue and garnish the wages of half of the people in the town they serve? How did we get to this point where American businesses have lost their competitiveness overseas because of health care costs? How did we get to a point where Starbucks spends more on health care than coffee beans and General Motors spends more on health care than steel? Or where some types of overtreatment have reached epidemic proportions, and medical error is a leading cause of death in the United States?

How did we arrive at this moment where pharmacists are contractually forbidden to tell a patient what's in their best interest, and middlemen work in a fog of transactions so opaque that a special law was passed to grant them exemption from antikickback laws? These money games become so accepted that ordinary people like Karen are getting charged $21,000 for an ineffective minor procedure, and meanwhile, she has no idea that she's a victim of the game.

Historically, hospitals were founded on an altruistic mission to serve their communities. They were sustained by charity and committed to great values of equality. My hospital was founded by Mr. Johns Hopkins. He described his mission in a March 10, 1873, letter, saying he would care for "the indigent sick of this city and its environs, without regard to sex, age or color, who may require surgical or medical treatment, and who can be received into the Hospital . . . The poor of this city and State of all races, who are stricken down by any casualty, shall be received into the Hospital without charge."[1] Like most hospitals in America, Johns Hopkins was founded on and dedicated to the principles of compassion and mercy.

The Johns Hopkins Hospital *operated in the red* for its first eight decades. The annual deficits were covered by gifts from trustees and by dipping into the endowment. Their commitment to serve the community was unwavering. Many landmark cases at Hopkins were performed at no cost. The pioneering craniofacial operations and the separation of conjoined twins connected at the head were done *gratis*. For free.

I'm inspired by the individual health care professionals who have sacrificed so much to improve the lives of patients. I think of Dr. Walter Dandy, a pioneer in neurosurgery who lived in the early 1900s. He developed the first ICU and performed the first vascular clipping of a cerebral aneurysm. Though considered a strict, firm-tempered man, he was also extremely generous.[2] He often paid the hospital expenses of indigent patients. On one occasion, when he learned that the mother of a patient could not afford the train fare to bring her child to Baltimore, he not only paid her way but refused to take any compensation. Dr. Dandy, known as the father of cerebrovascular neurosurgery, routinely declined to accept payment from teachers, police officers, or firemen. He was a dedicated and busy surgeon. He even wrote a letter to Dr. Harvey

Cushing on June 30, 1921, about the medical establishment of his day, saying that he was "very averse to joining societies of all kinds because I feel they are more social than beneficial and I cannot spare the time for them."

The day the polio vaccine was announced as safe and 90% effective, Jonas Salk refused to commercialize it or obtain a patent. He and polio vaccine developer Albert Bruce Sabin, a physician at Johns Hopkins, refused to make money from their discovery. Salk and Sabin had seen firsthand how polio paralyzed as many as 20,000 children each year, sentencing some to life in an iron lung machine. Our hospital had wards of them. But Salk and Sabin believed that the polio vaccine was the property of humanity. Because of their compassion, most of the world's children quickly had access to the medical breakthrough. *Forbes* estimates that Salk alone would have been richer by $7 billion if his vaccine had been patented. Salk and Sabin stayed true to their medical calling to help people and considered their vaccines to be donated for the benefit of mankind.

Dr. Benjamin Rush, son of a blacksmith, remembered his Philadelphia roots growing up in a family without much money. His dedication allowed him to become a physician and care for the poor regardless of their ability to pay. Serving as a voice for those with psychiatric disorders, he devoted his medical career to destigmatizing mental illness. He fought on behalf of those who couldn't fight for themselves, including people suffering from schizophrenia who were chained down in institutions because society did not understand their illness. Because having mental illness often meant living in extreme poverty, Rush would often serve his patients without being paid. But that didn't stop him. Considered the forefather of psychiatry, he held strong views on equality, even publicly calling for the abolition of slavery, declaring it a crime. Dr. Rush would later become one of five physician signers of the Declaration of Independence. He was at George Washington's side during the crossing of the Delaware, and he treated injured soldiers behind enemy lines. His duty to serve the sick and injured of society rose above any other allegiance. Dr. Rush was among the first to call for equal rights for women, free education and health care for the poor, citywide sanitation facilities, an end to child labor, universal public education, prison reform, and an end to capital punishment. He was highly critical of tobacco smoking and was known to call out physicians when he observed greed and incompetence among them.

Of all the signers of the Declaration, Rush would become the Founding Father most interested in diversity issues, stemming from his views on equality.[3] After his death, Thomas Jefferson said in a letter that he knew no one "more benevolent, more learned, of finer genius, or more honest." In comparing Benjamin Rush to Benjamin Franklin, President John Adams said, "Rush has done infinitely more good to America than Franklin. Both had deserved a high Rank among Benefactors to their Country and Mankind; but Rush by far the highest."

As we today struggle to address the issues in health care, doctors and other medical care professionals must remember the compassion that first drew us into the field. We need to remember the torch that Hopkins, Dandy, Sabin, Salk, and Rush passed on to us. Through their example and teachings, they bequeathed to us a mission of a healing profession that values equality. Regardless of circumstances, their mission was to take care of a fellow human being when they were vulnerable, and to be their advocate.

Honesty in Medicine

The contrast between the money games of medicine and the mission of our predecessors who worked so hard to earn the public trust couldn't be sharper. Today, health care's cost crisis has become an enormous blame game. People blame the arrogance of a Martin Shkreli and the gamesmanship of a Mylan Pharmaceuticals. People blame central line infections and surgical site infections. After all, it's easy to blame bacteria. These are easy targets. The problem is that these factors are minor compared to the major structural issues of health care's entrenched stakeholders.

People blame doctors, hospitals, payers, pharma, device companies, and even patients for not taking better care. But the money games are so established and the revenue stream they produce is so steady that experts don't want to discuss altering the business model. But every one of us in health care, every stakeholder, needs to look inward and address the waste in our own backyard.

After seeing so clearly that commonsense transparency reforms are needed to make health care affordable, I'm amused when I hear so-called health care experts blame one another for high prices. Nearly every one of these experts is beholden to one of health care's big stakeholders and is afraid to speak critically about the entire system. Experts are afraid to upset their bosses, who may promote them to leadership someday, or they fear upsetting stakeholders, who may pay their speaking fees. But a critical view of the whole ecosystem is exactly what we need. I've met so many people who speak on condition of anonymity about the waste in the system. At the same time, I've met health care minds unbeholden to the stakeholders. Some bold experts are unafraid to speak up. We need more honest critiques of the massive system.

We are at a critical moment in our nation's history. Delivering health care can be much more democratic, more methodologically honest, and more transparent.

A Call to Action

Health care is perhaps today's most divisive, territorial political issue. But many of the needed solutions are not partisan; they're American. We are at a pivotal juncture. Spending on health care threatens every aspect of American society. The time for commonsense reform has arrived. All of us can play a part in driving badly needed reforms, both in the marketplace and in the policy world. As Margaret Mead said, "Never doubt that a small group of thoughtful, committed citizens can change the world; indeed, it's the only thing that ever has."

One simple thing you can do: ask for a price every time you are considering a medical service. One hospital administrator I met during this journey told me that his hospital created a clear pricing sheet for delivering a baby, broken down for an uncomplicated vaginal delivery, for a C-section, for the epidural, and even for the car seat you can take home. That's a milestone event. That hospital decided to adopt fair and transparent pricing for baby delivery services because people asked. Most of health care can behave like any other marketplace in any other industry: it responds to customer demands for non-urgent services, which account for most health care services. A restaurant owner will be more likely to switch to organic foods if every customer asks the waiter "Is this food organic?" It's the same with hospitals. They respond to people who consistently ask good questions before choosing where to get their medical care.

As a society, we should embrace a basic set of patient rights, including a right to obtain a timely quote for a shoppable medical service. Lawmakers should look at the price transparency trails blazed by Florida, New Hampshire, and Maine. The prerequisite of any free market is viewable pricing information—not just inflated charges, but the actual amounts of settled bills. New policies should ensure a level playing field to make the free market functional again, to cut the waste and restore competition to the marketplace.

Physicians and hospitals can join the grassroots groundswell of physicians working toward a fair and functional health care system. The national Choosing Wisely[4] project, our Hopkins-based Improving Wisely[5] project, and the High Value Practice Academic Alliance[6] represent a few simple ways to get involved. Developing sound measures of appropriateness across thousands of areas of medical care requires input from clinicians on the front lines of medicine.

Hospital leaders should consider the tremendous demand in the market for increased honesty in health care. That includes being up-front about prices and making themselves available to discuss bills. Everyday Americans and business leaders are hungry for this kind of square dealing. Hospitals that respond to this demand will distinguish themselves as leaders in the health care landscape of the future. The market will soon reward hospitals that offer quality and price transparency. Dr. Keith Smith of the Surgery Center of

Oklahoma and other leaders of the free market medical movement have demonstrated how transforming a medical center to one that embraces transparency is not only feasible, but profitable.

Finally, billing quality is medical quality. Hospitals should be evaluated on their billing quality in patient navigation tools and hospital rankings. And when a hospital goes overboard to sue masses of low-income patients, going after their paychecks and putting liens on their homes, concerned citizens like you and I should respond by contacting the hospital's board of trustees to remind them that hospitals were built to be a safe haven for the sick and injured regardless of one's race, creed, or ability to pay. No patient should be at home sick and scared of going to a hospital for fear of price gouging. Reminding health care leaders of medicine's great public trust is the start of rebuilding a more honest and compassionate health care system.

So, the next time you have a conversation about health care, use a patient-centered vocabulary. By calling things what they are, we can avoid downplaying the crisis at hand. As Americans, we need to say enough is enough. Transparency's time has come. And for the sake of our patients, health professionals should lead this charge. It's central to our great medical heritage. As witnesses to birth, sickness, and death, we know that all humans are created equal and deserve to be treated with fairness and dignity.

Afterword

Just before this book was published, I gave an advance copy to a classmate from Harvard who was working in the U.S. Senate. To my surprise, she read it in one day and asked me for additional copies for her friends in Congress and the White House. Within weeks I found myself sitting in the offices of the nation's top political leaders (on both sides of the aisle).

I explained that the fundamental problem with health care is that it is a noncompetitive market, a problem magnified by mass hospital consolidation and distorted by clinical and administrative waste. When looking at all the abuses in a noncompetitive market, the natural temptation for a policymaker or consumer is to demand regulations to outlaw specific bad behaviors. But the lasting solution is to convert noncompetitive markets into competitive ones.

We walked through, among many other topics, the specifics of what a new price transparency policy for hospitals could look like, based on the model of a government policy to require nutrition labels on food. The new rule would require hospitals to post real cash prices for common shoppable services, to put a price estimator on their website, and disclose the secret discounts they give to each insurance company.

Remarkably, in a city where nothing gets done, the idea got momentum. The new rule was soon announced by the secretary of health and human services and immediately signed into action. Unsurprisingly, it had strong bipartisan consensus. After all, transparency is not a red or blue issue—it's an American value. The broad support was consistent with the recent Harvard study that found that 88% of the American public demand greater price transparency in health care.

But there was one opponent. The American Hospital Association immediately sued to block the new rule—it would shed light on the embarrassing price markup/discount game they play with insurers. Around this time, many hospital CEOs contacted me to tell me that they privately supported transparency even though their hospital and trade association did not. One said, "Who can really oppose transparency, even though our bulldog hospital lobbyists are opposing it; keep fighting for it."

The hospital lobby fought hard but ultimately lost two court challenges. In the second court challenge, the judge vehemently concluded that the new transparency rule was the fulfillment of the vague language in the Affordable Care Act stating that hospitals are required to show prices, a stealth provision of the landmark law that was never implemented or enforced.

Because the new rule also required full disclosure of the secret price discounts hospitals give to insurers, one prominent U.S. hospital opposed the policy. They argued that it would be a huge amount of work for them to look up their discounts for each insurer or group. They pointed out that they have over 3,000 contracts, each with a specified discount! I responded by saying yes, that's exactly the problem. Why do you have 3,000 different prices for the same medical service? Imagine all the time, money, and staff required to negotiate and write those 3,000 contracts and to price services differently depending on who's paying. Try having one price.

When doctors and consumer advocates pushed for a law requiring nutrition labels, the food industry pushed back with the same arguments the hospital lobby made. The food industry argued that it was too onerous and that the cost of adding nutrition labels would cause food prices to spike, resulting in more world hunger. They said they would be forced to lay off workers and that no one would use the information on nutrition labels. *None of those arguments were true.* Nutrition labels ignited competition around healthy ingredients. So when people argue against transparency in health care, remember that no industry has taken steps toward greater transparency and then realized it was a bad idea and reverted back.

Thanks to the many policymakers who took a bold step, pricing and insurance discount data for many U.S. hospitals is now in the public domain. Already people have told me they have used price estimator tools on hospital websites, a requirement of the new policy, modeled after the Mayo Clinic price estimator. Right now businesses are starting to scrape this information to make it easy for everyday Americans to digest.

The reward of watching ideas in this book being adopted into policy was counterbalanced by the agony of watching the coronavirus pandemic crash into a delicate health care system that was as fragile as a house of cards. Though this book was first published a few months before the pandemic, my warnings about flimsy supply chains putting the United States at risk of serious medical supply shortages were ignored. Tragically, the United States then found itself holding the bag, scavenging for protective personal equipment (PPE), ventilators, and critical medications in China.

At the start of the pandemic, when reports of coronavirus deaths in Wuhan began to emerge, I was struck by the sharp contrast between dire warnings from infectious disease experts and broader public complacency around the novel coronavirus. I had long talks with infectious disease doctors in late January and February 2020 and called doctors in Wuhan to get the real story. Convinced this was much bigger than the public realized, I took to the airways to sound the alarm.[1] I began urging hospitals, governors, and business leaders to begin contingency planning and, in the interim, stop all nonessential travel.[2] My pleas often falling on deaf ears, I took to begging the mainstream media to stop putting politicians and pundits on TV, and instead to use doctors.

By late February, Dr. Scott Gottlieb, myself, and a few others grew unabashedly outspoken, critical of how medical experts were being ignored as if scientific consensus was a political opinion.[3] I warned on one Sunday-morning talk show in March 2020 that "hundreds of thousands of Americans will die" from the virus.

I took a lot of arrows for that warning. Critics pointed to fewer than 500 total Covid deaths in the United States as of that date, less than that of seasonal flu. Their denialism was magnified by Twitter, Facebook, and cable news. I couldn't believe that pundits were talking about the probability of a pandemic like they were talking about their fantasy football picks. The denial was fueled by loud, highly opinionated public figures who knew nothing about medicine, epidemiology, or virology shouting on social media, which amplified their rhetoric.

If this virus has taught our country nothing else, its lesson should be humility. Humility is not something we can teach in a textbook; it's something we model with our behaviors and our approach to new information. Humility marks a great physician, nurse, trainee, businessperson, or teacher. It enables a clinician to deal with uncertainty and manage it appropriately. In my own specialty of surgery, the "captain of the ship" principle creates a chain of command necessary for emergency communications, but a good captain knows their limits and when to call for help. Students, residents, nurses, and staff all watch how we as physicians react to new information, and they notice our willingness to challenge groupthink and our own deeply held assumptions. As I have unexpectedly found myself at the center of coronavirus public policy, I have had to evolve my position on the virus with the arrival of new data.

It is clear now that our entire health care system was too slow and too rigid to respond swiftly to the coronavirus pandemic. It was also too dependent on foreign manufacturing and continues to be. The U.S. research infrastructure of the NIH and university procedures are too slow to respond to a health emergency. Of the $40 billion the NIH spent in 2020, almost none was awarded in grants to universities to study coronavirus. Instead, the funds were tied up by long review processes. Other barriers to a rapid response were what I call "self-inflicted wounds," including overly rigid institutional review boards that meet too infrequently to approve Covid research quickly, burdensome HIPAA-based policies that some institutions require for research that poses no risk to people, data-use agreements that slow down research, electronic health record systems that do not communicate with each other for proprietary reasons, and inadequate funding for clinical research that could have elucidated the basics of asymptomatic spread, masks, and airborne transmission.

For the reasons I give in chapter 8, the insistence on overly elaborate research designs prevented the medical community from studying the virus when we desperately needed to understand it. For example, we should have learned about the 30% mortality-reduction benefit of steroids (a drug that has been in every U.S. ICU for over fifty years) during the initial New York outbreak, rather than in June when the UK RECOVERY trial was completed. U.S. researchers had declined to participate in that trial because it did not meet their elaborate standards.

Throughout the first half of the pandemic, many doctors told me of great research questions they would have loved to have seen answered with simple studies.[4] When I asked them if they could conduct the study, they explained that there is little funding for field studies, public health research, or big data analyses and that applying for funding is needlessly complex. Having submitted government applications for Covid research myself, I agreed. In addition, medical journals took up to six months to review Covid research studies before publishing them. In so many ways, the old guard medical establishment failed us during Covid. In the future, we have to be able to adapt our peacetime research systems to meet the demands of war. Viral pandemics are not the only health emergency we need to be prepared for. Fires, hurricanes, and mass shootings will all require a more agile and resilient health care response.

Covid has ushered in telemedicine and shown us that relationship-based clinic models like ChenMed and Iora are the future. Liberated from the fee-for-service hamster wheel that burns out doctors and patients alike, ChenMed and Iora have thrived during the pandemic. Instead of being paid through the fee-for-service system, they are paid a steady annual revenue stream adjusted by the health outcomes of the people they serve. These clinics, and others delivering what has become known as value-based health care, quickly responded to the pandemic, putting their van pick-up service in reverse to deliver food and medications and switching to virtual visits long before Medicare approved it for fee-for-service clinicians. Meanwhile "fee-for-service medicine" was rushing the U.S. Congress, begging for a taxpayer bailout.

As I watch innovators disrupt health care and create better, I'm reminded that the best strategy for driving change in health care is to appeal to the best in people, reminding them of our great medical heritage of caring for those in need. You win more bees with honey than fire.

I've seen many examples of this strategy working, and they're not just limited to Covid-specific solutions. Since this book came out, I've been struck by the growing chorus of people in health care who want to bypass the middleman and go direct. Hospitals are signing more direct contracts with employer groups. Medical professionals are now calling for more appropriate care, asking how they can treat more diabetes patients with cooking classes instead of medication, how they can treat more back pain with ice and physical therapy instead of surgery and opioids, and how they can treat chronic conditions with conversations about better sleep and food as medicine instead of brief ten-minute checkups. In cancer research, we are now talking about environmental exposures instead of just talking about chemotherapy. We are witnessing a revolution in medicine and finally talking about the underlying problems that bring people to care rather than the care itself.

Businesses are stepping up as well. Many CEOs have asked me to point them to advisors who can help save them millions on their health care spend without cutting any corners on the benefits. I've now enjoyed watching many businesses save millions by switching to transparent brokers, swapping out their PBM, and changing their health care benefit design to make it smarter (with the same good coverage). Marshall Allen, an editor of this book, was so amazed at what we uncovered that he was inspired to write an excellent how-to book for everyday Americans to save money on their health care titled *Never Pay the First Bill*.

In the vast majority of my conversations with hospital leaders about predatory billing practices, I found that many of them were morally opposed to these practices, especially that of suing to garnish the wages of low-income patients who couldn't afford to

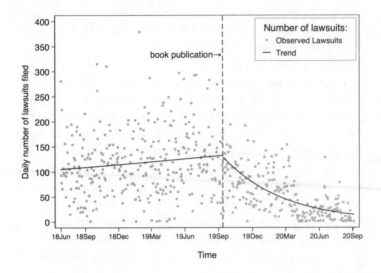

pay their bills. My team and I asked dozens of hospitals to stop suing patients with letters, phone calls, and even through the media. Nationwide, we were able to convince many hospitals to shut down or markedly reduce the practice of suing patients. Farah Hashim and Joseph Paturzo on my research team at Johns Hopkins did an analysis of hospital lawsuits before and after our national advocacy work over the summer months (my book's publication at the height of our work is indicated with a dashed line).[5]

Sometimes it was easy, such as when we spoke with the new CEO of Advocate Aurora medical center in Wisconsin, who instantly shut down the widespread practice of suing patients as soon as he learned about it. Sometimes it was hard, such as when we approached the University of Virginia (UVA). After alerting Kaiser Health News about the trend—which then ran a series of stories—we took to social media to ask alumni to contact the university's leadership. We met with doctors there and told them what their administration was doing (they were enraged to find out). The doctors began an uprising to demand an end to the practice, but when the hospital dug in, my students and I went to the big donors (whom we identified by researching the names on the buildings on campus). After a public battle, UVA finally decided to stop suing all patients.

The Leapfrog Group, a consortium of some of the nation's leading employers, is now working closely with my team to add billing quality to their hospital scoring system. Other ratings groups are similarly working with my team to add basic metrics of billing quality. Billing quality is medical quality. And financial toxicity is a complication. The American Medical Association gave this work a big boost by publishing standard billing quality metrics that I coauthored with Dr. Simon Matthews in the *Journal of the American Medical Association*—a set of measures my team is now working to implement with many different stakeholder partners in health care and in business.[6] Many hospitals perform well in their billing practice. The market should reward that good behavior. In the future, when you search for a hospital on the internet, you may not only see the facility's name, address, and consumer ratings. You may also see the facility's average price markup, a medical quality score by specialty, and a billing quality score.

The appropriateness-measures work described in this book has also blossomed into several national efforts, thanks to the leadership of entrepreneurs such as Drs. Daniel Stein and Matt Resnick of Embold Health in Nashville, Brandon Cady of AIM Specialty Health in Chicago, and Will Bruhn, a colleague I have mentioned throughout this book who is now leading Global Appropriateness Measures in Austin—a group with which I'm closely involved. They are using their business acumen to move health care markets by ushering in a new generation of appropriateness measures that will complement past quality-improvement efforts.

Most meaningful has been the greatest gift a university professor could ever receive—being inspired by the many young people who have told me that they are committed to working on these issues at their hospital, university, or business. If you know the millennial mindset, you know that these young people want to be a part of something larger then themselves. Unlike workers from past eras, millennials don't crave the traditional path of a big job, a big house, and retiring in luxury. They want to change the world. Social justice is a generational value.

To everyone who has worked on these issues with me, before me, and independently of me, thank you for your work to change health care to make it more honest, more equitable, more transparent, more efficient, and, most importantly, more caring.

Acknowledgments

A big thank-you to the Halsted surgery residents at Johns Hopkins who model patient-centered care better than anyone I know. I love you guys. And to my surgical mentors John Cameron, Andrew Warshaw, Charles Yeo, Robert Higgins, and Julie Freischlag. Thanks to my book club: Peter Hill, Redonda Miller, Stephen Sisson, Karen Davis, Daniel Brotman, Deb Baker, and Diana Ramsay for your incredible collegiality and teamwork that keeps work fun.

Thank you to Margeaux Van Horn and Tara Kennedy for your work on the book and coordinating with my crazy schedule and to my editors Marshall Allen, who helped me shape the book and encouraged me to go out into the field, and Nancy Miller, who believed deeply in this massive project and brought it to life. Thank you to the giant scholars of quality from whom I have learned a lot, Don Berwick, Bryan Sexton, Bruce Hall, Clifford Ko, Peter Pronovost, Atul Gawande, Maureen Bisognano, and Albert Wu. And special thanks to Elliot Fishman, Pamela Johnson, Josh Sharfstein, Tom Coburn, Katy Talento, John Hundt, Cynthia Fisher, Keith Lemer, Nathan Bays, Brian Blase, Zubin Damania, Peter Attia, Wendell Primus, Kavita Patel, Dick & Becky Cowart, Claire Haltom, Bill Frist, Jim Cooper, Annie Lamont, Angela Profeta, Danielle Lavey, Kathryn Weismantel, Mike Pykosz, Ryan Lee, Jason Davis, Adam Russo, Perla Ni, Suchi Saria, Lanalee Araba Sam, Nirav Shah, Chris Chen, Lydia Vogt, Andrew Ibrahim, Larry Van Horn, David Silverstein, Jeffrey Sachs, Robin Gelburd, Dean Sicoli, and Charlene Frizzera for your expertise and moral support.

Notes

Preface

1. M. H. Katz, D. Grady, and R. F. Redberg, "Undertreatment Improves, but Overtreatment Does Not," *JAMA Internal Medicine* 173, no. 2 (2013): 93.

2. E. S. Huang, "Potential Overtreatment of Older, Complex Adults with Diabetes," *Journal of the American Medical Association* 314, no. 12 (2015): 1280–81.

3. S. J. Katz, R. Jagsi, and M. Morrow, "Reducing Overtreatment of Cancer with Precision Medicine: Just What the Doctor Ordered," *Journal of the American Medical Association* 319, no. 11 (2018): 1091–92.

4. S. Wheeler, American Society of Clinical Oncology Quality Care Symposium, October 10, 2018, Phoenix, AZ.

5. A. W. Mathews, "Employer-Provided Health Insurance Approaches $20,000 a Year," *Wall Street Journal*, October 3, 2018.

6. N. Sood, A. Ghosh, and J. Escarce, "Health Care Cost Growth and the Economic Performance of U.S. Industries," *HSR: Health Services Research*, June 9, 2009.

Chapter 1: Health Fair

1. "$37 Million Settlement Reached in Unnecessary Heart Stent Case," WJZ CBS Baltimore, April 7, 2014.

2. The guidelines say there is not sufficient evidence to show the screening is beneficial for patients without symptoms. *Final Recommendation Statement: Peripheral Arterial Disease (PAD) and CVD in Adults: Risk Assessment with Ankle Brachial Index.* U.S. Preventive Services Task Force, December 2016.

3. A. Andras and B. Ferket, "Screening for Peripheral Arterial Disease," *Cochrane Database of Systematic Reviews*, 2014, issue 4, Art. No. CD010835, doi:10.1002/14651858.CD010835.pub2.

4. S. Wheeler, American Society of Clinical Oncology Quality Care Symposium, October 10, 2018, Phoenix, AZ.

5. P. Salminen et al., "Antibiotic Therapy vs Appendectomy for Treatment of Uncomplicated Acute Appendicitis: The APPAC Randomized Clinical Trial," *Journal of the American Medical Association* 313, no. 23 (2015): 2340–48.

6. J. F. Svensson et al., "Nonoperative Treatment with Antibiotics versus Surgery for Acute Nonperforated Appendicitis in Children: A Pilot Randomized Controlled Trial," *Annals of Surgery* 261, no. 1 (2015): 67–71.

7. H. C. Park et al., "Randomized Clinical Trial of Antibiotic Therapy for Uncomplicated Appendicitis," *British Journal of Surgery* 104, no. 13 (2017): 1785–90.

8. P. Salminen et al., "Five-Year Follow-up of Antibiotic Therapy for Uncomplicated Acute Appendicitis in the APPAC Randomized Clinical Trial," *Journal of the American Medical Association* 320, no. 12 (2018): 1259–65.

9. S. Di Saverio et al., "The NOTA Study (Non Operative Treatment for Acute Appendicitis): Prospective Study on the Efficacy and Safety of Antibiotics (Amoxicillin and Clavulanic Acid) for Treating Patients with Right Lower Quadrant Abdominal Pain and Long-term Follow-up of Conservatively Treated Suspected Appendicitis," *Annals of Surgery* 260, no. 1 (2014): 109–17.

10. D. A. Talem, "Shared Decision Making in Uncomplicated Appendicitis: It Is Time to Include Nonoperative Management," *Journal of the American Medical Association* 315, no. 8 (2016): 811–12.

11. Dr. Edward Livingston, deputy editor of the *Journal of the American Medical Association*, quoted in Steven Reinberg, "Appendicitis Can Often Be Treated with Antibiotics," *HealthDay*, June 16, 2015.

12. L. S. Lim et al., "Atherosclerotic Cardiovascular Disease Screening in Adults: American College of Preventive Medicine Position Statement on Preventive Practice," *American Journal of Preventive Medicine* 40, no. 3 (2011): 380–81.

13. W. E. Bruhn et al., "Cardiovascular Screenings at United States Churches" (forthcoming), Johns Hopkins University.

14. C. W. Hicks et al., "Race and Socioeconomic Disparities Associated with Peripheral Vascular Interventions for Claudication" (forthcoming), Johns Hopkins University, 2020.

15. C. W. Hicks et al. "Overuse of Early Peripheral Vascular Interventions for Claudication," *Journal of Vascular Surgery*, 2019.

16. S. Reddy, "Doctors Sound an Alarm Over Leg-Stent Surgery," *Wall Street Journal*, September 10, 2019.

Chapter 2: Welcome to the Game

1. B. D. et al., "Association of Hospital Prices for Coronary Artery Bypass Grafting with Hospital Quality and Reimbursement," *American Journal of Cardiology* 117, no. 7 (2016): 1101–06.

2. T. Xu et al., "Variation in Emergency Department Excess Charges in the United States," *JAMA Internal Medicine*, May 2017.

3. J. Harris, "I Tried to Find Out How Much My Son's Birth Would Cost. No One Would Tell Me," *Vox*, May 5, 2016.

4. A. W. Mathews, "Behind Your Rising Health-Care Bills: Secret Hospital Deals That Squelch Competition," *Wall Street Journal*, September 22, 2018.

5. J. Li, mock-up cover art for "Why Childbirth in the U.S. Is More Expensive than Other Countries," *Axios*, October 12, 2018.

6. NORC at the University of Chicago, "New Survey Reveals 57 Percent of Americans Have Been Surprised by a Medical Bill," *ScienceDaily*, August 30, 2018.

7. Ibid.

8. The New Mexico Office of Superintendent of Insurance and the University of New Mexico RWJF Center for Health Policy conducted the 2017 survey.

9. T. Xu et al., "Variation in Emergency Department Excess Charges in the United States."

10. S. Wheeler, American Society of Clinical Oncology Quality Care Symposium, October 10, 2018, Phoenix, AZ.

11. A. W. Mathews, "Employer-Provided Health Insurance Approaches $20,000 a Year," *Wall Street Journal*, October 3, 2018.

12. B. Herman, "Hospital Prices Are All Over the Board," *Axios*, August 30, 2018.

13. J. A. Sakowski et al., "Peering into the Black Box: Billing and Insurance Activities in a Medical Group," *Health Affairs* 28, no. 4 (2009): w544.

14. Xu T. et al., "The Potential Hazards of Hospital Consolidation: Implications for Quality, Access, and Price," *Journal of the American Medical Association* 314, no. 13 (2015): 1337–38.

15. M. A. Makary and G. Bai, "Revealing the Real Prices Insurers Pay Can Save Health Care," STAT News, May 2, 2019.

16. A. W. Mathews, "Behind Your Rising Health-Care Bills: Secret Hospital Deals That Squelch Competition."

17. A. Mehta et al., "The Impact of Price Transparency for Surgical Services," *American Surgeon* 84, no. 4 (2018): 604–608.

18. Federal Trade Commission, "Complying with the Funeral Rule," https://www.ftc.gov/tips-advice/business-center/guidance/complying -funeral-rule.

Chapter 3: Carlsbad

1. B. DiJulio et al., "Data Note: Americans' Challenges with Health Care Costs," Henry J. Kaiser Family Foundation, March 2, 2017.

2. West Health Institute and the NORC at the University of Chicago Report, "Americans Fear Crippling Medical Bills More than Illness," *HealthDay*, March 2018.

3. United States Federal Reserve Bank Board of Governors, "Report on the Economic Well-Being of U.S. Households in 2017," May 2018.

4. T. Tepper, "Most Americans Don't Have Enough Savings to Cover a $1K Emergency," *Bankrate*, January 18, 2018.

5. United States Department of Labor, Wage and Hour Division, https:// www.dol.gov/whd/regs/compliance/whdfs30.htm.

6. E. Cohen and J. Bonifield, "When Some Patients Don't Pay, This Hospital Sues," CNNHealth, September 10, 2019.

Chapter 4: Two Americas

1. W. E. Bruhn et al., "Prevalence and Characteristics of Virginia Hospitals Garnishing Wages for Unpaid Medical Bills," *Journal of the American Medical Association* (2019).

2. Ibid.

3. United States Department of Labor: May 2017 National Occupational Employment and Wage Estimates United States.

4. T. Xu et al., "Variation in Emergency Department Excess Charges in the United States," *JAMA Internal Medicine* (May 2017).

5. S. Simmons-Duffin, "When Hospitals Sue For Unpaid Bills, It Can Be 'Ruinous' For Patients," NPR.org, June 25, 2019, https://www.npr .org/sections/health-shots/2019/06/25/735385283/hospitals -earn-little-from-suing-for-unpaid-bills-for-patients-it-can-be-ru inous.

6. IRS Revenue Ruling 56-185, 1956-1 C.B. 202.

7. IRS Revenue Ruling 69-545, 1969-2 C.B. 117, which remains the current standard.

Chapter 5: The Ride

1. D. Rosato, "Air Ambulances: Taking Patients for a Ride," *Consumer Reports*, April 6, 2017.

2. K. Reece, "Snake Bite Victim Gets $30K Helicopter Bill," WFAA, ABC channel 8, Dallas, August 11, 2017.

3. G. A. Vercruysse et al., "Overuse of Helicopter Transport in the Minimally Injured: A Health Care System Problem That Should Be Corrected," *Journal of Trauma and Acute Care Surgery* 78, no. 3 (2015): 510–15.

4. Rosato, "Air Ambulances."

5. F. A. Habib et al., "Probable Cause in Helicopter Emergency Medical Services Crashes: What Role Does Ownership Play?" *Journal of Trauma and Acute Care Surgery* 77, no. 6 (2014): 989–93.

Chapter 6: Woman in Labor

1. D. L. Riddle et al., "Use of a Validated Algorithm to Judge the Appropriateness of Total Knee Arthroplasty in the United States: A Multicenter Longitudinal Cohort Study," *Arthritis and Rheumatology* 66, no. 8 (2014): 2134–43.

Chapter 7: Dear Doctor

1. American College of Mohs Surgery, "History of Mohs Surgery," https://www.mohscollege.org/about/about-mohs-surgery/history-of-mohs-surgery.

2. L. P. Casalino et al., "US Physician Practices Spend More than $15.4 Billion Annually to Report Quality Measures," *Health Affairs* 35, no.3 (2016): 401–406.

3. J. Albertini et al., "Evaluation of a Peer-to-Peer Data Transparency Intervention for Mohs Micrographic Surgery Overuse," *JAMA Dermatology*, published online May 5, 2019.

4. I. Ayres, S. Raseman, and A. Shih, "Evidence from Two Large Field Experiments That Peer Comparison Feedback Can Reduce Residential Energy Usage," NBER Working Paper No. 15386, September 2009.

5. www.improvingwisely.com.

Chapter 8: Scaling Improvement

1. *Social Science and Medicine* 211 (August 2018).

2. K. Kaczmarski et al., "Surgeon Re-excision Rates after Breast-Conserving Surgery: A Measure of Low-Value Care," *Journal of the American College of Surgeons* 228, no. 4 (2019): 504–12.

3. P. Wang et al., "Same-day Versus Different-day Elective Upper and Lower Endoscopic Procedures by Setting," *JAMA Internal Medicine*, published online May 13, 2019.

4. M. A. Makary et al., "Patient Safety in Surgery," *Annals of Surgery* 243, no. 5 (2006): 628–35.

5. M. A. Makary et al., "Operating Room Briefings: Working on the Same Page," *Joint Commission Journal on Quality and Patient Safety* 32, no. 6 (2006): 351–55.

6. M. A. Makary et al., "Operating Room Teamwork among Physicians and Nurses: Teamwork in the Eye of the Beholder," *Journal of the American College of Surgeons* 202, no. 5 (2006): 746–52.

7. M. A. Makary et al., "Operating Room Briefings and Wrong-site Surgery," *Journal of the American College of Surgeons* 204, no. 2 (2007): 236–43.

8. M. A. Makary et al., "Patient Safety in Surgery," *Annals of Surgery* 243 (2006): 628–35.

9. WHO Guidelines for Safe Surgery 2009: Safe Surgery Saves Lives. Available online at http://apps.who.int/iris/bitstream/handle/10665 /44185/9789241598552_eng.pdf;jsessionid=4C0514716CEEBE8D819E 2BFB223E7638?sequence=1.

10. American Society for Gastrointestinal Endoscopy, "Understanding Polyps and Their Treatment," https://www.asge.org/home/for-patients /patient-information/understanding-polyps.

11. J. A. Sparano et al., "Adjuvant Chemotherapy Guided by a 21-Gene Expression Assay in Breast Cancer," *New England Journal of Medicine* 379, no. 2 (2018): 111.

12. S. Reddy, "Doctors Sound an Alarm Over Leg-Stent Surgery."

Chapter 9: Opioids like Candy

1. J. Katz, "Drug Deaths in America Are Rising Faster than Ever," *New York Times,* June 5, 2017.

2. H. Hedegaard et al., "Drug Overdose Deaths in the United States, 1999–2016," NCHS Data Brief No. 294, December 21, 2017.

3. Hill et al., "Wide Variation and Excessive Dosage of Opioid Prescriptions for Common General Surgical Procedures," *Annals of Surgery* 256, no. 4 (2017): 709–14.

4. H. Overton et al., "Opioid Prescribing Guidelines for Common Surgical Procedures: An Expert Panel Consensus," *Journal of the American College of Surgeons* 227, no. 4 (2018): 411–18.

5. www.solvethecrisis.org.

6. M. A. Makary, "How Doctors Can Stop the Opioid Crisis at Its Source," *USA Today,* August 4, 2017.

Chapter 10: Overtreated Patients like Me

1. B. Lazarus et al., "Proton Pump Inhibitor Use and the Risk of Chronic Kidney Disease," *JAMA Internal Medicine* 176, no. 2 (2016): 238–46.

2. T. Carr, "Too Many Meds? America's Love Affair with Prescription Medication," *Consumer Reports*, August 3, 2017.

3. Ibid.

4. M. Ellenbogen et al., (forthcoming), Johns Hopkins University, 2019.

5. M. Favro, "Doctor Agrees with Steve Kerr's Advice to Avoid Back Surgery," NBC Bay Area, April 24, 2017.

6. Washington Health Alliance, "New Study Finds Hundreds of Thousands of Washington Patients Receive Unnecessary Tests, Procedures, and Treatments," https://wahealthalliance.org/new-study-finds-hundreds-of-thousands-of-washington-patients-receive-unnecessary-tests-procedures-and-treatments/.

7. K. R. Chhabra et al., "Surgical Decision Making: Challenging Dogma and Incorporating Patient Preferences," *Journal of the American Medical Association* 317, no. 4 (2017): 357–58.

8. High Value Practice Academic Alliance, www.hvpaa.org.

9. H. Lyu et al., "Overtreatment in the United States," *PLoS ONE* 12, no. 9 (2017) e0181970.

10. M. A. Makary et al., "A Call for Doctors to Recommend Antibiotic-Free Foods: Agricultural Antibiotics and the Public Health Crisis of Antimicrobial Resistance," *Journal of Antibiotics* 71, no. 8 (2018).

11. H. S. Ahn et al., "Korea's Thyroid-Cancer 'Epidemic'—Screening and Overdiagnosis," *New England Journal of Medicine* 371, no. 19 (2014): 1765.

12. S. Park et al., "Association between Screening and the Thyroid Cancer 'Epidemic' in South Korea: Evidence from a Nationwide Study," *British Medical Journal*, November 30, 2016.

13. *New England Journal of Medicine* commentary by Dr. Gilbert Welch of the Dartmouth Institute for Health Policy and Clinical Practice and Dr. Hyeong Sik Ahn of Korea University.

14. H. S. Ahn et al., "South Korea's Thyroid-Cancer 'Epidemic'—Turning the Tide," *New England Journal of Medicine* 373, no. 24 (2015): 2389.

15. S. Vaccarella et al., "Worldwide Thyroid Cancer Epidemic? The Increasing Impact of Overdiagnosis," *New England Journal of Medicine* 375, no. 7 (2016): 614–17.

16. Right Care series, *The Lancet*: https://www.thelancet.com/series/right-care. S. Brownlee, K. Chalkidou, J. Doust, A. G. Elshaug, P. Glasziou,

I. Heath, S. Nagpal, V. Saini, D. Srivastava, K. Chalmers, D. Korenstein, "Evidence for Overuse of Medical Services around the World," *Lancet* 390, no. 10090 (2017): 156–68.

Chapter 11: Starting from Scratch

1. F. Lambert, "Virginia Auto Dealers Are Suing Tesla and the State to Stop the Automaker from Opening a Store," *Electrek*, March 10, 2016.
2. A. Suderman, "Tesla Representative Booted from Auto Dealers' Board," Associated Press, January 24, 2018.
3. Medallia, Net Promoter Score: https://www.medallia.com/net-promoter -score/.
4. Kaiser Family Foundation, "An Overview of Medicare," April 2016, retrieved from http://www.kff.org/medicare/issue-brief/an-overview -of-medicare/.

Chapter 12: Disruption

1. Centers for Medicare and Medicaid Services, "Emergency Medical Treatment and Labor Act," https://www.cms.gov/Regulations-and -Guidance/Legislation/EMTALA/.
2. J. Curtis et al., "What Does the Affordable Care Act Say about Hospital Bills?" Hospital Accountability Project, June 15, 2015, https://www .communitycatalyst.org/resources/publications/document/CC -ACAHospitalBillsReport-F.pdf?1434480883.

Chapter 13: Buying Health Insurance

1. C. Isidore and M. Egan, "Wells Fargo under Siege," CNNMoney, September 13, 2016.
2. M. Egan, "Workers Tell Wells Fargo Horror Stories," CNNMoney, September 9, 2016.
3. "Fed Up with Rising Costs, Big US Firms Dig into Health Care," Reuters, June 11, 2018.
4. Employer Health Benefits 2018 Annual Survey, Kaiser Family Foundation, 2018.

Chapter 14: Pharmacy Hieroglyphics

1. M. Thompson, "Why a Patient Paid a $285 Copay for a $40 Drug," PBS, August 19, 2018.
2. Pharmacy Benefit Managers, "Health Affairs Health Policy Brief," September 14, 2017, doi:10.1377/hpb20171409.000178.

3. K. Van Nuys et al., "Frequency and Magnitude of Co-payments Exceeding Prescription Drug Costs," *Journal of the American Medical Association* 319, no. 10 (2018): 1045–47.

4. S. Lieberman et al., "A Billion Here, a Billion There: Selectively Disclosing Actual Generic Drug Prices Would Save Real Money," *Health Affairs*, August 8, 2018.

5. Ohio's Medicaid Managed Care Pharmacy Services, Auditor of State Report, August 16, 2018.

6. Ohio Pharmacists Association, "Ohio Auditor Releases Stunning Medicaid PBM Audit Report," https://www.ohiopharmacists.org/aws /OPA/pt/sd/news_article/184063/_PARENT/layout_interior_details /false.

7. M. Allen, "In Montana, a Tough Negotiator Proved Employers Don't Have to Pay So Much for Health Care," ProPublica, October 2, 2018.

8. S. Lupkin, "Patients Overpay for Prescriptions 23% of the Time, USC Analysis Shows," *Los Angeles Times*, March 14, 2018.

9. L. L. Gill, "Shop Around for Lower Drug Prices." ConsumerReports .org, April 5, 2018.

Chapter 15: 4K Screens

1. W. E. Bruhn et al., "Group Purchasing Organizations, Healthcare Costs, and Drug Shortages," *Journal of the American Medical Association*, November 2018.

2. Healthcare Supply Chain Association, "A Primer on Group Purchasing Organizations," https://c.ymcdn.com/sites/www.supplychain association.org/resource/resmgr/research/gpo_primer.pdf, accessed July 2018.

3. Premier Inc. Reports Fiscal 2017 Fourth-Quarter and Full-Year Results, August 21, 2017, 45.

4. M. Blake, "Dirty Medicine," *Washington Monthly*, July/August 2010.

5. U.S. Food and Drug Administration, "Statement from Douglas Throckmorton, M.D., Deputy Center Director for Regulatory Programs in FDA's Center for Drug Evaluation and Research, on the Agency's Response to Ongoing Drug Shortages for Critical Products," published June 2018, accessed July 23, 2018.

6. U.S. Government Accountability Office. "Drug Shortages: Certain Factors Are Strongly Associated with This Persistent Public Health Challenge," https://www.gao.gov/assets/680/678281.pdf, published July 2016, accessed July 19, 2018.

7. Committee on Oversight and Government Reform (2012), "FDA's Contribution to the Drug Shortage Crisis," https://oversight.house .gov/wp-content/uploads/2012/06/6-15-2012-Report-FDAs -Contribution-to-the-Drug-Shortage-Crisis.pdf, accessed July 22, 2018.

8. R. E. Litan et al., "An Empirical Analysis of Aftermarket Transactions by Hospitals," *Journal of Contemporary Health Law and Policy* 28, no. 1 (2011): 34.

9. R. E. Litan and H. J. Singer, "Broken Compensation Structures and Healthcare Costs," *Harvard Business Review*, October 6, 2010.

10. U.S. Government Accountability Office, "Group Purchasing Organizations: Research on Their Pricing Impact on Health Care Providers," published January 29, 2010, publicly released March 1, 2010, https:// www.gao.gov/new.items/d10323r.pdf.

11. D. Liljenquist et al., "Addressing Generic-Drug Market Failures— the Case for Establishing a Nonprofit Manufacturer," *New England Journal of Medicine* 78, no. 20 (2018): 1857–59, doi:10.1056/nejmp 1800861.

12. L. A. Johnson, "FDA to More Aggressively Tackle Disruptive Drug Shortages," Associated Press, July 12, 2018.

13. M. Hiltzik, "Supply Middlemen May Leave Hospitals Ailing," *Los Angeles Times*, April 14, 2005, accessed August 2018.

Chapter 16: Diagnosis: Overwellnessed

1. G. Claxton et al., "Employer Health Benefits 2017 Annual Survey," Kaiser Family Foundation, 2017.

2. Stern Speakers, "Dr. Peter Attia: Readdressing Dietary Guidelines," YouTube video, 1:19:04. Posted on Jan 28, 2015, https://www.youtube .com/watch?v=nhzV-J1hodo.

3. D. Mozaffarian et al., "The 2015 US Dietary Guidelines: Lifting the Ban on Total Dietary Fat," *Journal of the American Medical Association* 313, no. 24 (2015): 2421–22.

4. C. E. Kearns et al., "Sugar Industry and Coronary Heart Disease Research: A Historical Analysis of Internal Industry Documents," *JAMA Internal Medicine* 176, no. 11 (2016): 1680–85.

5. S. Zhang "Big Pharma Would Like Your DNA: 23andMe's $300 Million Deal with GlaxoSmithKline Is Just the Tip of the Iceberg," *Atlantic*, July 27, 2018.

6. K. Baicker et al., "Workplace Wellness Programs Can Generate Savings," *Health Affairs* 29, no. 2 (2010).

7. D. S. Hilzenrath, "Misleading Claims about Safeway Wellness Incentive Shape Health Care Bill," *Washington Post*, January 17, 2010.

8. M. A. Makary et al., "Operating Room Briefings: Working on the Same Page," *Joint Commission Journal on Quality and Patient Safety* 32, no. 6 (2006): 351–55.

9. M. A. Makary et al., "Operating Room Teamwork among Physicians and Nurses: Teamwork in the Eye of the Beholder," *Journal of the American College of Surgeons* 202, no. 5 (2006): 746–52.

10. M. A. Makary et al., "Operating Room Briefings and Wrong-site Surgery," *Journal of the American College of Surgeons* 204, no. 2 (2007): 236–43.

11. WHO Guidelines for Safe Surgery 2009: Safe Surgery Saves Lives, http://apps.who.int/iris/bitstream/handle/10665/44185/9789241598552_eng.pdf?sequence=1.

12. D. Lerner et al., "A Systematic Review of the Evidence Concerning the Economic Impact of Employee-focused Health Promotion and Wellness Programs," *Journal of Occupational and Environmental Medicine* 55, no. 2 (2013): 209–22.

13. A. McIntyre et al., "The Dubious Empirical and Legal Foundations of Wellness Programs," *Health Matrix* 27, no. 1 (2017).

14. A. E. Carroll, "Workplace Wellness Programs Don't Work Well. Why Some Studies Show Otherwise," *New York Times*, August 6, 2018.

15. Z. Song, and K. Baicker, "Effect of a Workplace Wellness Program on Employee Health and Economic Outcomes: A Randomized Clinical Trial," *Journal of the American Medical Association* 321, no. 15 (2019): 1491–1501.

16. www.choosingwisely.org.

17. www.vezahealth.com.

18. www.validationinstitute.com/.

Chapter 18: What We Can Do

1. N. Grauer, *Leading the Way: A History of Johns Hopkins Medicine* (Baltimore: Johns Hopkins University Press, 2012).

2. N. Grauer, *The Special Field: A History of Neurosurgery at Johns Hopkins* (Baltimore: Johns Hopkins University Press, 2015).

3. S. Fried, *Rush: Revolution, Madness, and the Visionary Doctor Who Became a Founding Father* (New York: Crown, 2018).

4. www.choosingwisely.org.

5. www.improvingwisely.org.

6. www.hvpaa.org.

Afterword

1. CNBC Squawk Box, "Johns Hopkins' Dr. Marty Makary On Coronavirus: All Americans Should Stop Nonessential Travel," video, 1:35. Posted on March 10, 2020, https://www.cnbc.com/video/2020/03/10/johns-hopkins-dr-marty-makary-on-coronavirus-all-americans-should-stop-nonessential-travel.html.

2. M. A. Makary, "COVID-19: Why I'm Very Concerned," MedPage Today, March 9, 2020. https://www.medpagetoday.com/infectiousdisease/covid19/85324.

3. CNBC Squawk Box, "Johns Hopkins' Dr. Marty Makary On Coronavirus."

4. P. Attia, "Video #12 (4/3/20)—The Most Important Experiment I Wish We Were Doing NOW," YouTube video, 8:44. Posted on April 3, 2020, https://www.youtube.com/watch?v=xdpwP4dK52Y.

5. Graph courtesy J. G Paturzo, F. Hashim, C. Dun, M. J. Boctor, W. E. Bruhn, C. Walsh, and M. A. Makary, Johns Hopkins University, 2021. Grant: Arnold Ventures.

6. ScienceDaily, "Physicians Propose Quality Measures to Improve Medical Billing," February 5, 2020. https://www.sciencedaily.com/releases/2020/02/200205103230.htm.

Index

The letter *f* following a page number denotes a figure.

A NOTE ON THE AUTHOR

Marty Makary, MD, MPH, is a surgeon and Professor of Health Policy at Johns Hopkins and a leading voice for physicians in the *Wall Street Journal* and *USA Today*. He was the lead author of the articles introducing a surgical checklist, later adapted by the WHO, and has published extensively on public health vulnerable populations, health care costs, and quality science. He served in leadership at the WHO Safe Surgery Saves Lives project and is a member of the National Academy of Medicine. The author of the *New York Times* bestseller *Unaccountable*, he lives in the Washington, D.C., area.